COMPETITION LAW

COMPETITION LAW

Beatrice Roxburgh

Published by

College of Law Publishing,
Braboeuf Manor, Portsmouth Road, St Catherines, Guildford GU3 1HA

© The University of Law 2024

British Library Cataloguing-in-Publication Data

A catalogue record for this book is available from the British Library.

ISBN 978 1 915469 61 8

Typeset by Style Photosetting Ltd, Mayfield, East Sussex

Tables and index by Moira Greenhalgh, Arnside, Cumbria

Preface

This introduction to competition law is a companion guide to the University of Law's competition law courses. As such, it has an emphasis on practical issues relevant to many of the law firms in which our students will qualify. It methodically works through the constituent elements of the main competition law prohibitions, covers elements of merger control that are most relevant in practice (including the acquisition of minority interests and joint ventures) and sets out the practical consequences of breach. It explains the latest developments in EU competition law and its UK mutations, covering for instance both EU and UK versions of the block exemptions for vertical agreements, and the horizontal guidelines.

The authors

Beatrice Roxburgh formerly practised EU and UK competition law at Linklaters LLP and in-house at BT Group plc, and is a Teaching Fellow at the University of Law.

Meytal McCoy and Angela Diveley Landry contributed to the US law sections of this textbook. Meytal McCoy is Special Counsel at Freshfields Bruckhaus Deringer US LLP. Angela Diveley Landry is Counsel at Freshfields Bruckhaus Deringer US LLP, where she advises clients on a range of antitrust law issues, including merger control, corporate compliance, and agency advocacy.

Contributors to past editions include Mhairi Morter, Trevor Tayleur, Thomas F Bush and Stephen Medlock.

Beatrice Roxburgh

The University of Law
London Moorgate

Contents

Table of Cases

Table of Primary Legislation

Page numbers in bold type indicate where legislation is quoted in part or in full. Further references may occur on the same page.

Table of Secondary Legislation

Page numbers in bold type indicate where secondary legislation is quoted in part or in full. Further references may occur on the same page.

Introduction to Competition Law

AIMS

This chapter introduces you to the broad economic policies that underpin the antitrust/competition law regimes that we shall be considering in this textbook. It will also provide you with background information on the legislation and institutions relating to these regimes.

OBJECTIVES

After studying **Chapter 1**, you should understand:

- the broad reasons for, and aims of, competition law;

- the core commercial conduct to which competition law applies;

- the objectives pursued by competition law, including the importance of single market integration for EU competition law;

- the basic legislative structure of the United Kingdom (UK), European Union (EU) and United States (US) competition regimes; and

- the institutions charged with upholding competition law in the UK, EU and US systems.

TERMINOLOGY

Before we consider the above objectives, a quick note about terminology. Antitrust is primarily a term of US law, whilst competition law is often used in the EU and in the UK. Both terms will be used throughout this textbook.

1.1 THE DEVELOPMENT OF COMPETITION LAW

Competition law is concerned with the functioning of markets. The prominence of competition law has increased significantly over the last decade. This can be put down to a number of factors, which include:

- The penalties that can be imposed for breaches of competition law are considerable and have been increasing. In the EU, fines run into billions of euros.

- Some systems of law, such as the UK's, include criminal sanctions on individuals for the most serious breaches.

- Competition authorities have extensive powers to detect anti-competitive behaviour, including unannounced 'dawn' raids.
- Many jurisdictions worldwide now have a competition law regime, including major economies such as China, India and Brazil. It has been estimated that there are now over 100 systems of competition law worldwide.
- Competition law is vigorously enforced in many privatised sectors formerly under state control. For example, in the UK, regulators overseeing the water, energy and communications sectors have a special role in competition law enforcement.

All these developments have seen a marked increase in competition law enforcement.

The main focus of this textbook will be on the system of competition law adopted by the UK and the EU, but comparisons will also be made with the US system.

The European Economic Area (EEA) has a system of competition law that mirrors the EU competition law regime. While this textbook generally refers to EU competition law only, EEA competition rules are generally the same.

1.2 ECONOMICS AND THE THEORY OF COMPETITION

Competition law is based on economic theory. Accordingly, any study of competition law must include consideration of the basic economic principles from which it derives.

Competition law is based upon the economic theory of the free market. Put at its most basic, the theory states that businesses operating in a competitive market will provide greater benefits to society as a whole than businesses that are protected from competition.

Economists understand competition at its simplest as the basic interaction between the supply of products and services to the market (for example, from manufacturers and traders) and demand for those products and services (for example, from raw material purchasers and final consumers). Purchasers and consumers will seek the best levels of price and quality for the goods and services they require. Competition is considered by many to be the best way to ensure that suppliers deliver the best response to this demand. For example, competition stimulates the efficient production and allocation of resources; and a wide choice, high quality and low price of goods and services for customers.

When considering the competitive dynamic on a market, economic theory starts from the position of considering a pure form of the free market called the 'perfect competition model'. The perfect competition model is comprised of a large number of small independent suppliers who, at its simplest, are all on a level playing field, subject to the same – overall beneficial – competitive pressures from each other and customers. In other words, each supplier in this market has to fight, or compete, for customers' orders. Given that there are so many suppliers, they must use their respective resources efficiently and provide customers with what they want in order to ensure their survival.

At the opposite end of the spectrum, economic theory also recognises a pure form of 'monopoly' market where one single supplier (the 'hypothetical monopolist') controls an entire market. The monopolist is the only supplier to a given market and is therefore able to act as it wishes, to the benefit of its own profits and the detriment of other players in that market, such as customers.

Of course, in reality, most competitive markets fall somewhere between the pure forms of perfect competition and monopoly highlighted above. Some markets will be dominated by a small number of powerful players ('oligopoly') or purchasers ('monopsony'), or they may look more like the perfect competition model discussed above. The basic role of competition law is to ensure that free markets operate freely for the benefit of consumers. This includes ensuring that parties operating on a market do not seek to remove or reduce the competitive dynamic.

Although competition law regimes will differ, they will all cover the following areas, which are also the focus of this textbook:

- anti-competitive agreements and concerted practices;
- abuses by undertakings that have market power or are dominant; and
- the regulation of transactions involving a change of control, such as mergers, takeovers and joint ventures.

In addition, some competition law regimes include rules relating to state aid or subsidy control. These are not covered by this textbook. The UK's market investigation regime is also not covered by this textbook.

Given the economic theory underpinning competition law, economists play an active role alongside lawyers when assessing the effects that certain actions will have on a market's competitive dynamic.

1.3 AN INTRODUCTION TO UK COMPETITION LAW

1.3.1 Main sources of UK competition law

In the UK, the main sources of competition law are:

- the **Competition Act 1998**;
- the **Enterprise Act 2002**;
- **Articles 101 and 102** of the Treaty on the Functioning of the European Union (TFEU). These provisions continue to be relevant notwithstanding the UK's departure from the EU on 31 January 2020 (an event referred to as 'Brexit'), to the extent set out in the European Union (Withdrawal) Act 2018 as amended by the European Union (Withdrawal Agreement) Act 2020.

In addition, secondary legislation and guidance set out the detail of the UK competition regime. We shall consider some of these additional sources throughout this textbook.

1.3.1.1　The Competition Act 1998

The UK's Competition Act (CA) 1998 is based on EU competition law. Its provisions mirror the two main prohibitions in Articles 101 and 102 TFEU: the prohibition on anti-competitive agreements (see **Chapter 2**), and the prohibition on abuse of dominance (see **Chapter 3**).

Since Brexit, the UK is no longer required to maintain consistency between how competition law is applied in the UK and how it is applied in the Member States of the European Union (see **4.3.1.2**). Nevertheless, the EU and UK regimes are expected to remain closely aligned for some time. Introducing inconsistencies between the two competition law systems is not usually seen as desirable, as it adds complexity and increases the burden of businesses that must comply with both EU and UK competition law. However, UK competition authorities are starting to tailor UK competition law to the particular situation of UK businesses and consumers.

1.3.1.2　The Enterprise Act 2002

The Enterprise Act (EA) 2002 contains the rules relating to the UK's merger regime. It has been amended by the National Security and Investment Act 2021 which contains special rules applicable to certain investments. See **Chapter 7**.

The EA 2002 also contains a criminal cartel offence for the most serious breaches of competition law. In addition, a director of a business found to have breached competition law can be barred from acting as a director. See **Chapter 4**.

The EA 2002 also contains provisions that enable the UK's competition authorities to investigate markets that are not functioning well for consumers. As mentioned above, the market investigation regime is not covered by this textbook.

The provisions of both the CA 1998 and the EA 2002 place the UK regime somewhere between the EU and US systems. In regard to the substantive law, the UK regime mirrors that of the EU system. In regard to enforcement, although based on EU principles, the UK regime has taken elements of the US law, namely the imposition of criminal liability on individuals.

1.3.1.3   Articles 101 and 102 TFEU

The European Commission, European courts and national competition or regulatory authorities of each EU Member State are the institutions responsible for enforcing Articles 101 and 102. As a general rule, the European Commission is the authority responsible for investigating the most serious pan-European breaches of Articles 101 and 102 TFEU, while the competition authorities in the different EU Member States investigate cases they are best placed to deal with locally. The exact allocation of Article 101 and 102 cases between the European Commission and the Member States' competition authorities is the subject of Council Regulation 1/2003 ([2003] OJ L1/1) ('Regulation 1') and its associated legislation and guides.

UK competition authorities may no longer apply Articles 101 and 102 TFEU, but these provisions remain relevant as they underpin retained EU law (see **1.3.3**).

The study of EU competition rules as they evolve continues to be of great importance for UK lawyers. Due to the extraterritorial reach of EU competition law (see **1.6**), many UK-based businesses continue to be subject to the EU's competition law regime.

1.3.2   UK competition law institutions

The main competition authority under the UK regime is the Competition and Markets Authority (CMA). Until 2014 the principal regulator was the Office of Fair Trading (the OFT); additionally the Competition Commission investigated mergers that gave rise to significant competition concerns (which were referred to it by the OFT) and also ruled on regulatory issues and market investigations. However, the Enterprise and Regulatory Reform Act 2013 provided for the establishment of the CMA as the UK's principal competition regulator. The Competition Commission and the competition functions of the OFT were thus merged into a unified authority, the CMA, which assumed its responsibilities on 1 April 2014.

The CMA investigates and pursues infringements under the CA 1998. The CMA is also concerned with the evaluation of mergers under the EA 2002. In addition to its roles under the main legislative provisions, the CMA provides information to businesses and legal advisers on its application of the UK's competition regime, as well as information on how to avoid breaches and the promotion of competition policy. In 2021, the CMA set up a new Digital Markets Unit to oversee online platforms and regulate companies with Strategic Market Status.

In addition to the CMA, specialist sectoral regulators within the UK also have powers (concurrent powers) to investigate breaches of the CA 1998. These regulators oversee certain sectors of the economy (most of which were formerly under public control). They include the Gas and Electricity Markets Authority (OFGEM), which regulates gas and electricity supply; the Office of Communications (OFCOM), which deals with the communications, broadcast and postal industries; the Water Services Regulation Authority (OFWAT), dealing with the water industry; and the Financial Conduct Authority (FCA), dealing with the financial services industry. In practice these regulators work closely with the CMA when assessing the appropriate action to take when a competition issue arises.

Prior to the UK's exit from the EU, the CMA and concurrent sectoral regulators also applied Articles 101 and 102 TFEU.

The following additional agencies are also involved in the UK competition regime:

* *Serious Fraud Office* – which also has the power to bring prosecutions for the criminal cartel offence under the EA 2002. However, prosecutions will generally be brought by the CMA.
* *The Competition Appeal Tribunal (CAT)* – considers competition and regulatory cases including appeals from decisions of the CMA and sectoral regulators under the CA 1998.

See also **4.7**, 'Private enforcement actions'.

1.3.3 Brexit

On 31 January 2020, the UK ceased being an EU Member State. However, until the end of the transition period on 31 December 2020 ('the Brexit transition period'), the UK was treated as if it remained a full member of the EU. The transition period is also known as the 'implementation period', and 31 December 2020 is referred to as 'implementation period completion day' (or 'IP completion day'). The end of the Brexit transition period on 31 December 2020 is when divergence between the UK and EU competition law systems begins.

The European Union (Withdrawal) Act 2018 (EUWA), as amended by the European Union (Withdrawal Agreement) Act 2020 (WAA), creates a new body of UK domestic law called 'retained EU law'. Retained EU law is the body of EU law in force at the end of the transition period, as amended by UK secondary legislation (statutory instruments) in order to operate appropriately in a UK legal context. In a competition law context, an important piece of secondary legislation amending retained EU law is the Competition (Amendment etc) (EU Exit) Regulations 2019 (the 'Competition SI').

The EUWA preserves the supremacy of retained EU law over pre-Brexit UK law. It even has a mechanism that ensures the supremacy of retained EU law over future UK legislation, which must be read and have effect subject to s 7A of the EUWA. Section 7A ensures that there is consistency with legislation passed 'from time to time' (in a similar way, s 2(1) of the European Communities Act 1972 used to ensure consistency with future EU laws). It would always be open to Parliament to override the mechanism in s 7A of the EUWA and pass a new statute that would take precedence over retained EU law.

When it comes to interpreting unmodified retained EU law, UK courts remain bound by retained case law which comprises retained domestic case law and retained EU case law. Lower courts, including the High Court, must interpret unmodified retained EU law in accordance with the decisions of the Court of Justice of the European Union (CJEU) made before IP completion day. Certain courts, namely the Supreme Court (or in Scotland the High Court of Justiciary), the Court of Appeal and certain other appellate courts are, however, able to depart from retained EU case law 'when it appears right to do'. As regards retained domestic case law, all courts are bound by the doctrine of precedent, with lower courts obliged to follow decisions of the higher courts and the Supreme Court able to depart from its own decisions 'when it appears right to do so'. It is thought that the UK courts are unlikely to diverge in their interpretation from that of the CJEU given the uncertainty this would create, except in areas where the EU pursues different objectives (such as single market integration). Nevertheless, differences may emerge. The UK courts are no longer able to refer questions of EU law to the European Court of Justice, an important driver for the consistent application of competition law throughout the EU.

1.4 AN INTRODUCTION TO EU COMPETITION LAW

UK competition law is best understood by studying the system of competition law in the EU, on which UK competition law is based. Outlined below is an overview of the sources and the rationale behind EU competition law. In addition, the institutions involved in the development of policy, legislation and enforcement of EU competition rules are considered.

Many of the UK's law firms continue to advise on EU competition law, with their competition law departments staffed by dual qualified lawyers (qualified in the UK and in an EU Member State).

1.4.1 Background to EU sources of law and institutions

1.4.1.1 EU Member States

The EU (or, as it was referred to then, the European Economic Community (EEC) and subsequently the European Community (EC)) was established by the Treaty of Rome in 1957 ('the Treaty' – subsequently renamed the European Community Treaty (the EC Treaty)). Initially there were six member countries (referred to as Member States), which membership over the years has increased to the present 27 countries. The current Member States of the EU are: France, Germany, Italy, Belgium, The Netherlands, Luxembourg, Denmark, Ireland, Greece, Spain, Portugal, Austria, Finland, Sweden, Estonia, Latvia, Lithuania, Poland, Czech Republic, Slovakia, Slovenia, Hungary, Cyprus, Malta, Bulgaria, Romania and Croatia.

The UK is no longer a Member State of the European Union, although EU competition law continued to apply during the Brexit transition period ending on 31 December 2020.

1.4.1.2 Treaty on the Functioning of the European Union

The original EC Treaty has been added to and amended over the years. These amendments have been numerous and beyond the scope of this textbook; however, for our purposes, it should be noted that two treaties (Amsterdam and Lisbon) had the effect of renumbering most of the EC Treaty articles. This can make the study of EU law, and hence EU competition law, rather confusing, as case law and publications may refer to the previous numbering system.

In terms of competition law, the only renumbering of which you need to be aware is that of the two main treaty articles we shall consider, which relate to (a) **anti-competitive agreements**; and (b) **abuse of dominance** (see **1.4.1.3**). Below is a table which explains the numbering changes to these treaty articles. Please note that the EC Treaty was renamed by the Lisbon Treaty and is now referred to as the Treaty on the Functioning of the European Union (TFEU). The EC was absorbed into the EU and ceased to exist as a separate entity.

	EC Treaty	**Treaty of Amsterdam renumbering**	**Lisbon Treaty renumbering (current)**
	1.1.1958 to 30.4.1999	1.5.1999 to 30.11.2009	1.12.2009 to present
Anti-competitive agreements	Article 85 EEC	Article 81 EC	**Article 101 TFEU**
Abuse of dominance	Article 86 EEC	Article 82 EC	**Article 102 TFEU**

The important thing to note regarding the renumbering outlined above is that the substantive wording (and hence law) has remained almost identical throughout these changes.

In this textbook, we use the current numbering – Articles 101 and 102 TFEU. However, please note that where previous numbering is used in an official document, such as secondary legislation or guidance note, the numbering will not be updated, unless it is an extract from a law report. This follows the approach of the European Commission.

1.4.1.3   The sources of EU competition law

The main provisions of EU competition law considered in this textbook are as follows:

- *Article 101 TFEU* prohibits '... agreements between undertakings, decisions by associations of undertakings and concerted practices which may affect trade between Member States and which have as their object or effect the prevention, restriction or distortion of competition within the internal market'.
- *Article 102 TFEU* prohibits '[a]ny abuse by one or more undertakings of a dominant position ... in so far as it may affect trade between Member States'.
- *The Merger Regulation 139/2004* provides that '[a] concentration which would significantly impede effective competition in the common market or in a substantial part of it, in particular as a result of the creation or strengthening of a dominant position, shall be declared incompatible with the common market'.

It is important to note that these three main provisions (or 'pillars') of competition law are a combination of Treaty articles and secondary legislation, such as the Merger Regulation, which was passed by the Council of Ministers. In addition to these three main legislative instruments, there is a huge amount of secondary legislation, guidance and policy notes which relates to EU competition law. We shall look at some of these other sources as we progress through the textbook.

1.4.1.4   The institutions of the European Union

These are some of the European Union's institutions:

- the Council of the European Union (often known as the Council of Ministers, or simply the Council);
- the European Commission;
- the European Parliament;
- the Court of Justice of the European Union.

Beyond the debate and creation of legislation, the European Parliament does not have a significant role to play in the field of competition law. We shall therefore concentrate on the other three institutions.

The Council of the European Union (the 'Council')

The Council is composed of one minister from each Member State. The Council is responsible for ensuring that the Treaty's objectives are attained, and is, with the European Parliament, the main legislative body of the EU.

The Council ensures the coordination of policies and, above all, takes decisions within the EU. This means that it is the Council rather than the Commission which is usually responsible for the final decision as to whether a piece of legislation should be passed.

However, in the field of competition law, the Council has delegated much of its decision-making powers to the Commission.

The European Commission (the 'Commission')

The Treaty requires the Commission to pursue infringements of EU law. It can, for example, take action before the European Court of Justice (see below) against Member States which breach EU law. It is also responsible for initiating European policy and legislation generally.

Each of the Commissioners is responsible for a particular area of EU competence. The Commission is divided into departments (known as Directorates-General) and executive agencies/services. DG COMP (formerly DG IV) is the Directorate-General that is responsible for competition law and is considered as one of the most important Directorate-Generals within the Commission.

The Directorate-General for Competition is itself divided into areas of responsibility according to the various fields of competition policy and enforcement, as well as along industry sectors. In this book, we shall, for ease of reference, refer to the Commission rather than DG COMP.

In the field of competition law, the Commission has been granted extensive powers to enforce EU competition policy, including the power to exact fines for any breach.

The Court of Justice of the European Union

The Court of Justice of the European Union (CJEU) was set up to ensure that EU law is observed throughout the Union. The CJEU consists of three courts, two of which hear competition cases. These are the Court of Justice, the highest court in the CJEU structure and commonly referred to as the 'ECJ', and the General Court (formerly the Court of First Instance (CFI)).

The CFI was established in the late 1980s because of the heavy workload faced by the ECJ. One of the areas assigned to the CFI was appeals from Commission decisions relating to competition law. It is possible to appeal the decision of the (now) General Court to the ECJ on a point of law only.

1.4.1.5   The European Economic Area (EEA)

The Agreement on the European Economic Area (EEA Agreement) came into force in 1994. It was entered into between the EU, all EU Member States and all European Free Trade Association (EFTA) States. Switzerland, although an EFTA State, failed to ratify the EEA Agreement and so is not part of the EEA. Following the accession of some EFTA States to the EU, the remaining non-EU Member States who are EEA members are Iceland, Liechtenstein and Norway.

The EEA Agreement contains competition provisions which follow those of the TFEU. Article 53 is the equivalent to Article 101 TFEU and prohibits anti-competitive agreements. Article 54 is the equivalent of Article 102 TFEU and prohibits abuse of a dominant position. Additionally, the rules provide for an equivalent system of merger control.

The EFTA Surveillance Authority and the Commission are responsible for enforcing EEA competition rules in the EEA. The EFTA Surveillance Authority enforces them in Iceland, Liechtenstein and Norway, and has equivalent powers and functions to those of the Commission, though the Commission handles all merger cases.

1.5   AN INTRODUCTION TO US ANTITRUST LAW

The most mature system of competition law is that of the United States, which began in 1890 with the enactment of the Sherman Antitrust Act, a response to the growing concentration of American industry in the last few decades of the 19th century. Much of this concentration took the form of trusts established to control corporations, hence the use of the term 'antitrust' in the US. United States antitrust laws were broadened, and the remedies for violations enhanced, in 1914 with the adoption of the Clayton Antitrust Act.

Initially, US courts interpreted the antitrust laws to promote a range of objectives, including not only the efficient operation of markets but also the elimination of large concentrations of economic power and the preservation of free choices for consumers and small businesses. Beginning in the 1970s, these objectives became more focused, as courts adopted the teachings of the 'Chicago School'.

This line of analysis, which is associated primarily with scholars and judges who have taught or studied at the University of Chicago, emphasises two major principles. First, the objective of the antitrust laws should be only to promote 'consumer welfare', defined as the benefits to consumers of an efficiently operating market, specifically lower prices and higher output. Secondly, intervention in the economy through the antitrust laws should be limited, because laws and judges generally are less effective in enhancing consumer welfare than the alternative of allowing the operation of the market to remove any imperfections.

In reaction to the rise of the Chicago School, a 'Post-Chicago School' has developed. This line of analysis largely accepts the first Chicago School principle, that antitrust laws should focus on promoting consumer welfare, but adherents of the Post-Chicago School are usually more inclined to find harm to consumers in certain conduct. They depart from the second principle, being less inclined to rely on market operations to eliminate harmful conduct. Today, debates over antitrust laws in the US are largely debates between these two schools of analysis.

1.5.1   Sources of US antitrust law

The major substantive provisions of US antitrust laws are found in the following statutes:

- *Section 1 of the Sherman Act* prohibits any 'contract, combination in the form of trust or otherwise, or conspiracy, in restraint of trade or commerce among the several States, or with foreign nations'. (15 USC §1)
- *Section 2 of the Sherman Act* makes it illegal to 'monopolize, or attempt to monopolize … any part of the trade or commerce among the several States, or with foreign nations'. (15 USC §2)
- *Section 7 of the Clayton Act* makes a merger or acquisition of shares or assets illegal if the effect of the transaction 'may be substantially to lessen competition, or to tend to create a monopoly'. (15 USC §18)
- *Section 8 of the Clayton Act* prohibits simultaneous service of an officer or director of a corporation on the board of a competitor, subject to certain exemptions (ie interlocking directorates).
- *The Robinson-Patman Act*, a 1936 amendment to the Clayton Act, makes it illegal 'to discriminate in price between different purchasers of commodities of like grade and quality' when certain effects on competition result. (15 USC §13(a))

These statutes are all federal laws and hence are applicable only to practices that affect commerce between the states and with foreign nations. Each of the 50 states also has enacted an antitrust law applicable to commerce involving that particular state. Most state laws include substantive provisions comparable to Sections 1 and 2 of the Sherman Act, or the courts of that state have determined that the applicable state law should be interpreted identically to its federal counterpart. Some states, however, either by statute or case law, diverge with federal law regarding certain issues. For example, Maryland (by statute) does not follow the federal approach regarding minimum resale price maintenance.

The US antitrust statutes are drafted with very broad language that gives little guidance to the actual application of these laws. The primary source of the meaning of these laws is the body of opinions issued by the federal courts that have interpreted and applied these laws over the course of more than a century. The most important opinions are those issued by the Supreme Court of the United States.

1.5.2   US antitrust law institutions

Four institutions have a major role in the enforcement of US antitrust laws:

- *The US Department of Justice* ('DOJ') is headed by the Attorney General, a member of the President's cabinet. Reporting directly to the Attorney General is an Assistant Attorney

General for the Antitrust Division, who has responsibility for both criminal and civil enforcement of the federal antitrust laws.

- *The Federal Trade Commission* (FTC) also has responsibility for the civil enforcement of the antitrust laws. Unlike the DOJ, the FTC is set up to operate independently of the President's administration. The Commission comprises five members, appointed to staggered seven-year terms. No more than three Commissioners may belong to the same political party. The FTC has primary responsibility for reviewing merger control filings under the Hart-Scott-Rodino Antitrust Improvements Act of 1976 (15 USC § 18a) for technical violations, although the FTC and DOJ have concurrent authority to review proposed transactions for any substantive antitrust concerns. The FTC also has the authority to enforce Section 5 of the Federal Trade Commission Act (FTC Act), which prohibits 'unfair methods of competition' and 'unfair or deceptive acts or practices' that affect commerce.

- *Private plaintiffs* are authorised by the Clayton Act, and by its counterparts under most state laws, to bring private suits for damages and injunctions. Unlike in most of Europe, private antitrust suits are prevalent in the United States. They play a major role in antitrust enforcement.

- *The attorneys general of the states* are responsible for both criminal and civil enforcement of the antitrust laws of their respective states. In addition, the state attorneys general have a right to bring civil suits under federal antitrust laws based upon injury to state government, to citizens of the state or to the general economy of the state. States also may review transactions, although merger control filings are not required at the state level. Some specific industries, such as health care and insurance, which varies by state, may have state level reporting requirements that contain antitrust considerations.

1.6 INTERNATIONAL ASPECTS

With the increasing globalisation of commercial markets, extraterritorial application of competition law regimes becomes inevitable. EU law applies wherever there is implementation in the EU or where there is an effect within the EU that is immediate, substantial and foreseeable (the 'qualified effects doctrine'). Thus an agreement between UK businesses which is implemented in the EU will be subject to EU competition law, even after Brexit.

Conduct occurring outside of the borders of the US can violate the Sherman Act. The Sherman Act applies to any conduct involving imports of goods or services into the US. If the conduct involves trade with foreign nations other than imports into the US, the Sherman Act applies only if the conduct has 'a direct, substantial, and reasonably foreseeable effect' on domestic US commerce or imports and if that effect gives rise to a Sherman Act claim (15 USC §6a).

In relation to merger cases, mergers affecting multiple jurisdictions can require several competition authorities to investigate the same merger. This can sometime cause friction between competition authorities, such as between US and EU competition authorities, about the correct analysis of mergers affecting both EU and US markets (see Boeing/McDonnell Douglas and GE/Honeywell). Post-Brexit, the UK CMA has also indicated an inclination to diverge from other authorities where it deems appropriate. Although some recent decisions have suggested an increase in authorities' willingness to reach divergent outcomes (see Microsoft/Activision), such friction between competition authorities remains relatively rare.

In addition to removing conflict, international cooperation has aided the detection and prosecution of worldwide infringements. Today, the cooperation and exchange of information between competition authorities has become one of the best methods of detection, and has resulted in prosecutions being made by numerous authorities for single worldwide infringements. Some of the main conduits for international cooperation relevant to the US, EU and UK are outlined below:

- *The International Competition Network* (ICN) has been established as a virtual network of competition authorities devoted exclusively to issues of competition law and policy. Its members now number more than 100 authorities worldwide.

- Many *bilateral and multilateral agreements* have been adopted between individual countries and jurisdictions. This includes two agreements between the EU and the US – the Cooperation Agreement of 23 September 1991 and the Positive Comity Agreement of 4 June 1998. Each year the Commission reports to the Council and the Parliament on the application of these agreements.

- The UK no longer benefits from the EU's bilateral agreements with other countries and is negotiating its own competition cooperation agreements. In September 2020, the UK and four other competition authorities signed a '*memorandum of understanding and model agreement*'. This sets out a framework for improving cooperation on competition investigations between the UK's Competition and Markets Authority (CMA), the Australian Competition and Consumer Commission (ACCC), the Competition Bureau of Canada (CBC), the New Zealand Commerce Commission (NZCC) and the Department of Justice (USDOJ) and Federal Trade Commission of the United States of America (USFTC).

- At the EU level, the *Commission notice on cooperation within the network of competition authorities* ([2004] OJ C101/43) (the 'Cooperation Notice') sets out the main elements of the cooperation between the Commission and the competition authority of the Member States in the European Competition Network (ECN). The most important aspect of the Cooperation Notice is how work is shared between the members of the ECN. The Cooperation Notice also deals with coordination, cooperation and information exchange between the authorities within the ECN. The UK's CMA is no longer part of the ECN.

- The *UK–EU Trade and Cooperation Agreement* is to be supplemented by provisions concerning the desirability of exchanging information in competition matters between the EU, the NCAs and the UK; and mutual assistance and cooperation in relation to enforcement proceedings.

CHAPTER 2

ANTI-COMPETITIVE AGREEMENTS, DECISIONS AND CONCERTED PRACTICES

AIMS

Chapter 2 introduces you to some basic concepts, focusing on the prohibitions set out in Chapter I of the Competition Act 1998 and Article 101 TFEU. It also briefly covers the approach under US antitrust law.

OBJECTIVES

After reading **Chapter 2**, you should be able to:

- appreciate in general terms the types of arrangements that are caught by the Chapter I and Article 101 prohibitions;

- appreciate that the UK's Chapter I is modelled on Article 101; and

- identify strategies for avoiding a breach of provisions prohibiting anti-competitive agreements.

2.1 THE ARTICLE 101 TFEU/CHAPTER I PROHIBITIONS

As Chapter I of the CA 1998 is modelled on Article 101 TFEU, we deal with Article 101 first.

Article 101 (see also **Appendix 1**) states:

1. The following shall be prohibited as incompatible with the internal market: all agreements between undertakings, decisions by associations of undertakings and concerted practices which may affect trade between Member States and which have as their object or effect the prevention, restriction or distortion of competition within the internal market, and in particular those which:

    (a) directly or indirectly fix purchase or selling prices or any other trading conditions;

    (b) limit or control production, markets, technical development, or investment;

    (c) share markets or sources of supply;

    (d) apply dissimilar conditions to equivalent transactions with other trading parties, thereby placing them at a competitive disadvantage;

    (e) make the conclusion of contracts subject to acceptance by the other parties of supplementary obligations which, by their nature or according to commercial usage, have no connection with the subject of such contracts.

2. Any agreements or decisions prohibited pursuant to this Article shall be automatically void.

3.   The provisions of paragraph 1 may, however, be declared inapplicable in the case of:

–   any agreement or category of agreements between undertakings;

–   any decision or category of decisions by associations of undertakings;

–   any concerted practice or category of concerted practices,

which contributes to improving the production or distribution of goods or to promoting technical or economic progress, while allowing consumers a fair share of the resulting benefit, and which does not:

(a)   impose on the undertakings concerned restrictions which are not indispensable to the attainment of these objectives;

(b)   afford such undertakings the possibility of eliminating competition in respect of a substantial part of the products in question.

2.1.1 Article 101(1) – the prohibition

The best way of dealing with Article 101(1) is to break it down into its constituent parts and to consider each in turn.

The same method should be used when considering the Chapter I prohibition under the CA 1998 as its provisions mirror those of Article 101(1) (see **2.2.2** for differences and **Appendix 2** for the text of the legislation).

2.1.1.1 Agreements between undertakings

Agreements and concerted practices

The term 'agreement' has been interpreted widely by the CJEU and covers all types of commercial arrangements, whether they are in writing or agreed verbally. The interpretation is wide enough to include arrangements that are non-legally binding. It also includes informal agreements. A meeting of minds or concurrence of wills is sufficient; for example it is sufficient that the undertakings concerned have expressed their joint intention to conduct themselves on the market in a specified way. Once there is an agreement, it is immaterial whether the intended course of action is followed through.

The term 'concerted practice' overlaps with that of 'agreement' in that both are used to describe informal agreements between undertakings. It is not legally necessary to distinguish between agreements and concerted practices since Article 101/Chapter I capture all collusion between undertakings, whatever the form.

However 'concerted practice' is a term of art, applied at the outmost boundary of conduct that will breach Article 101/Chapter I if the other elements of Article 101/Chapter I are present, to distinguish it from conduct that is independent and will not therefore breach Article 101/Chapter I. The classic description of a concerted practice is set out in the case of *Dyestuffs* (Case 48/69 *ICI v Commission* [1972] ECR 619), as being a form of coordination which '*knowingly substitutes practical cooperation ... for the risks of competition*'. Concerted practices, including *Dyestuffs*, are considered further at **2.1.1.3** below ('Boundary between concerted practices and parallel behaviour').

Undertakings

This term covers virtually all legal or natural persons carrying on economic or commercial activities. It therefore covers companies, partnerships and sole traders. It also includes non-profit making organisations (such as FIFA, the governing body of football in the Commission's case [1992] OJ L326/31) and public organisations carrying on economic or commercial activities (such as the Federal Employment Office in Case C-41/90 *Höfner and Elser v Macrotron GmbH* [1991] ECR I-1979).

Parent and subsidiary

For an agreement to come within Article 101/Chapter I, it must be between separate undertakings. Since parent and subsidiary cannot be expected to compete with each other, competition law takes a different approach to groups of companies than under many systems of company law. Under company law, each company will be regarded as a separate legal entity. Competition law looks at whether the undertakings form separate *economic* entities. As such, parent and subsidiary companies will generally be considered as one and the same economic entity, and therefore agreements between companies within the same group will not be 'between undertakings' for the purposes of Article 101/Chapter I. A subsidiary will form a single economic entity with its parent company if it does not enjoy autonomy to determine its own course of action on the market. In practice, the Commission and courts will look at the parent's level of control over the subsidiary, including shareholding, board representation and voting rights in determining whether the subsidiary does, or does not, operate as a separate economic entity.

Agency

On the same principle, 'pure' agency agreements, where the agent carries out the activity of the principal rather than acting as a separate economic entity, will generally fall outside Article 101/Chapter I (for more detail, see **6.2.2**).

Successor firms

The issue of successor firms concerns the extent to which the authorities can impose liability on undertakings that no longer exist, or which have become part of another organisation. Clearly, if an undertaking that has attracted liability can simply avoid the imposition of penalties by being merged into another entity, this would undermine the effectiveness of the regime.

Not unsurprisingly, the Commission and the CJEU have taken a robust approach with regard to successor firms. Where one entity succeeds another (for example in the case of a corporate reorganisation), the liability imposed on the former entity will be attributed to the successor firm (see Case 29, 30/83 *Compagnie Royale Asturienne des Mines SA and Rheinzink GmbH v Commission* [1984] ECR 1679). Needless to say, where a company proposes to take over another, it should ensure that extensive due diligence is undertaken to assess whether any latent liability for breaches of competition law exists.

2.1.1.2 Decisions by associations of undertakings

This category would include decisions taken by, for example, a trade association. Such decisions could clearly provide the potential for anti-competitive conduct by facilitating the coordination of market behaviour through, for example, price fixing. Once again, a decision by an association of undertakings need not be legally binding to be caught; a non-binding recommendation has been held to fall within Article 101 (see Case 96/82 IAZ *International Belgium NV v Commission* [1983] ECR 3369).

2.1.1.3 Boundary between concerted practices and parallel behaviour

As seen at **2.1.1.1**, the classic definition of a 'concerted practice' comes from the case of *Dyestuffs*. The ECJ described a concerted practice as a form of coordination between businesses which falls short even of an informal agreement, but which '*knowingly substitutes practical cooperation between them for the risks of competition*' (emphasis added).

The problem with establishing a concerted practice is one of evidence and intent. It can be very difficult to distinguish between coordinated conduct between undertakings capable of falling within Article 101/Chapter I, and independent, parallel behaviour by single undertakings which falls outside Article 101/Chapter I.

In terms of evidence, companies may well mirror the behaviour of a competitor. For example, imagine that there are two operators of cross-Channel ferry services from Dover (in South-East England) to Calais (in France). Every now and then, one of the operators raises its prices – these prices are publicly available. A few days later the other operator raises its prices broadly in line with the initial price rise. There may, of course, be a perfectly innocent explanation for this parallel behaviour, for example the cost of fuel has increased and the increase is passed on to passengers in higher prices. Alternatively, parallel pricing behaviour could be evidence of illegal cooperation between the two ferry operators, punishable under Article 101/Chapter I. This simple example gives some idea of the difficulties competition authorities have in gaining sufficient evidence to find concerted practices under Article 101/Chapter I.

There are two leading cases which illustrate the courts' approach to concerted practices and parallel pricing.

The first is *Dyestuffs*, which we have already mentioned. The Commission issued a decision finding that price increases in the dyestuffs industry were the result of concerted practices. Each increase was announced in advance by one of the companies in the industry and followed simultaneously by the others. The companies argued that this was not a concerted practice but was a merely an inevitable and acceptable reaction by firms to market conditions. They argued that the dyestuffs market was an 'oligopoly'; an oligopoly occurs where the market is controlled by a small number of undertakings. In an oligopoly, parallel conduct is often regarded as a natural economic phenomenon, and it does not breach Article 101/Chapter I. The ECJ analysed the dyestuffs market and details of a number of simultaneous price increases that had taken place over several years. Having identified the suspicious price increases, the ECJ then had to consider whether they constituted a prohibited concerted practice or whether, owing to the nature of the market, they were merely an acceptable reaction by one company to the others' price increases. Parallel pricing is not conclusive evidence of a concerted practice, but will be strong evidence of one if, having regard to the specific features of the market concerned, the conditions of competition, including the prices charged, are different from those which would normally be expected if there were effective competition. The ECJ found that the dyestuffs market was not an oligopoly and therefore concluded that the only plausible explanation for the parallel pricing was the existence of a concerted practice – that which 'knowingly substitutes practical cooperation' between competitors 'for the risks of competition'.

The other leading case is Cases 89 *et al*/85 *Ahlström Osakeyhtiö v Commission* [1993] ECR I-1307 (*Woodpulp*). The *Woodpulp* case involved several non-EU producers of woodpulp allegedly coordinating woodpulp prices in the EU. In reaching a decision against the woodpulp producers, the Commission had relied on simultaneous quarterly price announcements as evidence of a concerted practice. This decision was challenged before the ECJ. The ECJ concluded that the woodpulp market was an oligopoly. The market was very transparent, as woodpulp buyers shopped around and informed the producers what the other producers were charging. The businesses operating on the market therefore legitimately knew a lot about each others' terms and conditions, including their pricing strategies. In a true oligopoly, price competition will play a very limited role on the market. Accordingly the ECJ found that the woodpulp market was indeed an oligopoly and, as such, the coordinated pricing strategy could be explained by factors other than the existence of a concerted practice.

In conclusion, although parallel pricing might well be an indication of the existence of a concerted practice, the particular circumstances of the market must always be considered. Where the market is an oligopoly, evidence of parallel pricing will not be sufficient in itself to prove the existence of a concerted practice. Also, while a concerted practice can be a very loose arrangement, the judgment in *Woodpulp* does require some active, or knowing, cooperation between the parties. This cooperation does not have to be verbal, but can be made either directly or indirectly between the parties, and clearly can be made outside a formal or informal agreement.

2.1.1.4   Effect on trade between Member States

This requirement is specific to the EU system of law, although the UK system applies a similar requirement (effect on trade in the UK – see **2.2.2**).

The requirement for an effect on trade between Member States applies not only to Article 101, but also to Article 102 cases (see **Chapter 3**). The requirement is *'may affect trade'* and will be satisfied whenever there is a potential influence on the pattern of trade between Member States, as discussed below. An agreement does not necessarily have to have an actual effect. As such, this is a very low threshold which has been generously interpreted by the Commission and courts, thus ensuring that all anti-competitive behaviour that potentially impacts on the internal EU market is caught under Articles 101 and 102.

The effect on trade rule has practical consequences in terms of the competition authorities' jurisdiction. Where anti-competitive behaviour does not have an effect on trade between EU Member States, it will not be caught by Articles 101 or 102 but may still be caught by the domestic competition law of individual Member States. When national competition authorities of EU Member States apply domestic competition law and there is an effect on trade between EU Member States, they must also apply Articles 101 or 102 (see **4.3.1.2**).

To ensure that the concept of effect on trade is fully understood and applied consistently between the Member States, the Commission published *Guidelines on the effect on trade concept contained in Articles 81 and 82 of the Treaty*, Commission Notice [2004] OJ C101/81 (the 'Effect on Trade Guidelines'). The Effect on Trade Guidelines (as is common in all guidelines) in part reflect the case law but also set out the Commission's position. Note that Commission guidance notices are not legally binding on the CJEU, national courts and national competition authorities, though they are highly persuasive. However, the Commission is effectively bound by its guidelines in force in its everyday decision-making process, because it is likely to be estopped from imposing a fine or remedy in respect of activities which are effectively condoned in its notices.

'May affect trade'

The Effects on Trade Guidelines on 'may affect' largely echo the position in Case 56/65 *Société Technique Minière v Maschinenbau Ulm GmbH* [1966] ECR 235, [1966] CMLR 357, where it was held that:

> it must be possible to foresee with a sufficient degree of probability on the basis of a set of objective factors of law or fact that the agreement in question may have an *influence, direct or indirect, actual or potential, on the pattern of trade between Member States*. (emphasis added)

Note that the 'pattern of trade' between Member State is capable of being affected even if the agreement or conduct takes place within a single Member State, for example if its effect is to reinforce the compartmentalisation of national markets (Case 8/72 *Cementhandelaren v Commission* [1972] ECR 977, [1973] CMLR 7).

There may be an effect on trade even if parties are located outside the EU, where the agreement is implemented within the EU or the practice produces effects within the EU, and the agreement or practice is capable of affecting cross-border economic activity inside the EU (see para 101 of the Effect on Trade Guidelines). For example, agreements entered into between UK businesses that are implemented not only in the UK (as a non-Member State) but also within the EU may be caught by Article 101 (see **1.6** for the EU's qualified effects doctrine).

'Not appreciably affecting trade' (NAAT)

Of particular importance in the Effect on Trade Guidelines is the 'no appreciable affectation of trade' rule or 'NAAT' rule. This helpful rule applies in Article 101 cases: agreements are regarded by the Commission in principle not to appreciably affect trade if the combined market shares of the parties to the agreement do not exceed 5% on the relevant market, and:

(a)   in the case of horizontal agreements (between parties at the same level of trade), the parties' combined turnover in the EU does not exceed €40 million; or

(b)   in the case of vertical agreements (between parties at different levels of trade), the supplier's turnover in the EU does not exceed €40 million. (para 52 of the Effect on Trade Guidelines)

The NAAT rule applies to Article 101 cases and is not relevant to Article 102 cases.

Please note that the rules on effect on trade between Member States (including the NAAT rule), which are effectively rules to demarcate the EU's jurisdiction, differ from the substantive rules that consider whether agreements have an appreciable effect on competition (see **2.1.1.7**).

2.1.1.5   Object or effect

This section is relevant to both Article 101 and Chapter I.

It is crucial for legal practitioners to identify whether restrictions are 'by object' or 'by effect'.

If an agreement between undertakings has as its object the prevention, restriction or distortion of competition, it will be caught by Article 101/Chapter I. It will not be necessary to prove its effects on competition on the market (Case C-226/11 *Expedia Inc v Autorité de la Concurrence* [2013] 4 CMLR 14). This contrasts with 'effects' restrictions, where it must be shown that there is an appreciable effect on competition on the market for Article 101/Chapter I to apply (see further **2.1.1.7** below).

Restrictions of competition by object are those that are so injurious to competition that they are regarded by their very nature as producing negative effects on the market. These will include the most serious types of collusion between parties, and how they are assessed will depend on whether the relationship between the parties is horizontal or vertical (for more detail, see **Chapters 5** and **6**).

In regard to horizontal relationships, where the parties are actual or potential competitors (for example two manufacturers), restrictions by object include:

(a)   fixing prices, which can include exchanging pricing information;

(b)   market sharing;

(c)   bid-rigging; and

(d)   limiting output or sales.

In terms of vertical relationships, where the parties are non-competitors (for example a supplier and a distributor), restrictions by object include:

(a)   most forms of resale price maintenance; and

(b)   export bans (such as preventing a distributor from exporting goods outside its allotted territory).

The categories of restrictions by object are set out in the *Commission Staff Working Document Guidance on restrictions of competition 'by object' for the purpose of defining which agreements may benefit from the De Minimis Notice* (SWD (2014) 198 final). This does not preclude the Commission or CJEU from categorising new forms of agreement as restrictions by object and must be read in light of the subsequent case law of the CJEU.

Parties that engage in an objects restriction can attempt to justify their action under the Article 101(3)/CA 1998, s 9 exemption. It would be for the parties to prove that the pro-competitive effects of the arrangement outweigh any anti-competitive effect. In most circumstances this will be an extremely difficult burden to discharge; however, the possibility remains (see Case T-17/93 *Matra Hachette v Commission* [1994] ECR II-595). This differs from the US system (see **2.3.1** below), where the finding of a *per se* offence (the US equivalent of an objects infringement) is final in terms of imposing liability.

A restriction that does not fall within the category of a restriction 'by object' is a restriction 'by effect'. In respect of 'effects' restrictions, Article 101/Chapter I will apply to restrictions that can be shown to have the effect of preventing, restricting or distorting competition (see **2.1.1.6**) and this effect is 'appreciable' (see **2.1.1.7**).

The examples of prohibited agreements listed in Article 101(1)(a)–(e) (and in the UK, s 2(2) of the CA 1998) are just that – examples, rather than the starting point in an analysis. The list includes both object and effects restrictions.

2.1.1.6 Prevention, restriction or distortion of competition

Again, this section is relevant to both Article 101 and Chapter I.

Not all restrictions will be anti-competitive. Competition law is concerned with economic effects and not with all restrictions contained in commercial arrangements. For example, a confidentiality clause contains a restriction on revealing confidential information but this does not usually give rise to a restriction of competition. In the absence of a clear anti-competitive object (see restrictions by object, above), the effect of the arrangement as a whole needs to be considered, on competition in the relevant economic market(s) affected by the arrangement.

The terms 'prevention', 'restriction' and 'distortion' are used relatively interchangeably, and evidence of the least anti-competitive of the terms, a distortion, is still enough to trigger Article 101/Chapter I.

Restrictions that may prevent, restrict or distort competition are considered in detail in **Chapters 5** and **6**.

2.1.1.7 Appreciable effect on competition

This section is relevant to both Article 101 and Chapter I.

As indicated above (at **2.1.1.5**), outside the classification of an arrangement as an object infringement, it must be shown that there is an appreciable effect on competition on the market before Article 101/Chapter I can apply.

Again, please note that the question of whether agreements or restrictions have an appreciable effect *on competition* (considered in this section) is separate from the question of whether agreements or practices have an appreciable effect *on trade between Member States* (considered at **2.1.1.4**).

In Case 5/69 *Völk v Vervaecke* [1969] ECR 295, the first case to consider appreciability of effects on competition, or *de minimis*, the ECJ stated that:

> an agreement falls outside the prohibition in Article [101(1)] where it has only an insignificant effect on the market, taking into account the weak position which the persons concerned have on the market of the product in question.

The European Commission's *Notice on agreements of minor importance which do not appreciably restrict competition under Article 101(1) of the Treaty on the Functioning of the European Union (De Minimis Notice)* [2014] OJ C 291/01 (NAOMI) (an extract of which is reproduced at **Appendix 5**) outlines the parameters of the *de minimis* doctrine. As such it clears certain prima facie anti-competitive agreements from the scope of Article 101 if the parties' market share (and therefore the impact on competition) is insignificant, assessed by reference to the following market share thresholds:

(a)   agreements between actual or potential competitors (horizontal agreements) – the *aggregate* (combined) market share of the parties to the agreement does not exceed 10%; or

(b)   agreements between non-competitors (vertical agreements) – the market share *held by each* of the parties to the agreement does not exceed 15%.

These thresholds are also applied by the UK competition authorities. For instance, para 3.56 of the CMA's guidance on horizontal cooperation (see **5.3.1**) states:

> In determining whether an agreement is an appreciable restriction of competition for the purposes of the Chapter I prohibition, the CMA will have regard to the European Commission's approach as set out in its Notice on Agreements of Minor Importance (also known as the De Minimis Notice).

Note that the thresholds for vertical agreements are much more generous than those for horizontal agreements, which generally give rise to greater competition concerns (see **Chapter 5**).

It follows from the discussion of restrictions by object above (at **2.1.1.5**) that since object restrictions do not require an analysis of effects, an arrangement that contains object restrictions will not benefit from the *de minimis* doctrine. Accordingly, NAOMI does not apply to agreements that contain restrictions by object or hardcore restrictions, such as price-fixing or export bans. For the main restrictions by object, see **2.1.1.5** above. Restrictions that are listed as hardcore restrictions in a block exemption are also generally considered to constitute restrictions by object.

2.1.2   Article 101(2) – unenforceability

This section is relevant to EU and UK systems of competition law.

Article 101(2) provides that any agreement or decision in breach of Article 101(1) is automatically void; in other words, it is of no effect. Section 2(4) of the CA 1998 contains the equivalent UK provision. A strict construction of Article 101(2) would result in the whole agreement being declared void and unenforceable. However, the ECJ has held that the nullity only applies to any clause in the agreement affected by the prohibition. The agreement as a whole will be void only where those clauses are not severable from the remaining terms of the agreement, which will depend on the national rules as to severance under the governing law of the contract.

The sanction of nullity is important where parties seek to enforce their agreement before national courts. When the agreement contains a restriction caught by the Article 101(1) prohibition and is therefore null and void under Article 101(2), the courts may be prepared to sever the offending clause(s) and enforce the remainder of the agreement. The English law on severance, broadly speaking, ensures that illegal clause(s) can be severed if the remaining agreement still reflects accurately the agreement originally reached by the parties.

For example, many agreements between beer suppliers and pub landlords are in the form of property leases (beer leases) and require the tenant (the pub landlord) to purchase all of its beer exclusively from the beer supplier. This restriction on competition (known as the beer tie) may be caught by Article 101 and/or Chapter I. However, beer leases containing a tie caught by Article 101 have been enforced because the clause containing the tie could be excised (or struck out) under the blue pencil rule. The tie was not the 'heart and soul' of the agreement (*Inntrepreneur Estates Ltd v Mason* [1993] 45 EG 130; *Inntrepreneur Estates Ltd v Boyes* [1993] 47 EG 140).

It is worth noting that the sanction of nullity may be of no importance in certain cases, such as cartels, where the members count on their own mechanisms to enforce collusion. In such cases, the risk of investigation and imposition of fines will have a more dissuasive effect (see **Chapter 4**).

2.1.3 Article 101(3) TFEU – the exemption

As we have seen, although anti-competitive arrangements may potentially infringe Article 101(1), they may be exempted under Article 101(3). The CA 1998 contains equivalent provisions and the discussion below applies equally to the UK system.

To be exempted, an agreement must satisfy four conditions contained in Article 101(3)/CA 1998, s 9, two positive and two negative. The two positive conditions are:

(a) the agreement must contribute to an improvement in the production or distribution of goods or the promotion of technical or economic progress; and

(b) consumers will get a fair share of the resulting benefit.

The two negative conditions are:

(a) the agreement does not impose on the undertakings restrictions which are not indispensable; and

(b) the agreement will not afford them the possibility of substantially eliminating competition.

The important thing to note is that exemption under Article 101(3)/CA 1998, s 9 can be achieved in two different ways. The first is by an individual exemption where the conditions above will be applied to the terms of the agreement. Secondly, exemption can be achieved by way of a block exemption. Under a block exemption, the four conditions above are not expressly applied to the agreement; however, the terms of the block exemption will have taken these four conditions into consideration when being established.

Both of these exemptions are considered in more detail below.

2.1.3.1 Individual exemption

Under the system in force prior to May 2004, if an agreement was to benefit from the effects of an individual exemption, it had first to be notified to the Commission. This notification requirement was extremely resource intensive for the Commission and the parties, requiring the submission of a great deal of detailed economic and business information. It has now been replaced by a system of self-assessment.

This was achieved in the EU as part of the main implementing Regulation for Articles 101 and 102, Council Regulation 1/2003 ([2003] OJ L1/1) ('Regulation 1'), an extract of which is reproduced in **Appendix 4**. An equivalent amendment was made to the CA 1998.

2.1.3.2 Individual assessment

Agreements, decisions and concerted practices caught by Article 101(1)/Chapter I which satisfy all four conditions mentioned above at **2.1.3** are exempted from the prohibitions in Article 101(1)/Chapter I. Undertakings have to make their own assessment of the compatibility of their arrangements with the four conditions. It is for the undertaking or association of undertakings invoking the benefit of an exemption to prove that the four conditions are met.

The *Commission Guidelines on the application of Article 81(3) of the Treaty* (Commission Notice [2004] OJ C101/97) set out a framework of economic questions that parties should ask themselves for analysing whether the four conditions are met and that the agreement under consideration is therefore capable of exemption. Other guidelines contain further specific guidance, such as the EU and UK guidance on vertical agreements (see **Chapter 6**).

The outbreak of the novel coronavirus disease (COVID-19) has required forms of co-ordination which would normally be prohibited by Article 101(1)/Chapter I and are not capable of exemption under the four criteria in Article 101(3)/CA 1998, s 9. In such circumstances, there is no 'free pass' from the application of competition law. Some derogations, however, are possible. For example, the Commission has derogated from the application of competition law to allow cooperation in the agri-food sector during the outbreak of COVID-19 (4 May 2020 derogations under Article 222 of Regulation 1308/2013). In the UK, elements of the CA 1998 may be suspended by the UK government given exceptional and compelling reasons in the public interest under para 7(1) of Sch 3 to the CA 1998. For example, operators of ferries to and from the Isle of Wight were required to work together to manage staff absences while running an essential service despite reduced demand during the COVID-19 crisis.

2.1.3.3   Block exemption

Block exemptions outline a set of criteria within which an agreement is automatically exempted from Article 101(1)/CA 1998, s 2. Block exemptions are extremely useful for both the parties entering into an agreement and their legal advisers as they provide a measure of legal certainty. Should the parties' agreement fall within Article 101(1) (and/or CA 1998, s 2), it is automatically exempted under Article 101(3) (and/or CA 1998, s 9), provided the agreement is drafted in such a way as to meet the criteria of the block exemption. Block exemptions relate to a number of sectors and agreement types. It should be noted that many block exemptions are accompanied by guidelines which provide an invaluable source of information on how the authorities will interpret the exemption.

The Commission and EU Member States are empowered to withdraw the benefit of a block exemption regulation in certain situations. A Member State is entitled to do so when a particular agreement has effects incompatible with Article 101(1) in its territory, or in a part thereof, which has all the characteristics of a distinct geographic market. Under s 6(6)(c) of the CA 1998, the CMA may cancel a block exemption in respect of a particular agreement.

Block exemptions are time limited and are generally renewed after expiry, following consultation with stakeholders. Occasionally, new block exemptions are significantly different from their predecessors.

Prior to the end of the Brexit implementation period, UK agreements generally benefitted from the Commission's block exemptions under the CA 1998's regime for 'parallel exemptions'. EU block exemptions are no longer 'parallel exemptions' but are copied into UK law as 'retained exemptions' under s 10 of the CA 1998. For example, Regulation 316/2014 on technology transfer agreements, considered in **Chapter 8**, is a 'retained exemption' under s 10 of the CA 1998 and therefore continues to apply in the UK.

The UK is gradually replacing 'retained exemptions' with UK-specific block exemptions that are tailored to the needs of UK businesses and consumers. For example, the UK vertical block exemption, considered in **Chapter 6**, came into force on 1 June 2022. The equivalent EU vertical block exemption, which also came into force on 1 June 2022, is no longer a 'retained exemption' or part of UK law.

Block exemptions, all the accompanying guidelines and information relating to any consultation process can be found on the Commission's and CMA's websites.

2.1.4   Technique for avoiding the scope of the Article 101/Chapter I prohibitions

We have considered the various elements relating to Article 101/Chapter I, the accompanying secondary legislation and case law. We have seen that some arrangements, such as between parent and subsidiary, will generally fall outside Article 101(1)/Chapter I. We have seen that where there are no 'object' restrictions, Article 101(1)/Chapter I may not apply to restrictions 'by effect' if the agreement is *'de minimis'*. We then saw that agreements that do fall within Article 101(1)/Chapter I may benefit from a block exemption, or individual exemption, under Article 101(3)/CA 1998, s 9. In Article 101 cases, we considered the *'no appreciable affectation of trade'* rule.

Here we consider a methodology that a legal adviser may adopt when considering how to avoid the scope of Article 101/Chapter I when it appears that an agreement contains restrictions on competition.

2.1.4.1 Does the agreement have an appreciable effect on competition?

As outlined above (at **2.1.1.7**), outside an objects infringement, there must be an appreciable effect on competition before Article 101(1)/Chapter I may apply. Accordingly, when assessing an agreement, a legal adviser should assess whether the agreement might benefit from the Commission's De Minimis Notice (NAOMI). This will involve a consideration of the parties' market shares (see **2.1.1.7**).

If the agreement cannot benefit from NAOMI, for example because there are object restrictions or because the market share of the parties is too high, then the legal adviser will have to look for other ways in which the agreement may fall outside the scope of Article 101/ Chapter I.

The 'no appreciable affectation of *trade*' (NAAT) rule, which is separate from the 'appreciable effect on *competition*' rule, may also help in Article 101 cases.

2.1.4.2 Can the agreement benefit from a block exemption?

The next option for the legal adviser is to assess whether the agreement might benefit from a block exemption. As a general rule, block exemptions have higher market share thresholds than those contained in NAOMI. It is important that the legal adviser identifies the correct block exemption for the agreement in consideration. One of the most commonly applicable block exemptions is the Vertical Agreements Block Exemption considered in **Chapter 6**.

Generally, block exemptions will not apply where the agreement contains hardcore restrictions. If the agreement cannot benefit from either NAOMI or a block exemption, there is one last resort open to the legal adviser.

2.1.4.3 Can the agreement benefit from an individual exemption?

We have already considered the four elements contained in Article 101(3)/CA 1998, s 9 (see **2.1.3** above). Relying on an individual exemption under Article 101(3)/CA 1998, s 9 has the drawback that the parties must self-assess their agreement and bear the burden of proving that the criteria for an individual exemption are met. This may involve extra costs and there is no guarantee that the competition authorities or courts will follow the conclusion of the parties that the agreement qualifies for individual exemption. Accordingly, it is seen as a last resort. However, in the case where parties have large market shares, or even where the agreement contains hardcore restrictions, individual exemption is the only option (short of amending the agreement).

2.2 THE UK COMPETITION ACT 1998

The Competition Act 1998 (CA 1998) came into force on 1 March 2000 and introduced into UK law a competition law regime modelled on Articles 101 and 102.

Using powers in the European Union (Withdrawal) Act 2018 (EUWA), the Government passed the Competition (Amendment etc) (EU Exit) Regulations 2019 (the 'Competition SI'). The Competition SI amends legislation such as the CA 1998 to enable the transition to a UK domestic regime of competition law (see also **1.3.3**). The CMA issued Guidance on the functions of the CMA after the end of the Transition Period (CMA125) to explain these and other provisions.

2.2.1 The Chapter I prohibition

The Chapter I prohibition (reproduced at **Appendix 2**) is contained in s 2 of the CA 1998 and reflects Article 101. Accordingly, subject to the point covered at **2.2.2.1** below (effect on trade), the prohibition set out in s 2(1) is virtually word for word the same as Article 101. Also, s 2(4) provides that any agreement that breaches the Chapter I prohibition is void.

Until the end of the Brexit transition period, s 60 of the CA 1998 required that UK law should follow (where possible) the EU competition rules and case law. Section 60 has now been repealed.

A new s 60A now requires the competition authorities to ensure consistency with case law laid out by the TFEU and CJEU that pre-date the end of the transition period. The competition authorities must in addition have regard to decisions and statements made by the European Commission that pre-date the end of the transition period and have not been withdrawn. The competition authorities may depart from CJEU case law that pre-dates the end of the transition period where appropriate in certain circumstances, such as differences between UK and EU markets or developments in generally accepted principles of competition law analysis.

There is no requirement to ensure consistency with EU law applicable after the end of the transition period, although competition authorities may have regard to it. For example, the CMA has stated that it 'will have regard' to the European Commission's De Minimis Notice (see **2.1.1.7**) and Market Definition Notice (see **3.3.1**).

From the end of 2023, there is no longer any requirement on the UK competition authorities to follow general EU law principles, such as the principle of proportionality and the right to be heard (Retained EU Law (Revocation and Reform) Act 2023, s 4).

As in the EU system, the CMA (and before it the OFT) has produced numerous guides and notices outlining its approach to the application of the CA 1998. These are an invaluable source of information for parties affected by UK competition rules and can be obtained from the CMA's website.

2.2.2   Differences between the UK and EU systems

2.2.2.1   Effect on trade

The most obvious difference from Article 101 TFEU is that the CA 1998 applies to:

> agreements between undertakings, decisions by associations of undertakings or concerted practices which— (a) may affect trade within the United Kingdom ... (CA 1998 s 2(1))

The Chapter I prohibition applies only if trade within the UK is affected.

There may be an effect on trade in the UK even if the parties are not located in the UK, but their agreement is to be implemented in the UK (CA 1998, s 2(3)).

Does effect on trade within the UK need to be appreciable?

There has been some judicial disagreement as to whether the effect on trade within the UK needs to be appreciable. (Note that this is not the same question as whether the agreement or restrictions it contains have an appreciable effect on competition.) Since the EU doctrine 'not appreciably affecting trade' is primarily for jurisdictional purposes, there was arguably no necessity to import it into UK law. This was the CAT's view in *Aberdeen Journals Limited v The Office of Fair Trading* [2003] CAT 11. However, this view was put into question in two subsequent cases: *P&S Amusements Ltd v Valley House Leisure Ltd* [2006] EWHC 1510 (Ch) and *Pirtek (UK) Ltd v Joinplace Ltd* [2010] EWHC 1641 (Ch).

For practical purposes, the CMA's assessment will focus on whether an agreement has an appreciable effect on competition since, if it does, the agreement will also affect trade within the UK. The view of the CMA is set out in its Guide, OFT 401: Agreements and Concerted Practices: 'in practice it is very unlikely that an agreement which appreciably restricts competition within the United Kingdom does not also affect trade within the United Kingdom'.

The investigatory powers of the Commission and CMA are similar and will be considered in more detail in **Chapter 4.**

2.2.2.2 Points of divergence after Brexit

Significant points of divergence between the UK and EU systems are unlikely to emerge for some time given the similarities in competition law analysis between the two regimes, and the need to minimise the difficulty for businesses in complying with different (and potentially inconsistent) sets of rules.

Where EU documents expire, such as EU block exemptions which have a finite life, the UK has introduced new documents and some differences have emerged (see for example the vertical agreements block exemption regime discussed in **Chapter 6**).

2.2.2.3 Technique for avoiding the scope of the Chapter I prohibition

We considered above the methodology that legal advisers may apply to avoid a breach of Article 101/Chapter I (see **2.1.4**).

The UK system provides an additional method for avoiding some of the consequences of breach of the Chapter I prohibition. Section 39 of the CA 1998 provides a 'limited immunity' from the Chapter I prohibition for what it refers to as 'small agreements'. This means that the agreement is immune from penalties (ie fines) under s 36. A 'small agreement' is one where the parties' joint turnover does not exceed £20 million. It is very important to note, however, that a 'price-fixing agreement' cannot be a small agreement (s 39(1)(b)).

2.3 THE SHERMAN ACT, SECTION 1

The US counterpart to Article 101 is Section 1 of the Sherman Act (which is reproduced at **Appendix 3**), which prohibits any 'contract, combination in the form of trust or otherwise, or conspiracy, in restraint of trade' (15 USC §1). Two elements are necessary to find a violation of Section 1.

First, Section 1 requires some form of agreement or concert of action among two or more separate persons or entities. Unilateral conduct by a single firm cannot violate Section 1 (nor can it fall within Article 101 or within the Chapter I prohibition). The agreement does not need to be explicit or written, but rather can be implied. It can be horizontal, meaning that the parties are at the same level of distribution. It can also be vertical, meaning that the parties are at different levels, such as an agreement between a manufacturer and the retail dealers of its products. The parties must be separate entities. A corporation cannot violate Section 1 through agreements with its employees or its controlled subsidiaries.

Secondly, the agreement must form a restraint of trade. Recognising that all contracts impose some measure of restraint on trade, the Supreme Court ruled, early in the history of the Sherman Act, that Section 1 prohibited only 'unreasonable' restraints of trade (*Standard Oil Co v United States*, 221 US 1, 60, 65 (1911)). An agreement imposes an unreasonable restraint when its overall effect is to impair competition.

2.3.1 Per se violations

Some categories of agreements have been deemed *per se* violations of Section 1, which means that the agreement is of the type that is deemed to be so pernicious to competition and consumers that it almost always harms competition and can be deemed illegal without considering evidence of the purpose or effect of the particular agreement. No justification is possible for such agreement.

The most common form of *per se* violation is a cartel agreement: a horizontal agreement among actual or potential competitors to set the prices at which they sell their goods or services. Agreements among competitors that have the same purpose and effect as raising or stabilising prices, such as an agreement on the volume of sales or output, are also *per se* violations. Parties to cartel agreements cannot avoid liability by contending that their agreement was ineffective, that they set reasonable prices or that the agreement was necessary to avoid a purportedly greater harm, such as ruinous competition.

Other than cartels, courts apply the *per se* rule to only a few types of agreements. Among these are group boycotts, which are discussed at **5.4.2** below, and tying arrangements, which are discussed at **6.4.2** below. In general, the category of *per se* offences is small, and courts have shown reluctance to expand it, other than for variations on cartel agreements. In fact, even the nominal *per se* analysis for certain types of conduct have evolved to function more like the 'Rule of Reason' (discussed further below).

2.3.2   The Rule of Reason

Outside of cartel agreements, group boycotts and tying arrangements, courts rarely find that an agreement is *per se* unreasonable. Instead, courts consider evidence of the purpose and effect of the particular agreement, and find an antitrust violation only if on balance the effect of the agreement is more harmful to competition than beneficial to it. This analysis is known as the 'Rule of Reason'.

Certain forms of horizontal agreements have been held subject to the Rule of Reason, including the following:

(a)   joint ventures between competitors;

(b)   group purchasing arrangements;

(c)   industry self-regulatory bodies; and

(d)   sports leagues.

In the past, various forms of vertical agreements were deemed *per se* illegal. Under the influence of the Chicago School, the US Supreme Court has found virtually all forms of vertical agreements subject to the Rule of Reason, including agreements between a manufacturer and the wholesalers or retailers of its products that impose exclusive resale territories, exclusive classes of customers, maximum resale prices and even minimum resale prices (*Leegin Creative Leather Products, Inc v PSKS, Inc*, 551 US 277 (2007)). As discussed previously, some state laws, whether by statute or jurisprudence, diverge from the federal approach regarding certain issues, specifically minimum resale price maintenance.

In a Rule of Reason assessment, the plaintiff bears the burden of establishing that the alleged restraint has, or likely will have, a substantial anti-competitive effect. If established, the burden of proof then shifts to the defendant to establish that the alleged restraint or conduct at issue had pro-competitive benefits that outweighed any potential harm. To be successful, plaintiffs must counter defendants' arguments by establishing that the restraint was not reasonably necessary to achieve the intended benefits and that the harms outweigh any benefits.

Thus, in a Rule of Reason case, the court's job is to assess the extent to which the agreement both restrains competition and enhances competition. For example, in the case of a vertical agreement imposing exclusive territories on retailers, the agreement clearly restrains competition among retailers of the manufacturer's products, but it might enhance the competitiveness of those products against other brands by assuring retailers that they can invest in product promotion without the fear of nearby retailers taking a free ride on their investments.

In striking the balance in a Rule of Reason analysis, courts will consider whether the defendant possesses market power, meaning the ability to raise prices above the levels of a competitive market. If a defendant lacks market power, the court likely will conclude that its agreements do not have the capacity to harm competition and therefore do not violate the

Rule of Reason. Market power is determined by reference to market share, plus other factors such as barriers to entry and the general competitive conditions of the industry. No rules or presumptions exist on market share. In practice, courts likely will not find market power when a defendant holds less than a 30% share, and will usually require at least a 50% market share plus other indicia of market power.

Because the Rule of Reason depends ultimately on a balance of economic effects, its application is often imprecise. Some have argued that this imprecision tends to benefit defendants, because the party alleging a violation of Section 1, whether it is a government agency or a private plaintiff, bears the burden of proving that the negative effects on competition have the greater impact, and an inability to present sufficient evidence on that issue will result in the court dismissing the claim before trial.

ABUSE OF DOMINANCE

AIMS

Chapter 3 introduces you to the situations where competition laws seek to prevent dominant firms from using their dominant position in an anti-competitive manner. As the strength of a company (or 'undertaking') can be judged only by reference to the economic markets on which it operates, this chapter deals with the definition of markets as well as the concepts of dominance and abuse.

OBJECTIVES

After studying **Chapter 3**, you should be able to:

- understand in general terms how markets are defined;

- identify when an undertaking may be dominant;

- identify behaviour that may be abusive; and

- appreciate that the UK's Chapter II is modelled on Article 102.

3.1 WHY RULES ON ABUSE OF DOMINANCE?

There is something intuitively wrong about two or more firms agreeing to enter into a cartel, and very few people would argue in favour of such behaviour. We have already seen in **Chapter 2** the scope of the rules relating to such activity. However, it is arguably less obvious why competition rules need to address certain behaviour by a company that has a position of dominance. On one view, why should a company (or more correctly an undertaking) be prohibited from specific commercial activity just because it enjoys a dominant position? This seems particularly unfair where that undertaking became dominant by being the most competitive undertaking, or by introducing new and innovative products.

At the EU level, decisions made under the abuse of dominance rules have been some of the most controversial decisions made by the Commission and the courts. For example, Google was penalised for using its search engine to promote its own comparison shopping service, and for promoting its search engine on its own mobile operating system. Whether or not we agree with the rules, we can all appreciate that they can have severe implications for undertakings, as considered in **Chapter 4**. The types of practices that may constitute abusive conduct are considered at **3.4** below.

Lastly, in terms of introduction, it should be remembered that the rules relating to abusive conduct are in addition to the rules relating to anti-competitive agreements. Accordingly, an undertaking with a dominant position has to comply with both sets of rules.

3.2   THE ARTICLE 102 TFEU/CHAPTER II PROHIBITIONS

As Chapter II of the CA 1998 is modelled on Article 102 TFEU, we deal with Article 102 first.

Article 102 states:

> Any abuse by one or more undertakings of a dominant position within the internal market or in a substantial part of it shall be prohibited as incompatible with the internal market in so far as it may affect trade between Member States.

Contained within the prohibition are terms that are common to both Article 101/Chapter I and Article 102/Chapter II, and which will be interpreted in the same way. Accordingly, the types of businesses or entities that fall within the term 'undertakings' will be the same as those outlined at **2.1.1.1**. Note that unlike under Article 101/Chapter I, there is no need to have separate undertakings involved, and Article 102/Chapter II apply to conduct by one undertaking (so-called unilateral behaviour). Although unilateral behaviour will be the focus of this chapter, we shall also briefly consider a collective dominance held by more than one undertaking (see **3.3.5** below).

In addition to 'undertakings', Article 102 also refers to 'trade between Member States'. We have already considered this concept at **2.1.1.4** in the context of Article 101. Whether or not the abuse affects trade between Member States indicates the demarcation line between EU competition rules in this area and the domestic competition regimes of the EU Member States. The equivalent UK test is whether the abuse affects trade in the UK (see **2.2.2.1**).

Now we have considered some of the basic definitions, let us look at the substantive rules relating to abuse of a dominant position.

3.3   DOMINANCE

Establishing whether an undertaking holds a dominant position is crucial, because dominant undertakings may not engage in commercial activity that would be legal for non-dominant undertakings to engage in. For example, let us assume that a supermarket chain decides to enter into an aggressive sales drive in an attempt to get more customers to come to its stores rather than those of its competitors. In order to do this, it decides to sell some of its products at very low prices – so low in fact that the supermarket sells these products below the price it paid for them (this is referred to as 'below cost selling'). If the supermarket holds a dominant position on the market, this type of commercial activity may amount to an abuse (see 'Predatory pricing' at **3.4.2(a)** below) and therefore could result in extensive penalties being imposed (see **Chapter 4**). Conversely, if the supermarket is not dominant then its unilateral decision to sell a product below cost does not infringe competition law.

The ECJ laid down the legal test for dominance in Case 27/76 *United Brands v Commission* [1978] ECR 207:

> The dominant position thus referred to by Article [102] relates to a position of *economic strength* enjoyed by an undertaking which enables it to *prevent effective competition* being maintained on the relevant market by affording it the *power to behave to an appreciable extent independently of its competitors, customers and ultimately of its consumers*. (emphasis added)

Although the legal test was established over 40 years ago, it is still widely cited, including in later leading cases such as *Hoffman-La Roche* (cited below) and the Commission's Communication, *Guidance on the Commission's enforcement priorities in applying Article 82 of the EC Treaty to abusive exclusionary conduct by dominant undertakings* [2009] OJ C45/02 as amended ([2023] OJ C116/1)(the 'Exclusionary Conduct Guidelines'), considered further below.

The important point to note is that the test of dominance is based on the undertaking's ability to act independently of competitive constraints or, as the Exclusionary Conduct Guidelines state, 'largely insensitive to the actions and reactions of competitors, customers and, ultimately, consumers' (at para 10).

Indicative of an undertaking's ability to act independently is the market share that the undertaking enjoys on the market (although it is important to note that market share does not, in itself, establish dominance). This point was made in Case 85/76 *Hoffman-La Roche v Commission* [1979] ECR 461:

> [A]lthough the importance of the market shares may vary from one market to another the view may legitimately be taken that very large shares are in themselves, and save in exceptional circumstances, evidence of the existence of a dominant position.

Although we know that market share is not conclusive in establishing dominance, let us start by looking at how market share may be established.

3.3.1 The relevant market

In order to establish the market share of an undertaking, you have to start by defining the market (or markets) on which that undertaking operates. Generally, the wider the market is defined, the lower the market share figures of the undertaking will be. As a strategic matter, firms will often seek to define markets broadly to achieve desired outcomes, whereas claimants (for example a private claimant alleging dominance) will tend to argue for narrow markets. However, an undertaking's interest may lie in arguing that the relevant market is narrow, for example if the competition problem can be isolated to a narrowly defined market in which the undertaking is not present. Whatever the motives of the parties, the Commission's *Notice on the definition of relevant market for the purposes of Community competition law* [1997] OJ C372/03 (the 'Market Definition Notice') sets out the relevant framework for any analysis of the relevant market.

This is also the framework applied by the UK's competition authorities. The CMA's guidance is OFT 403, Market Definition, and the CMA also has regard to the Market Definition Notice as a statement of the European Commission for the purpose of s 60A of the Competition Act 1998.

The first point to note when establishing the relevant market is that in most cases it is broken down into the relevant product and geographic markets. These are considered in turn below.

3.3.1.1 The relevant product market

The Market Definition Notice states:

> A relevant product market comprises all those products and/or services which are regarded as interchangeable or substitutable by the consumer, by reason of the products' *characteristics*, their *price* and their *intended use*. (emphasis added)

Determining the relevant market requires a more detailed assessment, namely an analysis of:

(a) demand substitutability – the extent to which customers will switch to other sources of supply; and

(b) supply substitutability – the extent to which other suppliers can change their production to enter the market on which the firm operates.

In terms of defining the relevant product market, the Market Definition Notice states that it is the first of these restraints – demand substitutability – that is the most immediate and effective force on suppliers of a given product, and should therefore be given the most consideration.

Broadly speaking, demand substitutability defines the parameters of the market in which the products are sold. This can be best demonstrated by way of an example. Let us assume that we are considering a buyer of carton packaging (X). X has been buying carton packaging from the only supplier of the product for a number of years and has paid roughly the same price (excluding inflation). Recently, the price of carton packaging went up. When assessing demand substitutability, it is the options that X has at this point which are of interest:

- Does X have to continue to buy carton packaging, regardless of the price rise, as there are no alternative products that X can use? This is referred to as low demand-side substitutability.
- Conversely, faced with the increase costs of carton packaging, can X simply switch to another substitutable product (say non-carton packaging)? This is referred to as high demand-side substitutability.

Where there is low demand-side substitutability, this would indicate that carton packaging alone is the relevant product market, as consumers have no viable alternative. From an economic perspective, the supplier of carton packaging can raise its prices knowing that its customers have little option other than to buy expensive carton packaging.

Where there is high demand-side substitutability, it would indicate that the relevant market would be at least wide enough to cover both carton packaging and non-carton packaging. Here the supplier of carton packaging knows that if it raises prices too much, it risks losing many of its customers who will simply switch to purchasing non-carton packaging.

When looking at this dynamic, the Commission has adopted the SSNIP test, which stands for a **S**mall but **S**ignificant and **N**on-transitory **I**ncrease in **P**rice. Products will be considered to constitute a single market if a 'hypothetical monopolist' – the only seller of those products – could profitably impose and sustain a small but significant and non-transitory increase in price (usually 5%–10%). So in our example, if our supplier could get away with a price increase of this magnitude for a significant period of time, then carton packaging would be considered as a separate product market. Alternatively, if consumers switched supply to non-carton packaging, then the market would be at least as wide to include both carton packaging and non-carton packaging.

In Case T-83/91 *Tetra Pak v Commission* ('*Tetra Park II*') [1994] ECR II-755, [1997] 4 CMLR 726, the court decided that the relevant market did not include packaging materials other than carton. The evidence was that for packaging UHT milk products, non-carton packaging was not a viable substitutes for carton packaging because over a long period of time there had been only marginal substitution between the materials.

As well as 'demand-side substitutability', supply-side substitutability should also be considered (Case 6/72 *Continental Can v Commission* [1973] ECR 215), although greater weight is usually given to the former option. In the example of carton and non-carton packaging above, supply-side substitutability would involve considering whether suppliers of non-carton packaging were in a position to switch production to carton packaging, and market them in the short term without incurring significant additional costs and risks. If they could, the relevant product market would comprise both carton and non-carton packaging, even if buyers did not regard them as interchangeable. The Market Definition Notice gives the example of paper; if producers of one grade of paper could easily switch to producing different grades of paper, all such grades of paper will form part of the same relevant product market.

Note also that the relevant product market may be very narrow. In Case 22/78 *Hugin Kassaregister AB v Commission* [1979] ECR 1869, the issue was whether the product market was cash registers in general or spare parts for Hugin cash registers. Hugin was a Swedish manufacturer of cash registers; Liptons was a company based in London which serviced cash registers, including Hugin's. Hugin decided it wanted to start servicing its own machines and so stopped supplying Liptons with spare parts for its own machines. Consequently, Liptons could no longer service Hugin registers. The ECJ ruled that the product market was spare parts for Hugin cash registers; a firm servicing Hugin cash registers could not use spare parts made by anyone else because only Hugin spare parts could be used in Hugin registers.

3.3.1.2 The relevant geographic market

Once the relevant product market has been defined, it is also necessary to consider relevant geographic markets for that product. The relevant geographic market is the area where conditions of competition for the product in question are sufficiently homogeneous, ie the conditions of competition are sufficiently similar for everyone operating within that market. Relevant markets can be local, regional, national, EU/EEA-wide, worldwide or sometimes even defined by reference to a common language area.

The approach of the competition authorities is to initially look at variations in market shares and pricing between different geographic areas (usually different countries), and then to form a preliminary view of the relevant geographic market. The competition authorities will then test that initial assessment by examining more closely any national tendencies or preferences, current purchasing patterns by customers, product brands and other relevant factors. In this exercise it is the same dynamic described above with which the authorities will be concerned, although naturally this will be in the context of geographic substitution of supply. Looking at our example again, let us further assume that X is based in the Netherlands. How would X react to a price increase for carton packaging in that country? Would X buy carton packaging from Germany? If, for example, X would buy carton packaging elsewhere in the EU (or EEA), then the whole of the EU (or EEA) must be included in the relevant geographic market. If X would only buy carton packaging in the Netherlands, and other buyers behave in the same way, then the boundary of the relevant geographic market would be limited to the Netherlands.

Even if two products are not direct substitutes, they may be part of the same relevant market if there is a chain of substitution constraining each of the products between the extremes of the chain. For example, the prices in a petrol station in East London can constrain prices in a petrol station in West London because there are many petrol stations between them and each exercises a competitive constraint on the petrol stations nearest to it.

It is important to note the complexity of market definition in practice. The SSNIP test outlined above, for instance, may require consideration of hypothetical circumstances relating to the prices at which products are offered for sale and their impact on customer demand, since actual data is often unavailable. Customer surveys may need to be commissioned and models built by competition economists. The analysis involved is complex and opposing parties will submit contrary economic evidence. In some cases it may be possible to analyse markets in the alternative, leaving the market definition open, if this would lead to the same result. For example, a firm's market share may be 5% on a wide market definition, and 15% on a narrow market definition, ie in either case the firm is unlikely to be dominant.

3.3.2 Dominance – market share

Once both the product and geographic markets are defined, it will then be possible to estimate the undertaking's share of that market, which in turn will be indicative of whether that undertaking is dominant.

Given the fact that market share is only indicative of whether an undertaking is dominant, it is unsurprising that the competition authorities have not established any firm thresholds in this regard. However, a review of the case law of the CJEU and guidelines issued by the European Commission does provide some indication of the level of market share that would amount to dominance. An outline of the law in this area follows.

(a) Market share of 50% or more – presumption of dominance

In Case C-62/86 *AKZO v Commission* [1991] ECR I-3359, the ECJ stated that a market share of 50% or more would, in the absence of exceptional circumstances, give rise to a presumption of dominance. The presumption was applied by the CFI in Case T-30/89 *Hilti AG v Commission* [1991] ECR II-1439. Clearly, any presumption is capable of being rebutted; however, the higher the market share, the less likely that the presumption will be capable of rebuttal.

(b)   Market share between 40 and 50% – no presumption either way

In *United Brands* itself, a 40–45% market share was held to amount to a dominant position where there were additional factors that supported a finding of dominance.

However, smaller market shares than this range might still be held to represent dominance. Equally, higher shares might not. It is very important to look not only at the market share of the allegedly dominant undertaking, but also at the market shares of its competitors. The market shares of others in the market are also important because a share of 40%, for example, is less likely to give rise to dominance if there are two competitors with 30% each than if the next largest competitor has a share of 5%. In *United Brands*, the nearest competitors held market shares of 16% and 10%.

(c)   Market share below 40% – dominance unlikely

There have been few findings of dominance below 40%. In *Virgin/British Airways* [2000] OJ L30/1, the Commission found that British Airways held a dominant position in the UK for the procurement of air travel agency services, with a market share of 39.7%. This finding was upheld by the CFI, which noted that other factors on the market gave rise to the conclusion of dominance, not least BA's high market share compared to its rivals.

In addition to case law, the European Commission has stated in its Exclusionary Conduct Guidelines that, '[t]he Commission's experience suggests that dominance is not likely if the undertaking's market share is below 40% in the relevant market' (at para 14). However, the Commission goes on to state that dominance may be found where there are lower market share figures, and an assessment of all factors is necessary to determine dominance.

Factors that help to assess dominance include (this is not an exhaustive list):

- market share fluctuations over time;
- the strength and number of competitors;
- barriers to entry;
- countervailing buyer power;
- other factors, such as the undertaking's resources.

These are considered further below at **3.3.4**.

3.3.3   A substantial part of the internal market

In order to engage Article 102, an undertaking must be dominant 'within the internal market *or in a substantial part of it*' (emphasis added). In geographical terms this may be a very small area. Thus in Decision 94/19 *Sea Containers/Stena Sealink* [1994] 4 CMLR 513, [1994] OJ L15/8 (Holyhead), the Commission ruled that a single port may be a substantial part of the internal market; Holyhead, the port in question, was a major gateway between Great Britain and the Republic of Ireland and so was of considerable commercial importance.

The equivalent provision under s 18 of the CA 1998 is that an undertaking must be dominant in the UK, with the UK defined as 'the United Kingdom or any part of it'.

This is distinct from defining the relevant market. First of all, it is necessary to define the relevant geographic market. Once this has been defined then it is necessary to check that it forms a substantial part of the internal market.

3.3.4   Dominance – other factors

Below is a list of some of the factors, other than the parties' market shares, that the competition authorities will take into consideration when assessing whether an undertaking is dominant.

(a)   Market share trends and competitors

An undertaking must have been in a strong position over a period of time in order to be held to be dominant (see *United Brands*). If the undertaking has fluctuating market shares, doing well in some years and not so well in others, this may indicate that it is subject to competitive pressure. For example, in markets characterised by a small number of bids for large contracts (such as contracts to build a power station), an undertaking may win many bids in one year, gaining a high market share, but lose most of the bids the next year, when its market share will be low. Assessing competitors' corresponding market shares over time will provide valuable information about the undertaking's competitive position in the market.

Thus it not only the undertaking's market share that needs to be assessed, but also that of its competitors. The stronger and more numerous the competitors, the less likely it is that the undertaking will be dominant. At the extreme, if one undertaking has a 50% market share and another undertaking has another 50% market share, except in the limited circumstances where collective dominance may arise, neither undertaking will be dominant.

In some cases, an undertaking will hold a very large market share (or even have a monopoly) where it is the first to introduce a new product on the market. However, this high market share may be very short lived in markets where other undertakings can introduce competing products onto those markets relatively quickly. In these circumstances it is unlikely that dominance will be established. Assessing competitors' ability to introduce competing products involves a consideration of barriers to entry, discussed below.

(b)   Barriers to entry

Closely related to the above is the ability for other undertakings to enter the market – this is referred to as barriers to entry. Barriers to entry are high where, for example, any new entrant to the market has to gain access to intellectual property rights, or has to invest large amounts before it sees a return on its investment. In these circumstances the incumbent producer is effectively insulated from any competitive pressure that a new entrant might provide.

Thus an assessment of dominance will include consideration of whether there has been any recent market entry, and whether attempts to enter the market have been successful.

(c)   Countervailing buyer power

If customers enjoy buyer power (eg because there is a small number of large customers, each of which is critical to maintaining the volumes necessary for a plant to be profitable), this is a pointer against dominance.

For example a government procuring the purchase of a large power station may have countervailing buyer power, although this will depend on the circumstances.

(d)   Additional factors

Factors such as the financial resources and technological expertise of the undertaking may be relevant to a dominance assessment. For example, a company with deep pockets may sustain a strategy of pricing below cost in a way that a company that is tightly financially constrained would not be able to maintain. However, the mere availability of financial resources or technology will not be sufficient to establish dominance.

If an undertaking is capable of making profits that are excessive compared to the profits that should be charged in a competitive market, over a long period of time, this can be taken as an indicator that there are insufficiently effective competitive constraints and that the undertaking may be dominant. However, the mere presence of large profits is not sufficient. In *United Brands*, the ECJ said that large profits may be compatible with effective competition.

3.3.5 Collective dominance

A dominant position may also be held by several undertakings together. This is usually referred to as 'collective' (or 'joint') dominance.

In the *Italian Flat Glass* case [1990] 4 CMLR 535, the Commission found that three Italian companies jointly enjoyed a degree of independence from competitive pressures such that they were able to impede effective competition. Although the Commission's decision was overturned on appeal (on other grounds), the CFI confirmed:

> There is nothing, in principle, to prevent two or more independent economic entities from being, on a specific market, united by such *economic links* that, by virtue of that fact, together they hold a dominant position vis-à-vis the other operators on the same market. (emphasis added)

See Cases T-68/89 *Societa Italiano Vetro v Commission*; T-77/89 *Fabrica Pisana v Commission*; T-78/89 *PPG Vemante Pennitalia v Commission* [1992] 5 CMLR 302.

The CFI (now General Court) in Case T-193/02 *Laurent Piau v Commission* [2005] ECR II-209 stated that for there to be collective dominance, separate economic entities must 'present themselves or act together on a particular market as a collective entity'. Thus Article 102/ Chapter II may be capable of being invoked where there is a collective entity, albeit in circumstances where there is insufficient evidence of a concerted practice under Article 101 (see above at **2.1.1.3**).

The concept of collective dominance has also been considered in the context of EU merger control, under the former dominance test (which has now been amended). The essential characteristics of collective dominance were set out in the CFI (now General Court) decision in Case T-342/99 *Airtours v Commission* [2002] ECR II-2585. In that case the CFI held that, in order for undertakings to be collectively dominant, those undertakings must:

> consider it possible, economically rational, and hence preferable, to adopt on a lasting basis a common policy on the market with the aim of selling at above competitive prices, without having to enter into an agreement or resort to a concerted practice within the meaning of Article [101] and without any actual or potential competitors, let alone customers or consumers, being able to react effectively.

In addition, the CFI raised the evidential burden for establishing collective dominance, requiring evidence of, amongst other things, effective deterrents to prevent deviation from the common course of conduct and the inability of competitors and customers to react.

Few cases have been pursued as joint dominance cases, perhaps because in practice it is highly unusual for companies to present themselves as a collective without also engaging in a concerted practice. In Case C-395/96 P *Compagnie Maritime Belge Transports SA v Commission* [2000] ECR I-1365, the ECJ upheld a Commission decision that the collectively dominant members were found to have engaged in practices attempting to eliminate competition, such as selective price-cutting and the grant of loyalty rebates. These practices fell short of a concerted practice which would have enabled the Commission to pursue a case under Article 101.

3.4 ABUSE

Holding a dominant position in the relevant market will not of itself breach Article 102/ Chapter II. It is the abuse of that position that will be unlawful. As we have seen (see **3.3** above), conduct that a non-dominant firm may legitimately engage in may be problematic when engaged in by a dominant firm. In Case 322/81 *Michelin v Commission* [1983] ECR 3461, the ECJ stated that a firm in a dominant position 'has a special responsibility not to allow its conduct to impair undistorted competition on the common market'. Abuse of a dominant position occurs when a dominant firm in a market engages in conduct that is intended to exploit its dominant position, or to eliminate or discipline a competitor, or to deter future entry by new competitors, with the result that competition is adversely affected. As will be discussed below in greater detail, 'abuse cases' are often highly complex, and it is sometimes difficult to distinguish ordinary competitive behaviour from abuse.

Examples of practices that may constitute an abuse are given in Article 102/CA 1998, s 18 (reproduced in **Appendix 1** and **Appendix 2**). The list is not exhaustive though. In *Hoffman-La Roche v Commission* (see **3.3** above), the ECJ provided further guidance and defined an abuse as:

> an objective concept relating to the behaviour of an undertaking in a dominant position which is such as to influence the structure of a market where, as a result of the very presence of the undertaking in question *the degree of competition is weakened* and which, *through recourse to methods different from those which condition normal competition* in products or services on the basis of the transactions of commercial operators, has the effect of hindering the maintenance of the degree of competition still existing in the market or the growth of that competition. (emphasis added)

Abuse is an objective concept which generally does not depend on a party's intent. In practice, the Commission will investigate the rationale underlying an undertaking's decisions. Typically, the Commission will be in possession of evidence from the company subject to investigation (for the Commission's powers to compel evidence, see **Chapter 4**), for example minutes from board meetings or presentation slides used by senior management to explain their policies to the board. This will often constitute powerful evidence that an abuse has been committed, for example if an undertaking's ability to increase prices without suffering a loss in profits is acknowledged to have a detrimental impact on consumers. As an exception to the rule, in cases of predatory pricing (see **3.4.2(a)**), a company's intention is relevant to the assessment of abuse.

Abuses under Article 102/Chapter II are typically broken down into two broad categories of conduct:

(a)   exploitative abuses; and

(b)   exclusionary abuses.

These will be looked at in turn below, although it should be noted that there is no clear demarcation between the categories, and some abuses may be both exploitative and exclusionary. What is important is to analyse the harm to competition, rather than to categorise conduct as one type of abuse or another.

3.4.1   Exploitative abuses

This category of abuse relates to ways in which the dominant undertaking can exploit others on the market. For example:

(a)   Charging excessive prices

The most obvious way in which a dominant undertaking can abuse its position is to charge its customers an excessive price, ie a price that is unfair by comparison with the economic value of the product (*United Brands*). Although this may appear to be an obvious abuse, in practice it raises some difficult questions, not least what price may be viewed as an excessive price.

Thus, in *United Brands*, the Commission failed to prove that the company's prices were excessive.

In *Advanz Pharma* (Case 50395, 29 July 2021, Liothyronene), the CMA imposed over £100 million in fines after Advanz inflated the price of thyroid tablets, causing the NHS and patients to lose out. The company engaged in a strategy of sustained and repeated price increases, involving an overall price increase for some tablets of 6,000% despite no significant increase in costs. The CMA's decision was upheld by the CAT (*Advanz Pharma and others v Competition and Markets Authority* [2023] CAT 52), although some of the appellants' fines were reduced.

(b)   Excessively low price by a dominant buyer

It should be noted that the dominant undertaking on the market will not always be the supplier. In some markets, the dominant undertaking will be the buyer, who may demand unreasonably low prices from its suppliers which could amount to an abuse.

3.4.2   Exclusionary abuses

Exclusionary abuses include a wide range of practices. The main ones are considered below. Where relevant, reference is made to the Exclusionary Conduct Guidelines (see **3.3** above), which are not intended to summarise the law but provide some useful guidance on the Commission's priorities in enforcing Article 102. Rather than taking a formalistic approach, the Commission's focus is on conduct that is most harmful to consumers, and it will aim to safeguard the competitive process, rather than merely protecting competitors.

(a)   Predatory pricing

This type of practice aims to reduce prices to such a level that a competitor (or competitors) is forced to exit the market as it cannot match the very low prices being offered. In theory, once all competition is removed from the market, the dominant firm can then raise prices in the knowledge that customers cannot use an alternative source of supply.

Case C-62/86 *AKZO Chemie v Commission* (above) provides a classic example of predatory pricing. AKZO, the dominant undertaking, and ECS, a small English competitor, both produced benzoyl peroxide, a product used in both the plastics and flour markets. Initially, ECS only sold the product in the flour market, but then decided to expand into the plastics market. AKZO responded by aggressively targeting ECS's customers in the flour market and cutting its prices to below the cost of production. Its aim was clearly to drive ECS out of the plastics market.

The court set out some useful rules for the assessment of predation. Broadly speaking:

- If an undertaking prices above its total costs of production, then its conduct cannot be predatory.
- If an undertaking prices below its average variable costs, then a presumption arises that its intent must be to eliminate competition. This is because no rational commercial undertaking would price at a level where it cannot recover the variable cost of producing an additional unit of its products (unless there are special circumstances, such as a temporary promotion or a mistake: thus the presumption can be rebutted).
- If an undertaking prices below total costs but above its average variable costs of production, then for predatory pricing to be established, it must be proved that the undertaking's intention is to eliminate competition – this can no longer be presumed. There can be many reasons for undertakings to charge below their total costs of production, as long as they cover their variable costs. For example an undertaking may attribute non-variable costs that are common across all of the company's activities (eg the costs of running the Chairman's office) onto products that face less competition.

In Decision AT.39711 *Qualcomm (Predation)* (OJ C 375/25, Commission decision of 18 July 2019, appeal pending), the Commission fined Qualcomm €242 million for selling three of its chipsets (used for smartphones and tablets to connect to mobile networks) below cost. The Commission found that price concessions were targeted to maximise the adverse impact on a smaller competitor. The Commission also found that the company's rationale was anti-competitive. The Commission concluded that Qualcomm's conduct reduced competition, stifled innovation and ultimately reduced choice for consumers. This case illustrates the significant penalties that may be imposed on companies that price below cost (including, in this case, average variable costs) where their rationale for so acting is anti-competitive.

Note that it is not necessary for a smaller competitor to be eliminated from the market in order for a finding of predatory pricing to be made, although in *Qualcomm (Predation)* the smaller competitor was acquired by another company and its relevant business was wound down.

(b) Exclusive dealing

A dominant firm may restrict competition by insisting that its customers do not use any other supplier. This can be done by requiring the customer to purchase all or most of its requirements from the dominant firm. In these circumstances, other suppliers (competitors of the dominant firm) cannot sell their products to the customers or can do so to a lesser extent. Where a customer is required to purchase more than 80% of its requirements from the dominant firm, this is usually treated in the same way as exclusivity (by analogy with the definition of 'non-compete' in the vertical block exemptions; see **6.2.7.1**).

A short-term exclusivity requirement is unlikely to foreclose competition since smaller firms can compete with the dominant firm once the exclusivity period has ended, and if the exclusivity period is short it is unlikely to have a detrimental effect on competition. However, in *Prokent-Tomra* COMP/38113 [2009] 4 CMLR 101, a six-month exclusivity period was considered abusive in the particular circumstance of the case.

A long-term supply agreement, even if it is not completely exclusive, may have the effect of foreclosing competition. For example, a long-term gas supply contract which is not exclusive may nevertheless deter competitors from entering the market or make it more difficult for them to compete. A supply agreement which is longer than five years is generally considered long term, although shorter-term agreements could also be considered abusive depending on the circumstances.

Exclusive dealing can take many other forms, for example through loyalty rebates – see **(f)** below.

(c) Refusal to supply

Competition may also be affected where a dominant firm refuses to supply its products. This can be particularly problematic where the dominant firm's refusal impacts on a 'downstream' market. This may be demonstrated by an example. Say that A is dominant in the supply of flour. B, its subsidiary, obtains flour from A in order to make cakes. C, another cake producer, needs flour in order to compete with B. A's refusal to supply C with flour would make it more difficult for C to compete with B on the downstream cake market.

The cases of *Hugin* (as described above) and *United Brands* provide examples of refusals to supply. In the latter case, United Brands stopped supplying a distributor which had taken part in a competitor's advertising campaign. The ECJ ruled that a dominant undertaking 'cannot stop supplying a long-standing customer who abides by regular commercial practice if the orders placed by that customer are in no way out of the ordinary' (para 182). United Brand's conduct would have deterred other distributors from buying bananas from its competitors, thereby entrenching the company's dominance.

Refusal to supply can be a 'constructive refusal to supply' in circumstances where the dominant firm does not refuse to supply outright, but makes supply conditional on terms that are unreasonable, for example at prices that are too high.

Existing/new customers

Although the case law does not distinguish between refusing to supply an *existing* customer and refusing to supply a *new* (potential) customer, the distinction is of practical importance. Where there is an *existing* customer supply relationship which is broken off by the dominant firm, it may be relatively easy to discern an anti-competitive rationale for the refusal (as in *United Brands* itself). Where the dominant company merely exploits its legitimate property rights by refusing to make its products available to any customer (who may be a competitor), an abuse is more difficult to establish. In such cases there are two broad situations in which a refusal to supply may be abusive:

- A dominant company which supplies an 'essential facility' may be required to provide access to that essential facility (for example, access to a port of embarkation at reasonable prices). Where a facility may reasonably be replicated by a competitor (such as a private parcels distribution network), it will not be considered an essential facility (Case C-7/97 *Bronner v Mediaprint* [1998] ECR I-7791, [1999] 4 CMLR 112).

- A dominant company which fails to meet demand on a distinct economic market may be required to supply, where needed to develop a new market for the benefit of consumers. This line of cases is discussed in **Chapter 8** as they relate to the licensing of intellectual property (see *Microsoft* at **8.4**). Note, however, that the principle is not limited to licensing.

As a practical matter, the Commission has published guidance on its enforcement priorities in relation to Article 102 (the Exclusionary Conduct Guidelines referred to at **3.3**), where it states that it will take action where the refusal to supply:

- relates to a product or service that is objectively necessary to be able to compete effectively on a downstream market;

- is likely to lead to the elimination of effective competition on the downstream market; and

- is likely to lead to consumer harm.

(d) Tying

A typical example of tying or 'bundling' abuses involves requiring that a buyer, when purchasing one product, is also required to purchase a second (different) 'tied' product. Tying arises where the two products are distinct, rather than components of a single product. For example, the supply of zips on trousers is not tying, whereas a requirement that manufacturers of mobile operating systems must install the dominant company's search engine may amount to a tying abuse by a dominant company. In *Google and Alphabet v Commission* (*Google Android*) (Case T-604/18) (14 September 2022), the General Court largely confirmed the Commission's finding of a tying abuse, in circumstances where mobile device manufacturers who purchased Google's Android mobile operating system were also required to pre-install Google Search and the Google Chrome browser.

Case C-53/92P *Hilti AG v Commission* [1994] ECR I-667 is an early leading case on tying abuse. Hilti was dominant in the market for nail cartridges which it made. It required its customers of nail cartridges also to buy its nails, although other competing manufacturers made compatible nails. In a subsequent case, Case T-201/04 *Microsoft v Commission* [2007] ECR II-3601, the CFI stated that the Commission was entitled to base its findings of a tying abuse on the following factors:

(i)   the tying and tied products must be two separate products;

(ii)   the supplier must be dominant in the market for the 'tying' product;

(iii) the supplier does not give customers a choice to obtain the tying product without the tied product; and

(iv)   tying must foreclose competition.

Where customers have a choice to obtain the tying product without the tied product, but the price of the bundled products purchased together is more favourable than the price of the products purchased separately, this is known as 'bundling' (sometimes called 'mixed bundling'). Bundling is another form of tying but is less likely to be found abusive as the bundling may reflect efficiencies. For example, the dominant firm's bundled pricing may reflect costs savings achieved by selling the products together.

(e)   Price discrimination

Price discrimination may arise where a dominant undertaking charges different prices to different customers for the same product without justification on the grounds of quality, quantity or other characteristics (or charges identical prices to different customers for goods which should be priced differently by virtue of different quantities/characteristics or dissimilar circumstances).

Discriminatory practices that segregate customers on a national basis are particularly objectionable. In *United Brands*, the company charged its German customers more than its Irish customers, even though the cost to it was the same. The company imported the bananas into ports in the EU, and the buyers then paid the transport costs to their home State.

The issue of discriminatory pricing has also arisen in the context of airport landing fees. Some airports charged different landing fees depending on the origin of the flight. The Commission argued that this was discriminatory and unjustifiable as the services provided by the airport were the same, irrespective of where the landing plane had originated. The ECJ upheld the Commission's arguments in Case C-163/99 *Portugal v Commission* [2001] ECR I-2613.

Discriminatory pricing may, however, be economically justified and will not always amount to an abuse. For example, in Case C-209/10 *Post Danmark A/S v Konkurrencerådet* (27 March 2012), the Court of Justice considered whether Post Danmark was entitled to charge different prices to three major customers acquired from Post Danmark's main competitor. The charges appeared discriminatory because the costs of supplying these customers were the same, while the prices to these customers were different. However, the Court held that this was not sufficient to constitute an abuse. It is also necessary to consider whether the pricing policy has an exclusionary effect. The purpose of competition law is not to protect less efficient competitors.

Therefore, simply charging different prices to different customers will not be abusive; all the circumstances of the case need to be considered.

(f)   Fidelity rebates/discounts

These comprise special financial rebates or discounts offered to the customers of a business in return for loyalty to that business. The ECJ considered them an issue in Case 85/76 *Hoffmann-La Roche AG v Commission* [1979] ECR 461. Roche granted substantial 'fidelity' discounts to customers who bought from it all or most of their vitamin requirements. The ECJ held that Roche had abused its dominant position.

It is standard commercial practice for suppliers to give their customers discounts in return for larger volume orders. However, a dominant undertaking may be prohibited from offering such discounts if the discounts are not purely linked to costs savings from offering large volumes but have the intention of dissuading a customer from obtaining the product elsewhere. If a rebate is expressed as a percentage of a customer's requirements, it is not being measured by reference to the savings incurred by the supplier. While a dominant supplier is able to offer its customers a discount if they buy a large volume of goods from it, it cannot, say, offer its customers a 25% discount if they buy 90% of their requirements from it. The latter approach is designed to restrict sources of supply and deny other producers access to the market and so constitutes an abuse.

Case C-413/14P *Intel v European Commission* (6 September 2017) sparked a debate on exclusivity rebates – loyalty discounts that have a similar effect to exclusivity – and whether the economic effects of discounts should be considered as well as their form. The General Court took a somewhat formalistic approach which was quashed on appeal. Intel had been fined €1.06 billion in circumstances where it was granting discounts for its computer chips in return for exclusivity. Intel was also granting discounts in return for customers delaying the launch of products using chips from Intel's main competitor, AMD. The Court of Justice found that the test of abuse should involve a full assessment of the circumstances, including how competition was being foreclosed. In particular, Intel's argument that a competitor as efficient as itself ('equally efficient competitor') would not be excluded from the market should have been addressed. The case was remitted to the General Court.

(g)   Margin squeeze

A margin squeeze occurs where a dominant undertaking which also operates in the downstream market is only willing to supply its downstream competitors on unfavourable terms, for example at such a high price that competition in the downstream market is rendered difficult or impossible.

(h)   Refusals to license intellectual property rights

This is discussed at **8.4**. Note that a refusal to license IP rights cannot be got around by an undertaking simply charging a very high licence fee instead of refusing to license its IP rights, as this may constitute a constructive refusal to supply or a margin squeeze.

The above are some of the more common forms of abuses, but they do not cover the whole field.

3.4.3   Objective justification

Certain types of behaviour carried out by a dominant undertaking may be commercially legitimate and not caught by Article 102/Chapter II. This will be the case if the conduct of the dominant firm can be justified as being objectively necessary (ie reasonably needed to protect its commercial interests) and proportionate to the objective (ie not more restrictive than necessary to achieve the objective). For example, a dominant undertaking may have objective justification in refusing to supply where the undertaking concerned has a poor credit rating and/or history. Where an objective justification is put forward, it is for the dominant firm to support its arguments with evidence. If the Commission disagrees, it must then show why it cannot accept the evidence and arguments that have been put forward.

For example, in Hilti, the company's defence – that the tie was objectively justifiable for reasons of safety and reliability – was dismissed by the ECJ. It was the responsibility of the public authorities to determine the safety of the competitors' nails, not Hilti's.

3.5   ABUSE ON DIFFERENT MARKET TO DOMINANCE

The abuse will usually occur on the market (or markets) on which the undertaking is dominant. However, in certain circumstances, liability may be imposed under Article 102/Chapter II where the abuse occurs on an associated market, but not on the actual market where that undertaking holds a dominant position. In Case T-83/91 *Tetra Pak v European Commission* [1994] ECR II-755, it was held that Tetra Pak's activities on one market amounted to an abuse of its dominant position on a distinct (but closely associated) market.

In practice it is important that an undertaking which holds a dominant position on one market ensures that its activities cannot amount to an abuse on any of the markets on which it operates.

3.6   POINTS OF DISTINCTION BETWEEN ARTICLE 102/CHAPTER II AND ARTICLE 101/CHAPTER I

The main difference between the two main prohibitions is that the Article 102/Chapter II prohibition applies to unilateral conduct by a single undertaking (bar the exceptional circumstances of collective dominance), whereas the Article 101/Chapter I prohibition applies in cases of collusion between at least two undertakings.

Under Article 102/Chapter II, once it has been established that there has been an abuse of a dominant position, there is no possibility of any exemption from the prohibition. This is in contrast with the situation under Article 101/Chapter I where it is possible for an agreement to be exempted under Article 101(3) (and the equivalent UK provisions) (see **2.1.3**). It has sometimes been asked whether there is an efficiency defence under Article 102/Chapter II, similar in concept to an exemption. However, in an Article 102/Chapter II case, whether conduct results in harm to competition and customers, or on the contrary would result in efficiencies, is assessed as part of the test for abuse and not as a specific defence.

Another point of difference is that, under Article 101/Chapter I, agreements that are *de minimis* (usually by reference to market share thresholds) may fall outside Article 101/Chapter I, provided that they do not contain object restrictions. Article 102/Chapter II apply to dominant companies with significant market shares, and as such the *de minimis* doctrine is not relevant in the same way (there may be cases where a company is dominant in one market and the abuse takes place in a second market but the effects in that second market are not economically significant: *Streetmap v Google* [2016] EWHC 253 (Ch)).

Note that the doctrine of effect on trade between EU Member States applies to both Article 101 and Article 102 (except the NAAT rule which only applies to Article 101). The doctrine is not relevant to UK law since its purpose is to demarcate the EU's jurisdiction.

3.7 THE UK COMPETITION ACT 1998

3.7.1 The Chapter II prohibition

Section 18 of the CA 1998 contains the UK prohibition on abuse of a dominant position (reproduced in **Appendix 2**). The prohibition is referred to as the 'Chapter II prohibition' and mirrors Article 102. As with Article 101, the only substantive difference between the two pieces of legislation is that the Chapter II prohibition relates to abusive conduct that 'may affect trade within the *United Kingdom*'.

Before the end of the Brexit transition period, Regulation 1 and s 60 of the CA 1998 required the CMA to follow the European interpretation of the rules. Regulation 1 no longer applies to the UK and s 60 has been repealed. The new s 60A of the CA 1998 sets out the more limited requirements for consistency with retained EU law (see **2.2.1**). The upshot is that **3.1–3.6** above largely reflect the UK position as well as the position under EU law.

3.7.1.1 Dominance

Dominance is assessed in the same way as it is under Article 102, and market share will often be the most significant factor. The CMA has indicated that, as a rule of thumb, it will usually treat undertakings with market shares of 50% and over as dominant; undertakings with market shares of less than 40% are unlikely to be seen as dominant (see CMA Guides: Abuse of a dominant position, OFT 402; Market definition, OFT 403; and Assessment of market power, OFT 415 – these were originally OFT guides, but have been adopted by the CMA).

3.7.1.2 Abuse

Like Article 102, the CA 1998 gives specific examples of types of conduct that are likely to be considered an abuse (eg imposing unfair purchase or selling prices). However, this list provides guidance only and is not exhaustive. Given the requirement for the consistent application of UK laws with EU laws in force prior to the end of the Brexit transition period, the UK rules follow the position under the EU rules described above. After the end of the Brexit transition period, divergences may start to emerge over time.

As with EU rules, undertakings will not have abused their dominant position where there is objective justification for their actions.

3.7.2   Limited immunity under the Chapter II prohibition

There is no exemption for the Chapter II prohibition under UK law. However, unlike the EU system, s 40 of the CA 1998 provides for limited immunity from fines for conduct of minor significance. The conduct may still be abusive and the company may still be investigated, but the immunity avoids the imposition of fines on undertakings that have a turnover that does not exceed £50 million a year. The CMA may, however, withdraw the immunity from fines. In addition, the immunity is only in relation to UK law; there is no immunity for breaches of Article 102.

3.7.3   The UK market investigation regime

A particular feature of the UK competition law regime, which is not currently present in the same form in EU competition law, is the ability of UK competition authorities to investigate market sectors and impose remedies to prevent any adverse effect on competition that is identified. The market investigation provisions are contained in the Enterprise Act 2002 and are outside the scope of this textbook.

3.7.4   Special regimes

Special regimes govern specific industrial sectors. A common feature of these regimes is that regulators have the power to intervene 'ex-ante' before problems occur, rather than 'ex-post' after the competition or other problems have manifested themselves. These special regimes include:

- *Regulated industries* – regimes covering regulated industries, such as Ofcom's powers to impose obligations on communications companies designated as having 'significant market power' (a concept similar to dominance).
- *Digital markets* – the UK's proposed pro-competition regime for digital markets, which will empower the CMA's Digital Market Unit to designate firms as having 'strategic market status'.

   The EU has also developed a new competition tool to address structural or behavioural problems in on-line digital markets (the Digital Markets Act), for example where conduct by 'gatekeepers' who are not yet dominant companies could monopolise markets, or where there is widespread use of algorithmic pricing that easily allows alignment between competitors without them agreeing prices.

These provisions are not discussed further.

3.8   THE SHERMAN ACT, SECTION 2

In the US, Section 2 of the Sherman Act prohibits any action to 'monopolize or attempt to monopolize, or combine or conspire with any other person or persons, to monopolize any part of the trade or commerce among the several States, or with foreign nations' (15 USC §2) (see also **Appendix 3**).

A Section 2 violation may be, and typically is, based on the conduct of a single, large firm.

3.8.1   Monopoly power

To find that a company has committed illegal monopolization, the evidence must show that the company possesses monopoly power, which is the power to control prices above what the market will bear and to lower output in a market unilaterally without the constraints of competition (*United States v EI du Pont de Nemours & Co*, 351 US 377 (1956)). Monopoly power is not specifically defined under the US antitrust laws, but it is understood that it requires something greater than market power. Monopolization claims are determined on the basis of a large share of a relevant market and other relevant factors.

3.8.1.1 Market definition

The first step in determining monopoly power is defining the relevant product and geographic markets. Product market is defined as all products that compete for sales with the defendant's products, including identical products and products that are reasonably interchangeable. Geographic market is defined as the physical territories in which competitors of the defendant are located and to where customers reasonably can turn for sources of supply.

3.8.1.2 Market shares

Although no exact thresholds have been established, the courts typically find monopoly power in Section 2 cases when the defendant's market shares exceed 70%, but never find monopoly power at market shares below 50%. Between those two figures, the court's findings vary with the particular facts and circumstances of each case, including the specifics of the industry involved.

3.8.1.3 Other relevant factors

A high market share alone is not sufficient to establish monopoly power. The evidence must also show that the defendant's ability to control prices and lower output is not impaired by other factors, such as the ability of fringe competitors to expand their output or of new competitors to enter the market, consumers' ability or willingness to pay more, or the presence of powerful purchasers.

3.8.2 Exclusionary conduct

Simply possessing monopoly power is not illegal, neither is 'abusing' the power by charging higher prices or imposing harsh sales terms. A company that obtains a monopoly by innovation, by luck, by patents or other legal grants of a monopoly, or by driving its competitors out of business through legitimate means, is free to enjoy the fruits of its monopoly. A Section 2 violation occurs only where the company has acquired, enhanced or maintained its monopoly power through 'exclusionary conduct', which means practices intended to prevent or impair competition rather than to win the competitive battle legitimately (*United States v Grinnell Corp*, 384 US 563 (1966)).

In reality, many of the practices which will amount to an abuse for the purposes of Article 102 will also amount to exclusionary conduct under US law.

Among the practices that have been found to be exclusionary, and that constitute a violation of Section 2 of the Sherman Act when a monopolist engages in them, are the following:

(a)   Predatory pricing, which occurs when a company sells its products below its marginal or long-run average variable costs, for the purpose of driving out competitors. A US court will find predatory pricing, however, only when the proof shows not only sales below costs but also that the defendant is likely to recoup its investment in predatory prices through higher prices in the future, after competition has been eliminated (*Brooke Group v Brown & Williamson Tobacco Corp*, 509 US 209 (1986)).

(b)   Efforts to prevent customers or suppliers from dealing with actual or potential competitors of the monopolist, through exclusive dealing terms or refusals to deal with a disloyal customer or supplier, without a legitimate business reason.

(c)   Tying, which is the conditioning of a customer's purchase of one product or service on its purchase of another product, without a legitimate business reason.

(d)   Obtaining patents through fraud on the patent office.

In *Verizon Communications, Inc v Law Offices of Curtis Trinko*, 540 US 398 (2004), the US Supreme Court appears to have narrowed the scope of exclusionary conduct, at least in regulated markets. In accordance with the teachings of the Chicago School, a monopolist, like any other firm, has the right to choose the parties with whom it does business, even if the exercise of that right to choose results in a significant impairment of competition. The Court in Trinko ruled that the company with a monopoly on the local telephone service in the state of New York did not violate Section 2 by refusing to provide rival telecommunications companies interconnections to the local telephone exchanges, notwithstanding the rivals' need for these interconnections and the defendant's obligation to provide them under existing regulations. Trinko has created uncertainty about the continuing validity of many earlier decisions by lower federal courts finding that defendants had violated Section 2 by refusing to deal with certain customers or suppliers.

3.8.3 Attempted monopolization

A company that does not currently possess monopoly power can violate Section 2 of the Sherman Act through attempted monopolization (Spectrum Sports, Inc v McQuillan, 506 US 445 (1993)). Essential elements of an attempt offence are as follows:

(a)   Exclusionary conduct, which has the same meaning for an attempt claim as for a monopolization claim. The defendant must engage in some practice designed to prevent or impair competition rather than to win the competitive battle legitimately.

(b)   Specific intent to achieve a monopoly. This intent is established primarily on the basis of inferences from the defendant's exclusionary conduct, ie a finding that the most likely reason for the defendant engaging in a particular practice is to prevent or impair competition. Statements in internal documents and in the testimony of employees can also be relevant.

(c)   A dangerous probability of success in achieving monopoly power through its exclusionary conduct. This element will usually be found where the defendant starts with a very high market share and engages in exclusionary conduct that could be sufficiently effective in preventing or impairing competition to result in monopoly power.

CHAPTER 4

ENFORCEMENT

AIMS

Chapter 4 provides an overview of the enforcement of competition law in three important jurisdictions: the EU, the UK and the US. This overview starts with the rules that operate within the EU. The UK rules are largely based on the EU rules and are very similar.

OBJECTIVES

After reading **Chapter 4**, you should have a basic understanding of:

- the authorities' powers of investigation in the UK, EU and US;

- the sanctions for breaching competition rules;

- the role of national courts and competition authorities, as well as private litigants, in competition law enforcement;

- leniency programmes; and

- the importance of competition law compliance programmes.

4.1 HOW DO THE AUTHORITIES BECOME AWARE OF POTENTIAL INFRINGEMENTS?

Before we look at the various enforcement regimes, let us consider how the authorities become aware of a potential infringement. In the context of competition law, the ability to detect potential breaches is particularly onerous on the authorities as the most serious infringements take place in secret. Below is an outline of some of the ways in which authorities may become aware of potential infringements.

(a) Leniency regimes – whistleblowing

Parties involved in anti-competitive behaviour can receive a substantial reduction in, or indeed immunity from, fines for bringing infringements to the notice of the authorities. This partial or total immunity has provoked numerous applications and provided evidence of anti-competitive behaviour used to support findings of infringement. This will be looked at in more detail at **4.6** below.

(b)   Information from other authorities

As we have seen in **Chapter 1** (see **1.6**), there is increasing cooperation and communication between the various competition authorities around the world. Accordingly, illegal activity found by one authority may result in subsequent investigation under other competition regimes. Indeed, some of the biggest investigations under the European rules have been as a result of investigations started by the US authorities. There are numerous examples of authorities launching parallel investigations and coordinating their dawn raids on the same day in order to keep the element of surprise.

(c)   Third parties

Another very good source of detection is that of complaints by parties who are the victims of anti-competitive activity. Competition authorities will be particularly attentive to complaints from customers, suppliers and consumers of the product or service which is the subject of anti-competitive behaviour. Competition authorities will also receive complaints from competitors. Although competitors can be best placed to provide information to the authorities about anti-competitive behaviour, authorities will be mindful that competitors' interests are often to weaken their rivals.

Where third parties bring an action before the courts (see **4.7**), this may tip off the authorities as to anti-competitive behaviour.

(d)   Other investigations

The authorities themselves may uncover anti-competitive behaviour as a result of their market monitoring activities.

In addition, investigations launched on the basis of one type of illegal activity can sometimes find evidence of other infringements. If these other infringements do not fall within the scope of an investigation which the Commission has opened, the Commission will need to open a new investigation and request the evidence to be produced afresh.

4.2   ENFORCEMENT BY THE EUROPEAN COMMISSION

4.2.1   Introduction

As we have seen in **Chapter 1** (see **1.3.1.3**), the Commission is the body responsible at the EU level for competition law. This includes the investigation and enforcement of competition law.

Regulation 1 (an extract of which can be found at **Appendix 4**) is the main EU regulation implementing Articles 101 and 102. It contains the Commission's power to investigate, impose interim measures and penalise undertakings for breaches of Articles 101 and 102. Additionally, Regulation 1 permits the EU Member States' national authorities and courts to enforce Articles 101 and 102. As a result of the sharing of the enforcement of Articles 101 and 102, the Commission can focus its attention on international cartels, other serious infringements of EU competition law and cases it is best placed to deal with (see **4.3.1** below for more detail).

The UK enforcement provisions are largely similar to EU enforcement provisions and are dealt with at **4.4**.

4.2.2   The powers of the European Commission

4.2.2.1   Enforcement

Articles 4 and 7 of Regulation 1 contain the Commission's power to make an infringement decision relating to a breach of Articles 101 or 102, either acting on a complaint (see above) or acting on its own initiative. The Commission acts by addressing a reasoned decision to the business entity or entities concerned. Before reaching that decision, and to support its reasoning, the Commission will have had to amass sufficient evidence upon which to base its conclusions. So how does the Commission go about collecting evidence?

(a)   Requests for information

In order to carry out its duties to enforce competition law, the Commission has the power under Article 18 of Regulation 1 to request businesses to provide all necessary information. This may be by way of 'simple request' or by way of a formal decision. In either case, the Commission must state the legal basis for its request, the penalties it may impose (in Articles 23 and 24) and provide the business concerned with a time limit to respond. Parties will have every incentive to comply even with a simple request, since, if they do not, a formal decision is likely to follow.

Under Article 19, the Commission is able to interview any person who may be in possession of useful relevant information and to record the statements made, whether or not that person is employed by the company under investigation, provided that the person consents to be interviewed (but see the Commission's power to interview individuals during dawn raids, below).

(b)   Inspection – 'dawn raids'

A crucial part of the Commission's evidence-gathering powers is its ability to carry out on-the-spot unannounced investigations within the territory of the EU (Articles 20 and 21). The Commission will either proceed by way of written authorisation (Article 20(3)), or more commonly by way of formal decision requiring the undertaking to submit to the investigation (Article 20(4)). Although the press tends to describe compulsory Commission investigations as 'dawn raids', the inspectors in fact arrive within normal business hours as they need to be reasonably certain that key personnel will be there. The officials will normally go to the reception desk and ask for a director or other senior officer of the company, usually by name. The inspectors will explain how they wish to proceed, and will usually ask for an explanation as to where and how relevant documents and information are kept and how they are organised.

The Commission has other powers associated with the inspection. These include the power:

(a)   to examine and take copies of books and other records related to a business, irrespective of the medium on which they are stored. Under Article 21, the Commission has powers to inspect other premises, land and means of transport where such information may be held, including homes of directors and management;

(b)   to seal any business premises and books or records for the period of the inspection; and

(c)   to ask any representative or member of staff of the undertaking or association of undertakings for explanations of facts or documents relating to the subject matter and purpose of the inspection, and to record the answers.

There may, from a company's point of view, be a concern that Commission inspectors will embark on a 'fishing expedition' and examine documents which are unrelated to the subject matter of the investigation. It is open to a company to refuse the inspectors access to information that is outside the scope of the Commission's written authorisation or decision, or information that benefits from legal professional privilege in the EU. Nevertheless, refusing the Commission access can be a high risk strategy. If the Commission agrees that the information is outside the scope of its investigation, it can hold a fresh investigation and order the documents to be produced by a certain date, backed up with the threat of a fine. In addition, any refusal to produce documents that are later found within the scope of the investigation could be interpreted as hindering the investigation, and subsequently could result in a higher fine being imposed (see **4.2.4** below).

In practice, where there is a disagreement during a dawn raid as to whether documents should be produced, these documents can be held by agreement with the Commission in a sealed envelope or in electronic form, to be reviewed at a later stage when relevance or the applicability of the rules on legal professional privilege can be decided.

Since the end of the Brexit transition period, the Commission no longer has the power to conduct dawn raids within the territory of the UK.

4.2.2.2   Interim measures

As a general rule, the Commission will need sufficient evidence from its investigation before it can move to the next stage of the enforcement process. The only exception to this general rule is that the Commission can, in limited circumstances, impose interim measures (see Article 8 of Regulation 1). Interim measures allow the Commission to take action where there is urgency, and waiting for a full investigation could result in 'serious and irreparable harm' to competition. For example, assume that a small company is the subject of a predatory pricing infringement by a dominant undertaking under Article 102 (see **3.4.2(a)**). If the Commission waits, the company could simply be forced out of business by the time a full investigation is completed, causing irreversible damage to the competitive dynamic on the market. In this context, an interim measures order (such as banning the dominant firm's pricing policy) would be put in place, subject to a full investigation and possible infringement decision.

In Case AT.40608 – *Broadcom* (16 October 2019), the Commission imposed interim measures to prevent serious and irreparable damage to competition arising from exclusivity clauses. The measures ensured that Broadcom did not require customers to purchase certain types of chips for TV products exclusively, or near exclusively, from Broadcom pending investigation.

Where a complainant wishes the Commission to act urgently to prevent serious and irreparable harm to competition, it should consider whether national measures could be more effective.

The UK's Competition and Markets Authority can adopt interim measures when there is a risk of significant harm (a lower threshold than the EU's serious and irreparable harm threshold): see **4.4.1.3**. In addition, private enforcement action in the UK courts (see **4.7**) could include seeking an injunction to prevent harm to competition from occurring pending trial.

4.2.2.3   Post-investigation options

Putting aside interim measures outlined at **4.2.2.2** above, having amassed sufficient relevant information to proceed, the Commission will have a number of options.

(a)   Infringement decisions

Many cases that are investigated will end in the Commission issuing an infringement decision. An infringement decision will be the last stage of the investigation process which is governed by Commission Regulation 773/2004 *relating to the conduct of proceedings by the Commission pursuant to Articles 81 and 82 of the EC Treaty* ([2004] OJ L123/18) (the 'Conduct of Proceedings Regulation').

One of the most important issues within the investigation procedure is that the parties subject to the process must be aware of the case against them and have an opportunity to answer that case. As such, the Conduct of Proceedings Regulation provides (at Article 10) that the Commission should issue a 'statement of objections'. The statement of objections effectively outlines the case for the Commission. The parties have the right to access the Commission's file so that they may see the evidence against them. The parties can then make written submissions in reply to the case contained in the statement of objections, and they also have the option of attending an oral hearing (see Articles 10–12). A great deal of skill goes into both oral and written submissions, including how to craft a defence which disposes of the case rather than aiding the Commission to simply write a second, better reasoned statement of objections which is less vulnerable to appeal.

If at the end of the investigation process (and after considering the parties' arguments) the Commission is still minded to issue an infringement decision, it can do so under Article 7 of Regulation 1. In addition to an infringement decision, the Commission may issue fines under Article 23 and may, under Article 7, order the undertaking to bring the infringement to an end (see **4.2.3**).

(b)   Commitments

As an alternative to proceeding to a full infringement decision, the Commission can accept binding commitments from the parties subject to an investigation (see Article 9 of Regulation 1). This has advantages for both parties. From the Commission's perspective, binding commitments can be an efficient way to resolve competition concerns. From the perspective of the parties giving commitments, this can remove the possibility of sanctions being imposed by the Commission in an infringement decision. Many investigations are resolved through the commitments procedure.

(c)   Settlement in cartel cases

The Commission may enter into a settlement agreement with parties that have been involved in cartel activity. The procedure is contained in Article 10a of the Conduct of Proceedings Regulation.

If the Commission considers that a case is suitable for settlement, the Commission will ask the parties if they are interested in settlement discussions before it issues its statement of objections. The parties that are under investigation then have an opportunity to review the Commission's evidence. If, when confronted with this evidence, they conclude that there is little chance of defending the case, the parties can opt to enter into a settlement agreement with the Commission. In return for settling the case, the party will receive a 10% reduction in the level of any fine imposed.

From the Commission's perspective, there are a number of advantages in settling the case. First, settlement removes the need for written or oral submissions (see (a) above), which can involve tying up significant resources of the Commission. Secondly, the fact that the party has admitted its involvement means that there is no question of appeal of the Commission's infringement decision. Given the large fines imposed under EU competition rules, a very high number of Commission decisions are appealed, largely in an attempt to reduce the level of the fine. The settlement procedure helps the Commission in committing its resources to the detection of anti-competitive behaviour, rather than to the appeals process. For the parties, the settlement procedure involves an element of a gamble. The requirement to admit the infringement means opening themselves to third party private enforcement action (see **4.7** below). However, such private enforcement action will present itself in any event should the parties lose their case with the Commission and in the courts.

4.2.2.4   Rights of defence and rights of third parties

Undertakings have rights conferred by the European Convention on Human Rights, which the CJEU has recognised must apply to the conduct of proceedings by the Commission, for example when conducting an inspection and before finding that an undertaking has infringed competition law. There are also general principles of EU law that apply, rights provided for by the Treaty and rights in Regulation 1 itself, which provide important limitations to the Commission's powers. In enforcement proceedings by the Commission, the most common include:

(a)   In a dawn raid, the right to consult a lawyer. The Commission will not be required to wait for a lawyer to attend before conducting a raid, although it may allow a short time provided business records are not at risk of being disturbed. Many law firms provide their clients with a dawn raid quick reference guide to ensure that help is at hand as quickly as possible.

(b)   The right not to make self-incriminating statements, for example when questioned by the Commission, where the answer would constitute an admission of the infringement. There is, however, no right to silence in Commission proceedings, and the undertaking has a duty of 'active cooperation'.

(c)   The right to be heard. On this basis the Commission is required to put its case to the defence before deciding to take punitive action. Hence if a company has put forward cogent arguments chipping away at the Commission's case as set out in its statement of objections, the Commission may need to restate its case or supplement its statement of objections to enable the defence to be heard in relation to the restated case.

(d)   The right to have access to the Commission's file. The Commission is required to provide the defence with the evidence on which the Commission relies for its case. This may enable parties to put forward an alternative explanation of a document, for example if the Commission uses a business presentation to demonstrate the company's intent but that presentation does not reflect the intentions of management.

(e)   The right to privacy. The Commission is under an obligation not to disclose 'business secrets', which covers confidential information, the disclosure of which would be severely harmful to legitimate interests of the parties or of competition.

(f)   The Commission's duty to give reasons. This will enable parties to build a legal challenge of the Commission's decision before the courts should they wish to do so.

(g)   The requirement for the Commission to act proportionately and in a non-discriminatory manner. This may be invoked, for example, to challenge a proposed behavioural or structural remedy. Where the commitments procedure is used (see **4.2.2.3(b)** above), the Commission must ensure that the commitments are proportionate and no more onerous than required to address the competition concerns identified.

Third parties, primarily complainants, are often involved in the Commission's investigation. They too have rights, although these are not as extensive as the rights of the undertakings that are being investigated. For example, third parties may have a legitimate interest in making their case at an oral hearing. They may also be able to review submissions made by the undertakings that are being investigated, suitably redacted for confidentiality to respect the parties' right to privacy.

Third parties also have obligations, for example to respond to Commission requests for information truthfully and in a timely manner. Responding to Commission requests can be onerous, time consuming and costly, and businesses which complain to the Commission need to be prepared to devote substantial resources to the investigation process. This is usually less onerous, however, than private enforcement action, dealt with at **4.7** below.

Third party complainants are often unable to persuade the Commission to devote its limited resources to taking on their case. The Commission has no obligation to take on a complaint, although it must consider whether there could be an infringement that falls within the Commission's investigative priorities (Case T-24/90 *Automec v Commission ('Automec II')* [1992] ECR II-2223, [1992] 5 CMLR 431).

4.2.3   Consequences of breach

The consequences of breaching Articles 101 and 102 can be severe. The following will usually be of most relevance to business clients (including those in the UK):

*   *Fines.* As part of its infringement decision, the Commission will impose fines, which can be extremely high, to a maximum of 10% of an undertaking's turnover (see (a) below).
*   *Void.* An agreement in breach of Article 101 is void, and conduct prohibited under Article 102 may not be enforced by the courts (see (b) below).
*   *Damages.* Private enforcement action may be taken by affected third parties, which may result in damages being awarded (see **4.7**).

- *Orders.* Following an investigation, the Commission may order undertakings to bring an infringement to an end (see (c) below). This may involve behavioural or even structural remedies.

- *Reputation/expense.* Apart from penalties and enforcement action, there may be other 'softer' consequences, such as the impact on a company's reputation and even its stock market valuation. Firms will also be mindful of the time and expense taken in defending an investigation.

There may be other consequences in the particular circumstances, such as enforcement action by other competition authorities or interim measures.

(a)   Fines

This is by far the best known penalty that may be imposed. Under Article 23(2) of Regulation 1, the Commission can impose fines not exceeding 10% of the worldwide turnover of the undertaking. The fact that fines relate to turnover means that the level of fines can be very high. For example, Alphabet Google was fined over €4.1 billion for an infringement of Article 102 involving its search engine and its Android operating system (see **3.4.2(d)**), the highest competition law fine so far. Some of the highest fines are for cartels, and in 2016/17 the participants in a trucks cartel were fined a collective €3,807,022,000 (or approximately €3.8 billion). The Commission publishes annual statistics on the level of fines imposed for cartel activity under Article 101. A brief review of these statistics underlines the trend for a rise in fine levels.

Note that the Commission also has power under Article 24 of Regulation 1 to impose penalty payments for non-compliance with its infringement decisions. For example, in 2006 Microsoft was fined €280.5 million for non-compliance with a Commission decision imposing remedial obligations on it as a result of an Article 102 infringement.

(b)   Void

Agreements that breach Article 101(1) are automatically void under Article 101(2) (see **2.1.2**). This is not a penalty imposed by the Commission, but it is one that arises automatically. Its consequence is that agreements in breach of Article 101(1) will not be enforced by national courts. As seen at **2.1.2**, if the offending provisions are capable of being severed under national severance rules, the remainder of the agreement, without the offending provisions, may be enforced.

The courts will not generally enforce provisions in an agreement that would constitute abusive conduct prohibited by Article 102. For example, a patent licence with an abusive royalty clause may be challenged by the licensee.

As a result, commercial contract litigation may involve parties raising a competition law defence or counterclaim, using competition law tactically where provisions in an agreement may breach Article 101 or amount to an abuse under Article 102. This occurred for example in the beer tie cases referred to at **2.1.2**. In *Inntrepreneur Estates Ltd v Mason* [1993] 45 EG 130, the pub landlord sued for possession and payment of arrears. The pub tenant resisted by claiming that the effect of the beer tie was to render the entire lease void.

(c)   Order to cease the infringement

The Commission's infringement decision does not have to make any specific orders requiring an infringement to be terminated, as continuing the infringement would be a continued breach of Articles 101/102. However, the orders that may be imposed include the following.

Article 7 of Regulation 1 allows the Commission to order that the infringement is brought to an end immediately. In practice most undertakings that become subject to enforcement proceedings will stop the infringement in any event. This is especially relevant where the undertaking seeks leniency from the imposition of fines, where the termination of illegal activity is a condition of any leniency award.

The Commission can also make an order to prohibit behaviour to a like effect. For example, in Case T-30/89 *Hilti AG v Commission* [1991] ECR II-1439, measures 'having an equivalent effect' were prohibited.

Article 7 of Regulation 1 also allows the Commission to impose behavioural and structural remedies that are proportionate to the infringement and necessary to bring the infringement to an end. Behavioural remedies are the most common and can provide clarity as to the types of behaviour that may not continue. For example, in *Commercial Solvents* [1974] ECR 223, [1974] 1 CMLR 309, the dominant undertaking that breached Article 102 by discontinuing supplies was ordered to resume supplies. Sometimes behavioural remedies involve a level of complexity that requires the appointment of an expert 'monitoring trustee' to ensure that the remedies are complied with.

At the extreme, remedies can be structural. For example, a business that is both a manufacturer and distributor may have the incentive to degrade its products when selling to competing distributors. The only way to effectively remove this incentive may be to split the company between its manufacturing and distribution businesses. Such a measure would, however, be drastic and likely to be challenged if the competition concern can be addressed by less restrictive measures such as behavioural remedies.

If an undertaking does not comply with an order of the Commission, the Commission may impose periodic penalty payments of up to 5% of its average daily turnover (Regulation 1, Article 24).

4.2.4   Setting the level of the fine

The Commission methodology for setting the appropriate level of fine is contained in its *Guidelines on the method of setting fines imposed pursuant to Article 23(2)(a) of Regulation No 1/2003* ([2006] OJ C210/2). Under the Guidelines, it first determines the basic amount of the fine, which is based on a proportion of the party's value of sales in the relevant market sector (depending on the degree of gravity of the infringement and capped at 30%), multiplied by the number of years of infringement. In its assessment of gravity, the Commission takes into account the nature of the infringement, the combined market share of the undertakings concerned, the geographic scope of the infringement and whether or not the infringement has been implemented. In addition, the Commission will add a sum of 15 to 25% of the value of sales by way of a deterrent.

After the basic amount of fine has been established, the Commission will adjust this amount to take account of any aggravating or mitigating factors. Examples of aggravating circumstances are repeated infringements of the same type by the same undertaking, refusal to cooperate with the Commission and being the leader or instigator of the infringement. Examples of mitigating circumstances include termination of the infringement as soon as the Commission intervenes and negligent (as opposed to intentional) infringements.

Lastly, the Commission will make any adjustment to ensure that the fine imposed does not exceed the maximum of 10% of worldwide turnover.

4.3   THE RELATIONSHIP BETWEEN THE EUROPEAN COMMISSION AND NATIONAL COMPETITION AUTHORITIES/COURTS

4.3.1   The European Commission and EU Member States' national competition authorities

This section discusses the relationship between the European Commission and the national competition authorities of EU Member States.

Since the end of the Brexit transition period, the UK's relationship with the European Commission is that of a third country outside the Commission's European Competition Network. See **1.6**.

4.3.1.1 EU Member States' national competition authorities ('NCAs')

NCAs may be called on to assist with Commission inspections or to conduct an investigation on behalf of another national authority (Regulation 1, Articles 18–22). In addition, NCAs are enabled under Article 5 to apply Articles 101 and 102 in individual cases and are given the full range of powers to enforce a finding of infringement. This gives NCAs a very important role in the 'decentralised' enforcement regime of Regulation 1. Unless the context suggests otherwise, NCAs includes the EU Member States' national courts and regulatory authorities empowered to apply competition laws.

4.3.1.2 Requirement for consistency

To ensure a coherent system of competition law in the EU, Regulation 1 contains provisions that are intended to reflect the primacy of Articles 101 and 102 and ensure the consistent application of competition laws throughout the EU:

(a) *Duty to apply Article 101 and 102.* Under Article 3(1) of Regulation 1, when NCAs apply their own competition laws, they must also apply Articles 101 and 102 (where these are applicable, ie there must be an 'effect on trade between Member States' – see **2.1.1.4**).

(b) *Convergence.* Under Article 3(2) of Regulation 1, NCAs cannot prohibit agreements under their national competition laws which would be allowed by Article 101(1) or by an exemption under Article 101(3). This is known as the 'convergence' rule. The rule does not apply to Article 102: stricter national laws can apply to unilateral conduct, for example national laws requiring a dominant undertaking to compete fairly.

(c) *Different objective.* Stricter national laws are also permissible where they predominantly pursue an objective different from that pursued by Articles 101 and 102 (Regulation 1, Article 3(3)), for example legislation prohibiting unfair or disproportionate contract terms (Regulation 1, recital 9). Merger control laws can also diverge (although the EU has exclusive jurisdiction over certain mergers – see **Chapter 7**).

The requirement for consistency has particular relevance in cases that are pending before the Commission and then come before a national authority. In such cases the general rule is that the national authorities of EU Member States (including the courts) should not take decisions that would 'run counter' to the Commission. This means that where proceedings are taken before the national courts of EU Member States in relation to a matter under consideration by the Commission, the proceedings will usually be stayed (see **4.3.2** below).

Case allocation between the Commission and NCAs

The intention is that the Commission should be able to concentrate on only the most significant cases that present a real threat to the EU's interests in terms of competition policy. The European Competition Network ('ECN') has been set up as a forum for national authorities and the Commission to agree on case allocation, exchange information and assist each other in their investigations.

Whether the Commission or an NCA investigates an alleged breach of Articles 101 or 102 is outlined in Article 11 of Regulation 1 (further guidance is available in the Commission *Notice on cooperation within the network of competition authorities* [2004] OJ C101/43). If the Commission acts on a case, this relieves the NCA of its competence to deal with the matter.

4.3.2 The role of the national courts

It has long been established that Article 101 and Article 102 have direct effect. This means that they can be enforced by individuals and businesses before the national courts of their EU

Member State. Article 6 of Regulation 1 provides that national courts in the EU Member States have the power to apply Articles 101 and 102 (in their entirety). Further rules relating to the relationship are included in Article 15 of Regulation 1, including the exchange of information. The importance of uniform application of EU competition rules is outlined in Article 16. Guidance on the relationship between the Commission and national courts of EU Member States may be found in the Commission's *Notice on the cooperation between the Commission and the courts of the EU Member States in the application of Articles 81 and 82 EC* ([2004] OJ C101/54) (discussed at **4.7.1**).

As a general rule, an infringement decision by the Commission may be used by a private claimant in the context of national litigation in EU Member States. Accordingly, the claimant is generally required to prove only that it was affected by the infringement and to establish the amount of damage caused. Therefore the burden of proving the infringement is removed from the claimant in such circumstances. See further **4.7** below.

Where the Commission is already considering a matter that is then brought before the courts of an EU Member State, the court should consider whether it would be appropriate to stay the proceedings (see Article 15 of Regulation 1). Given that courts of EU Member States must avoid giving a decision that runs counter to a Commission decision, a stay will usually be appropriate.

In practice this means complainants deciding early on whether to bring a complaint to the Commission or in the alternative to bring proceedings before the courts.

4.4   ENFORCEMENT BY THE UK COMPETITION AUTHORITIES

4.4.1   Introduction

In regard to the substantive law, as we have seen, UK law mirrors the system under Articles 101 and 102 (see **Chapters 2** and **3**), and the two systems are likely to remain aligned for some time, with some differences emerging as the UK starts to implement its own regime and adapt it to the UK situation

In regard to the procedure, the UK provisions contained in the CA 1998 are similar to those under EU law although not always the same. Until the end of the Brexit transition period, the CMA had a duty under s 60 of the CA 1998 to deal with 'questions arising in relation to competition' consistently with how they would be treated under EU law. This requirement for consistency applied not only to substantive issues but extended to procedural issues such as the CMA's obligation to act in a procedurally fair manner, including the rights of a complainant to be heard (Case 1017/2/1/03 *Pernod-Ricard v OFT* [2004] CAT 10). The UK is no longer required to follow EU principles (see **2.2.1**), although these have permeated the UK's procedural rules and as such remain relevant.

It is now possible for both the EU and the UK to use their respective competition powers with regard to the same suspected anti-competitive conduct.

In regard to the decisions that may be taken by the UK competition law authorities, these are broadly similar to the decisions that may be taken by the European Commission, including interim measures, penalties, directions (behavioural or structural), commitments and the settlement procedure.

Where the UK system differs from that of the EU, and where it has taken aspects of the US regime, is in relation to fines and imprisonment for individuals when addressing the most serious infringements, and the disqualification of company directors.

The enforcement powers will be outlined with regard to both the CA 1998 and the criminal cartel offence under the EA 2002. The CMA has published a number of guidance notes relating to these powers, the most relevant being its Guidance on the CMA's investigation procedures in Competition Act 1998 cases – CMA8, which can be found on the CMA's website.

4.4.1.1 Investigations – CA 1998

As seen at **1.3.2**, the CMA is the UK's main competition authority, which exercises competition law powers concurrently with the sector regulators. The Guidance on the CMA's investigation procedures in Competition Act 1998 cases (CMA8) sets out the approach and procedures used by the CMA when exercising its powers.

The CMA can conduct an investigation if there are 'reasonable grounds for suspecting' that either of the prohibitions have been breached (CA 1998, s 25). As seen above (see **4.1**), competition authorities may launch infringement proceedings as a result of a leniency application, information received from other competition authorities, a complaint received from a third party, or as a result of its own investigations into a particular market or sector of industry.

In addition to these ways of detecting anti-competitive behaviour, the CMA operates a policy whereby it can pay up to £250,000 for information leading to the identification and the ability to take action against illegal cartels.

The way in which the CMA gathers evidence includes the methods available to the Commission, namely information requests, 'dawn raids' and interviews, as seen above (see **4.2.2.1**). However, and mainly as a result of the introduction of the criminal cartel offence, the investigatory powers of the CMA are more extensive and include the power to conduct covert surveillance.

(a)   The written procedure – section 26 notices

Once the CMA has established that it has 'reasonable grounds for suspecting' an infringement under s 25 (which is a low threshold for intervention), s 26 of the CA 1998 enables the CMA to request in writing that a business produce a specified document or provide information that it considers relevant to its investigation.

The CMA's request is in the form of a 'section 26 notice', triggering statutory obligations to respond within the deadline set by the CMA. There are statutory penalties for failing to respond or for providing false or misleading information. In Case CE/9742-13 Pfizer was fined £10,000 for failing to comply with a section 26 notice without reasonable excuse.

A section 26 notice can be very onerous for businesses to respond to, with some requests generating hundreds of thousands of documents. Relevant documents are typically gathered by the business's legal, regulatory or compliance functions and then sifted to exclude documents benefitting from legal professional privilege, or those outside the scope of the investigation, which do not have to be submitted to the CMA.

(b)   Inspection – 'dawn raids'

Either in conjunction with or instead of the written procedure, the CMA may carry out a so-called 'dawn raid', which is an unannounced inspection made by CMA officials at business premises (and sometimes homes and vehicles of senior executives).

Before carrying out a 'dawn raid', the CMA must first establish that it has reasonable grounds to suspect a breach of competition laws under s 25 of the CA 1998. It then has one of two statutory routes:

- *section 27 investigations.* On-site investigations may be made without a warrant (CA 1998, s 27) and may involve giving prior notice to the business being investigated.
- *section 28 investigations.* Alternatively, on-site investigations may be made with a warrant (CA 1998, s 28). The CMA must have reasonable grounds for suspecting that documents would be destroyed or tampered with if they were requested under a section 26 notice. A

section 28 investigation with warrant has the advantage of enabling the CMA to force entry if required. The CMA also has the power to take away original documents, not only copies. The CMA may also obtain a warrant authorising its officers to inspect domestic premises (CA 1998, s 28A).

As under EU rules, the CMA is not permitted to exceed the scope of its authorisation and undergo a 'fishing expedition' into the business concerned. As in dawn raids carried out by the European Commission, officials will have forensic tools at their disposal enabling them to access and download relevant documents, and they will ask to be taken to where documents can be accessed. The CMA may also ask for explanations of documents which are produced.

The process is similar to that followed by the European Commission, although there are greater safeguards in place when the CMA also acts under its powers to investigate individuals.

(c)   Compulsory interviews of individuals

The CMA has the power to interview any person 'with a connection to' an undertaking being investigated. This includes current and former employees and management. The CMA can exercise this power at any stage of an investigation, including during a dawn raid (CA 1998, s 26A). The CMA may impose civil fines on individuals who refuse to answer questions (CA 1998, s 40A). There are certain safeguards, including a privilege against self-incrimination.

(d)   Further powers

In addition to the traditional investigatory tools outlined above, the CMA is one of the agencies allowed to use powers under the Regulation of Investigatory Powers Act (RIPA) 2000. It can engage in the following investigatory techniques:

- direct surveillance – such as watching a person's office (RIPA 2000, s 28); and/or
- covert human intelligent sources – such as the use of informants (RIPA 2000, s 29).

4.4.1.2   Investigations – Enterprise Act 2002

The Enterprise Act 2002 (EA 2002) introduced the criminal cartel offence. In practice, an investigation under the EA 2002 will run in parallel with the CA 1998, and many of the rules relating to the CA 1998 will also apply to the EA 2002. The CMA can launch an investigation under the EA 2002 where it has reasonable grounds for suspecting that a criminal infringement has taken place (EA 2002, s 192(1)). The CMA can use the following investigatory powers only in the context of an EA 2002 investigation (EA 2002, ss 199, 200):

- Intrusive surveillance – which allows the CMA to undertake covert surveillance in residential premises (including hotels and vehicles). Covert surveillance may be made either by an individual being present on the premises to hear or see what is happening, or by way of a surveillance device(s).
- Property interference – this is closely related to the intrusive surveillance power described above and allows the CMA to enter premises (which would otherwise involve an element of trespass) in order to install surveillance devices.
- Access to communications data – which allows the CMA to obtain information about, for example, records of telephone numbers called.

4.4.1.3   Interim measures

As seen at **4.2.2.2**, interim measures are an important tool in competition law enforcement to prevent harm to the competitive process before an investigation is completed and to ensure the effectiveness of any decision to bring infringements to an end. The CMA can make an interim measures direction under s 35 of the CA 1998. The test for obtaining interim measures is that the CMA has started, but not completed, an investigation under s 25 of the CA 1998; and that it is necessary for the CMA to act as a matter of urgency, either in order to prevent significant damage, or in order to protect the public interest. The CMA must also consider that the interim measures are proportionate and the least intrusive measure to achieve their purpose, considering the same 'balance of interest' between the parties as applied by the High Court for interim injunctions.

Interim measures were imposed in Case 50616 *Atlantic Joint Business Agreement* (17 September 2020) in the unusual circumstances of the COVID-19 pandemic. The CMA needed to address an enforcement gap to protect the public interest after the expiry of 10-year commitments made to the European Commission. The parties were required to reduce their cooperation on certain city-pair routes, as the CMA could not be confident that new proposed commitments would address competition concerns until it had more time to assess the impact of the pandemic on the agreements.

4.4.2   Post-investigation options

Putting aside interim measures outlined at **4.4.1.3** above, having amassed sufficient relevant information to proceed, the CMA will have a number of options.

(a)   Infringement decision

In the investigation, the CMA will analyse the documents and information in its possession. In the event that there is sufficient evidence, the CMA may proceed to an infringement decision and any appropriate directions, for example to terminate the infringement.

Until the end of the Brexit transition period, due to the operation of Article 3 of Regulation 1, the CMA also acted under Article 101 and/or Article 102 where these applied.

Before issuing its infringement decision, the CMA will need to respect the rights of the defence, which involves issuing a statement of objections and allowing the parties to which it has been addressed to respond to the statement in writing and/or orally at a hearing (CA 1998, s 31). As in the EU process, the parties have the right to access the CMA's file so that they may see the evidence against them. Third parties have similar rights as under the EU process.

(b)   Commitments

Under s 31A of the CA 1998, the CMA can accept binding commitments from the parties instead of proceeding to a full infringement decision. As seen at **4.2.2.3(b)**, the commitments procedure can be an efficient way to resolve a competition law investigation. A party may voluntarily offer commitments to the CMA, which triggers a period of consultation following which the CMA may adopt a decision making the commitments binding. The case is then closed without a finding of infringement. The party accepting commitments thus does not admit any breach of competition law. The procedure, despite its advantages, has not been used as frequently as under the EU process.

Since the end of the Brexit transition period, commitments to the CMA can no longer relate to CMA investigations under Articles 101 and 102. The CMA can only investigate and accept commitments under the CA 1998.

(c)   Settlement

The settlement process enables a party to admit that it has breached competition law and benefit from a reduced penalty. The CMA will adopt a streamlined procedure, which will include a statement of objections and an infringement decision but with a reduced administrative burden on the CMA and the parties. The CMA's settlement procedure is operated pursuant to rule 9 of the Competition Act 1998 (Competition and Markets Authority's Rules) Order 2014 (SI 2014/458).

Where a settlement is reached before the statement of objections, parties are eligible for a discount of 20% on the fine imposed, while they are eligible for a discount of 10% if a settlement is reached afterwards.

(d)   Pursuing individuals

The CMA has primary responsibility for the prosecution of the criminal cartel offence in England and Wales and Northern Ireland (the Lord Advocate is responsible for prosecutions in Scotland). Prosecutions may also be brought by the Serious Fraud Office, which used to be the primary prosecution authority. The criminal cartel offence is further considered at **4.4.3.2**.

The CMA is also responsible for seeking company disqualification orders, considered at **4.4.3.3**.

4.4.3   Penalties and other consequences

4.4.3.1   CA 1998

The following penalties may be imposed on undertakings by the CMA in the context of an infringement of the CA 1998. The list below is essentially the same as in **4.2.3**.

(a)   Fines

The CMA has the power to impose a fine of up to 10% of an undertaking's worldwide turnover. Like the European Commission, the CMA has a broad discretion on how to impose fines and has issued guidance on the appropriate level of penalty under s 36 of the CA 1998. The CMA considers factors in a six-stage process. The starting point is based on the seriousness of the infringement (up to 30% of turnover in the relevant infringement market). There are then a further five stages, including the duration of the infringement, aggravating and mitigating circumstances, and adjustments for deterrence and leniency. The CMA must not exceed the legal maximum of 10% of turnover.

(b)   Void

Infringements of the Chapter I prohibition will render the agreement automatically void under s 2(4) of the CA 1998 (although the remainder of the agreement may be enforceable once the restrictive provisions fall away). A court will not enforce conduct prohibited under Chapter II.

(c)   Damages

Damages or other forms of relief may be imposed by the courts. Private enforcement actions are discussed at **4.7**.

(d)   Directions

The CMA may address directions to a party or parties that have breached the CA 1998 (s 32 in relation to agreements and s 33 in relation to conduct). These directions may involve the requirement to cease the activity in question and may also require a party to modify its conduct. Both behavioural and structural remedies may be imposed.

(e)   Other consequences

There are other consequences of infringing the Chapter I and Chapter II prohibitions. These include 'softer' consequences, such as reputational damage and investors' reduced appetite for buying shares or investing in a company. See **4.2.3**.

In the UK, the criminal penalties and directors' disqualification regime also acts as a powerful incentive for individuals to comply (see **4.4.3.2** and **4.4.3.3** below).

4.4.3.2   Criminal cartel offence – EA 2002

The EA 2002 introduced a new criminal offence, the 'cartel offence', and penalties. These are imposed on the individual for the most serious forms of anti-competitive behaviour.

Section 188 of the 2002 Act (as amended) provides that an individual is guilty of an offence if they agree with one or more other persons to engage in prohibited cartel activity, namely:

(a) price-fixing;

(b) limiting supply or production;

(c) market-sharing; and

(d) bid-rigging.

There has been an amendment to the law to remove the previous requirement that an individual must be acting dishonestly. Under the previous law, only two cases proceeded to trial, of which only one led to a conviction. The perception was that juries were unwilling to find anything dishonest about individuals struggling with competitive pressure and colluding in the innocent belief that they were not doing anything wrong. The Enterprise and Regulatory Reform Act 2013 accordingly removed the requirement to prove dishonesty. In response to criticism that this could criminalise innocent mistakes, the 2013 Act created two defences.

Defences under the EA 2002

The first defence open to an individual accused of the criminal cartel offence is that the individual did not intend the arrangements to be concealed from customers or from the CMA. The second defence is that the defendant disclosed the arrangements to legal advisers for the purpose of obtaining advice (EA 2002, s 188B).

In addition the CMA published guidance on the principles it will adopt for deciding whether a person should be prosecuted for the offence (under s 190A) – CMA9, published in March 2014.

Penalties for the cartel offence under the EA 2002

An individual may be imprisoned for up to five years for the cartel offence. In addition, an individual may be subject to an unlimited fine (EA 2002, s 190).

For example, in June 2008, three British businessmen were imprisoned for terms between two-and-a-half and three years for a series of cartel infringements relating to marine hoses (used to transport oil from tankers to storage facilities). They were also disqualified from acting as directors for periods between five and seven years. This case was decided before the removal of the requirement of dishonesty from the cartel offence.

4.4.3.3 Director disqualification – EA 2002

A director of a company which has been found to have breached the competition rules may be disqualified from acting as a director for up to 15 years. The requirements are that the company has breached competition law (Article 101 or 102; and/or CA 1998, Chapter I or Chapter II) and that this makes the director unfit to be concerned in the management of a company (EA 2002, s 204, which amends the Company Directors Disqualification Act 1986). The CMA published Guidance on Competition Disqualification Orders, CMA 102, in February 2019.

Thus, disqualification orders may be made in respect of any type of breach of competition law and not just the infringements which could give rise to imprisonment or the imposition of a fine described above. In 2018, estates agencies in Somerset were fined for participating in a cartel, and the CMA accepted undertakings from two of their directors not to act as directors of any UK company for three and three-and-a-half years respectively. Disqualification orders and undertakings have become increasingly common.

As well as criminal penalties and disqualification, individuals can face severe consequences for being involved in a breach of competition law in terms of disciplinary action from their employers, suspension pending investigation and ultimately dismissal.

4.5 GOVERNMENT ENFORCEMENT OF US ANTITRUST LAWS

4.5.1 Criminal enforcement for cartel agreements

Although Sections 1 and 2 of the Sherman Act were both drafted to provide for criminal penalties for any violation, in practice, criminal prosecutions are reserved to egregious cartel offences. Criminal antitrust prosecutions typically focus on situations where the government has evidence that competitors met and agreed to fix prices or to suppress competition among themselves. The United States Department of Justice (DOJ) Antitrust Division has recently indicated its intent to enforce Section 2 criminally, but has since only brought one enforcement action, an attempted-monopolization action relating to an 'invitation to collude'.

The DOJ is solely responsible for the criminal enforcement of federal antitrust laws. Most state antitrust laws charge the state's attorney general with responsibility for the criminal enforcement of state laws, generally by procedures similar to those used by the DOJ. However, criminal enforcement is much less common at the state level than at the federal level.

The tools available to the DOJ to investigate criminal antitrust violations include grand jury subpoenas to compel witness testimony and production of documents. The DOJ can also ask a court for permission to execute a warrant to search private premises for evidence or to install a wiretap to uncover evidence of illicit activity. Search warrants and wiretap authorisations usually impose specific restrictions on the scope of the search or the listening. Due to restrictions in the US Constitution, law enforcement officials cannot execute a procedure equivalent to a dawn raid under EU law. The DOJ can utilise Mutual Legal Assistance Treaties with foreign countries to request that foreign competition agencies collect documents outside of the United States to aid an ongoing cartel investigation in the United States. In addition, the DOJ often coordinates informally with foreign competition agencies with respect to multi-jurisdictional cartel investigations.

The maximum corporate criminal fine is $100 million, or double the loss or gain from the offence, whichever is the greater. The US Sentencing Guidelines, which are not binding on courts, but are frequently used as a reference in setting criminal fines, calculate fine levels based on factors including the volume of commerce affected by the cartel, whether the corporation is cooperating with the government's investigation, and whether the corporation has previously been found to have violated US antitrust laws. As of September 2023, 35 corporate fines of over $100 million had been imposed, including 13 of $300 million or more.

Individual executives can be prosecuted criminally for entering into anti-competitive agreements with competitors, directing subordinates to do so, or, in the case of senior executives, being aware of the company's participation in a cartel and doing nothing to stop it. Individual employees who participated in the offence face both large fines and imprisonment; the maximum sentence is 10 years. Under the US Sentencing Guidelines, when determining the length of an individual's prison sentence and the extent of an individual criminal fine, courts consider factors including whether the individual has a prior criminal history and whether the individual is cooperating with the investigation. The maximum individual fine is $1 million, or double the loss or gain from the offence, whichever is the greater.

A number of foreign nationals have been sentenced to prison terms. In 2014, the DOJ completed the first-ever successful extradition of a foreign national for a violation of the Sherman Act. The DOJ has considerable tools at its disposal to convince foreign nationals to travel to the United States and face criminal antitrust charges, including indicting foreign nationals under seal, issuing Interpol Red Notices for foreign nationals charged with antitrust offences, and seeking extradition under the 'dual criminality' provisions of extradition treaties.

4.5.2 Federal agency civil enforcement in non-cartel cases

For non-cartel restraint of trade cases and monopolization cases, both the DOJ and the Federal Trade Commission (FTC) have civil enforcement responsibilities. These agencies will investigate and bring actions to enjoin the continuation of conduct that violates the antitrust laws. The agencies typically seek structural relief (ie, the break-up of the alleged monopoly or divesting an exclusive contract), but the FTC is generally more favourable to behavioural or conduct remedies (ie, setting up firewalls to ensure that information is not inappropriately shared).

Aside from the fact that the DOJ is the criminal enforcer, the other primary distinction between the agencies is that the DOJ seeks relief in federal court. Settlements of investigations or enforcement actions are filed in federal court and reviewed and/or adjudicated by a US federal judge. Investigations and enforcement actions before the FTC typically are resolved by consent decrees or via administrative proceedings brought before the Commission.

The FTC also enforces Section 5 of the Federal Trade Commission Act, which declares 'unfair methods of competition' to be 'unlawful' (15 USC §45(a)(1)). Under this statute, the FTC may prohibit conduct that does not constitute a Sherman or Clayton Act violation but which the Commission determines, based on the evidence in the particular case, is harmful to competition. Historically, the Commission has used the broad power of Section 5 sparingly, but its use in competition cases has been resurrected. On November 10, 2022, the FTC issued a Policy Statement 'restor[ing its] policy of rigorously enforcing the federal ban on unfair methods of competition' via the application of Section 5 of the FTC Act. The Policy Statement outlines the general principles that the FTC will apply to determine whether conduct constitutes an unfair method of competition in violation of Section 5. On August 16, 2023, the FTC settled a complaint brought as a result of a merger investigation that involved, for the first time, stand-alone claims brought under Section 5 of the FTC Act. The claims alleged that the parties inappropriately shared confidential and competitively sensitive information between them to the detriment of consumers and other competitors. On January 5, 2023, the FTC issued a notice of proposed rulemaking declaring nearly all employer/employee non-compete agreements to be 'unfair methods of competition' and thus a violation of Section 5. At the time of writing, the rule has not been finalised or implemented. Critics of the rule have questioned whether the FTC indeed has the authority to issue such a rulemaking. Details of these policies and of the notice are available from the FTC's website.

While no formal division exists between the civil enforcement responsibilities of the DOJ and the FTC, the agencies tend to investigate matters where one has history or experience in that industry. The agencies have established a clearance procedure to ensure that only one of them proceeds with an investigation of a particular violation.

4.5.3 Civil enforcement by state attorneys general

The attorneys general of most states have powers to enforce their state's antitrust laws similar to the DOJ's civil enforcement powers under federal laws. In addition, state attorneys general have a range of enforcement rights under the federal antitrust laws.

(a) State government plaintiff

When the state government suffers an injury from a federal antitrust violation, such as when a cartel overcharges a state agency on its purchases, the attorney general can sue on behalf of the state government for treble damages in the same manner as a private plaintiff.

(b) Injunctions

The attorney general can sue for an injunction against a federal antitrust violation that threatens injury either to the state government or to the general economy of the state.

(c) *Parens patriae*

The attorneys general may sue to collect treble damages on behalf of natural persons residing in their states who have been injured by a federal antitrust violation, in a manner similar to a class action.

Using these processes, the attorneys general of several states have become very active antitrust enforcers.

4.6 LENIENCY PROGRAMMES

Outlined below is an overview of the leniency systems in the EU, UK and US. As indicated above, leniency programmes have proved to be an invaluable tool in the detection of anti-competitive behaviour, and as such have been introduced in most of the competition regimes worldwide.

A common feature of leniency programmes is that they encourage a race among cartel participants to be the first to report a cartel to the relevant competition authorities, knowing that only the first participant qualifies for total immunity, ie zero fines. Being second, even by a few minutes, can result in paying significant penalties, sometime in the hundreds of millions of euros. This inevitably instils a sense of urgency among leniency applicants.

4.6.1 The EU leniency programme

The European Commission has implemented a number of leniency programmes, the latest version of which was introduced in 2006 and can be found in the Commission *Notice on immunity from fines and reduction of fines in cartel cases* ([2006] OJ C298/17) (the 'Leniency Notice').

The Leniency Notice is broken down into two parts, the first relating to a 100% reduction in the level of fine (or immunity), and the second dealing with reductions in the level of fine.

4.6.1.1 Immunity

Immunity from fines will be available for the first undertaking in a cartel to submit information to the Commission to allow it to carry out an inspection or to find an infringement of Article 101(1). The undertaking must also make a corporate statement outlining all relevant information. To qualify for immunity, the undertaking must not have coerced the other undertakings to take part in the cartel. In addition, the undertaking must also comply with the following conditions:

(a)   to provide genuine, continuous and expeditious cooperation;

(b)   to terminate its involvement in the cartel (unless agreed with the Commission that for evidence-gathering reasons it should continue to give the appearance that it is still part of the cartel); and

(c)   not to destroy, falsify or conceal any relevant information.

A 'marker system' operates under the EU system. Under this system, an undertaking will approach the Commission in circumstances where it does not have sufficient available information to make a full immunity application. Where the Commission accepts the marker, the undertaking will be given a specific period in which to 'perfect' the marker by providing all relevant information. If the undertaking manages to do this, the application date is deemed to be the date on which the marker was granted (this is significant, as other undertakings may have approached the Commission in the meantime, and it is only the first that can obtain immunity).

4.6.1.2 Reduction in the level of fine

If an undertaking does not qualify for 100% immunity (or it is not the first to make an application), it can still obtain a reduction in the level of any fine. Again, a reduction is dependent on providing the Commission with evidence, and in particular evidence which represents 'significant added value'. Reductions in fines will be made at the end of the administrative procedure on the following bases:

(a) first to provide significant added value – reduction of 30–50%;

(b) second to provide significant value – reduction of 20–30%; and

(c) subsequent undertakings which provide significant added value – reduction of up to 20%.

4.6.2 The UK leniency programme

The UK system for leniency is more complicated than that of the Commission, primarily as it has to deal with leniency for both undertakings and individuals. Below is a brief overview of the main points (for further information, please refer to the OFT publication, now adopted by the CMA – *Applications for leniency and no-action in cartel cases* – OFT 1495 (July 2013)).

The UK system outlines a number of grades (or types) of *immunity* (100% reduction) and *leniency* (partial reduction) which may be granted by the CMA:

- Type A immunity – provides immunity from fines and immunity from prosecution for all directors and employees where the undertaking is the first in and no investigation was underway.

- Type B immunity/leniency – provides *discretionary* immunity from fines and immunity from prosecution for all directors and employees, or a reduction in penalties, where the undertaking was the first in but an investigation was already in progress.

- Type C leniency – provides for a reduction of up to 50% in the level of fine whether they were first in or otherwise, and is not dependent on whether an investigation was in progress.

In order for an undertaking and/or individual to qualify for any of these types, they must meet the conditions of immunity/leniency. In the case of Type B immunity/leniency, these conditions include that the applicant should not have coerced another undertaking into taking part in a cartel. If an applicant is a coercer, only Type C leniency is available. In Type B and C leniency, since an investigation has already started, an applicant must provide significant added value to the CMA's investigation in order to qualify for leniency.

The conditions to be met to qualify for any type of immunity or leniency are set out in para 2.7 of the OFT 1495 Guide. The applicant must be prepared to confess. They must provide sufficient information to the CMA and cooperate on an ongoing basis. They must terminate the cartel unless the CMA directs them not to, for example where this would tip off other participants.

Individuals that qualify for immunity from prosecution under 'blanket' immunity will be issued with a 'no-action letter' if they need it. Other individuals may also seek immunity by way of a 'no-action letter' being issued by the CMA.

In addition, an applicant may benefit from 'Leniency Plus'. If a company is already cooperating with the CMA in relation to a cartel and that company's internal investigations uncover a second cartel, an incentive is provided for reporting that second cartel to the CMA. An applicant may benefit from immunity or leniency not just in relation to the second cartel, but it may also benefit from additional leniency (Leniency Plus) in relation to the first cartel already being investigated (OFT 1495, para 9).

As under the EU programme, there is a 'marker' system to enable companies to establish their place in the queue pending their full application being developed.

4.6.3 The US leniency program

Under the Corporate Leniency Program of the DOJ, a member of a cartel can obtain complete amnesty from criminal penalties – no fines for the corporation and no fines or prison sentences for its employees – if it ceases its participation, reports the cartel to the DOJ and meets several other requirements designed to assist the DOJ in prosecuting the other participants. The key requirement is that the company must be the first member of the cartel to report and request amnesty. The rule is one grant of amnesty per cartel, given to the first company to request and qualify for it. The objective of the Leniency Program is to sow distrust among cartel members and to encourage companies to act vigilantly to uncover cartel agreements and to report them promptly.

Benefits in private treble damages actions also flow from a grant of leniency. Provided that the company cooperates with the plaintiffs, it will be assessed only single, not treble, damages, and it will be relieved from joint and several liability, so that its damages will be measured only on its own sales.

A company that fails to win the race for amnesty can obtain benefits under another DOJ program, known as Amnesty Plus. If that company reports a second criminal antitrust violation, and is the first to report that violation, it will receive not only complete amnesty for that second violation, under the normal terms of the Leniency Program, but also a reduction of its penalties for the first. Under a variation of this program known as Penalty Plus, if a company is under investigation for one criminal antitrust violation and it fails to disclose its participation in a second violation, the DOJ will seek substantially enhanced penalties for the second violation.

The DOJ updated its Leniency Policy in April 2022. The update affirms the DOJ's continued commitment to criminal antitrust enforcement. Among other things, the policy clarifies the DOJ's requirements for prompt notification to the DOJ once a violation has been identified, for remediating the harm caused by the violation, and for revising internal compliance programs to avoid recidivism.

4.7   PRIVATE ENFORCEMENT ACTIONS

Public and private enforcement

So far we have considered the public enforcement of competition rules. An individual or undertaking affected by anti-competitive behaviour may also bring a private enforcement action before the courts.

Public authorities encourage private enforcement actions as they are an important element of deterrence against anti-competitive conduct. Since the private enforcement of EU competition law takes place in the national courts of EU Member States (and not in the EU appeal courts), the EU introduced measures to facilitate private enforcement action in national courts (see **4.7.1**). The UK has also introduced measures to facilitate private 'class' (or collective) enforcement action against companies breaching competition law (see **4.7.2**).

Public and private enforcement actions are usually in the alternative rather than concurrent. Competition lawyers will need to advise their clients as to the advantages and disadvantages of either option in the circumstances of the case. This can be a difficult balancing act. In a complaint to the authorities, there is no guarantee that the authorities will take up the case (they will take into account the availability of private enforcement action). Even where the authorities open an investigation (for example because the case is within one of their enforcement priorities), the process can be slow. In addition, any fines are paid to the state, rather than damages being awarded to the victims. Nevertheless, private enforcement action can be significantly more expensive than a complaints procedure before the authorities.

Historical background

Public enforcement was for many years by far and away the predominant method of enforcing competition law; it was not until 2001 that the ECJ ruled that a victim of anti-competitive behaviour had the right to claim damages for breaches of EU competition law (*Courage v Crehan* [2001] ECR I-6297, although sadly for the claimant the House of Lords ultimately ruled that the defendant had not actually breached Article 101 (*Crehan v Inntrepreneur Pub Co* [2006] UKHL 38)). In contrast, the English courts had already accepted in *Garden Cottages v Milk Marketing Board* [1984] AC 130 that damages were in principle available for breaches of EU competition law. With the EU's 2014 Damages Directive (see **4.7.1**), private undertakings have a greater incentive to take matters into their own hands through litigation in national courts. Law firms specialising in private enforcement actions have emerged, as have companies that specialise in funding private enforcement actions in return for some of the proceeds.

Types of private enforcement actions

Private enforcement actions can be 'follow-on' actions, where the aggrieved parties launch a damages action after a public finding by a competition authority; however, this assumes that a finding of infringement has indeed taken place. If so, the main advantage of 'follow-on' actions is that the infringement decision is taken as fact and need not be proved again (see **4.7.3.1**).

Outside such circumstances, an aggrieved party wishing redress for anti-competitive behaviour will need to take a 'stand-alone' private enforcement action in its national courts, ie an action not made on the back of an infringement decision by a competition authority.

In practice, private enforcement actions may involve elements of 'follow-on' and elements of 'stand-alone', for example where there is a prior infringement decision which covers only some of the anti-competitive practices affecting the claimant. It can also be difficult to establish how much of the infringement decision is binding on the national court.

4.7.1 EU legislation

This section sets out some of the EU texts relevant to private enforcement.

European Union legislation that is 'directly effective' (such as Regulations) may be invoked by individuals before their national courts. Regulation 1 outlines some of the bases for cooperation between the Commission and national courts of EU Member States, including the following:

- Article 6 – establishes that Articles 101 and 102 may be enforced by national courts.
- Article 15 – allows for cooperation between the Commission and the national courts.
- Article 16 – requires that national courts cannot take decisions that run counter to a decision made by the Commission. This effectively allows a claimant to use a Commission decision as the basis of a subsequent damages action.

This cooperation is further developed in Commission *Notice on the co-operation between the Commission and the courts of the EU Member States in the application of Article 81 and 82 EC* ([2004] OJ C 101/54).

The EU passed *Directive 2014/104/EU on certain rules governing actions for damages under national law for infringements of the competition law provisions of the Member States and of the European Union* ([2014] OJ L 349/1) ('the Damages Directive'). The Damages Directive provides for the partial harmonisation of Member State rules and procedures that apply in competition damages actions. It is complemented by a package of measures including a Recommendation and accompanying Communication on collective redress and a Communication on quantifying harm in competition damages cases. The Commission's package is based on the principle that victims of anti-competitive behaviour should be able to obtain full compensation for the loss they have suffered. It establishes a number of presumptions that are helpful to claimants in private enforcement actions. The Commission has also issued guidelines for national courts of the EU Member States on how to estimate the share of overcharge passed on to indirect purchasers.

4.7.2   UK legislation

The Damages Directive was implemented in the UK by the Claims in respect of Loss or Damage arising from Competition Infringements (Competition Act 1998 and Other Enactments (Amendment)) Regulations 2017 (SI 2017/385) on 9 March 2017.

The Consumer Rights Act 2015 aims to facilitate private actions by consumers and small businesses so that any person or business who has suffered loss flowing from unlawful anti-competitive behaviour can bring a claim. It made it easier to bring collective actions following a breach of competition law. It also expanded the jurisdiction of the UK's specialist competition law tribunal, the Competition Appeal Tribunal ('CAT'), so that private enforcement actions may be brought before the CAT, not just the High Court.

4.7.3   Private enforcement in the UK

4.7.3.1   Follow-on actions

A claimant may bring a follow-on action in the UK where there is a prior infringement decision by one of the UK's national competition authorities. It is no longer possible to bring a follow-on action in the UK courts based on a decision of breach of Articles 101 or 102 TFEU.

A follow-on action is brought under s 47A of the CA 1998. The CMA or a concurrent regulator must have taken a decision establishing a breach of Chapter I or Chapter II of the CA 1998. Generally, the time limit for appeal of any decision by the regulator will have to have elapsed before a damages action can be initiated.

The main advantage of a follow-on action is that the court is bound by the prior infringement decision and so the claimant does not have to prove that the defendant has breached competition law (CA 1998, s 47A); the case can move straight on to the issues of causation and whether the claimant has suffered loss. The claimant may bring the claim in either the High Court or the CAT.

4.7.3.2   Stand-alone actions

Where there is no prior finding of infringement, the claimant must bring a stand-alone action and must first prove that the defendant has breached competition law, before moving on to the issue of whether the claimant has suffered loss. Before the Consumer Rights Act 2015, stand-alone actions had to be brought in the High Court. The 2015 Act extended the CAT's jurisdiction to cover them.

4.7.3.3   Injunctions

A claimant may seek interim relief from the court, such as an injunction requiring the defendant to cease the anti-competitive activity in question. This is a valuable remedy as a victim of anti-competitive conduct will often be as anxious to stop the offending conduct as to obtain damages. Although interim relief is available as a remedy from the European Commission or the CMA, in practice applications take time and are rarely successful.

The test for granting an interim injunction in competition cases is to decide which course (ie the grant or refusal of the injunction) would involve less risk of injustice if it transpires to be wrong (*AAH Pharmaceuticals Ltd v Pfizer Ltd* [2007] EWHC 565 (Ch)). The court will consider other factors as well, such as urgency, whether damages would be an adequate remedy and the strength of the parties' case if it proceeds to trial.

4.7.3.4 Damages

Proof of harm

In follow-on actions or stand-alone actions, once the competition law breach has been proven, a claimant will need to establish that the infringement has caused the damage or harm. The burden of proof is on the claimant to prove on the balance of probabilities that the infringement has caused it harm.

While this may sound straightforward, in practice it is very hard to prove causation and to quantify the loss suffered. Even when there is a prior infringement decision, it will not usually involve a finding that the infringement has caused harm or quantify such harm. Accordingly, provisions brought in to implement the Damages Directive make it easier for victims of anti-competitive conduct to prove not only infringement, but also causation and loss.

Under para 13 of Sch 8A to the CA 1998, for cartel infringements, there is a rebuttable presumption that the cartel infringement caused harm. The burden of quantification of harm remains with the claimant, but procedural rules must not make quantification 'practically impossible or excessively difficult'. Significantly, courts have the power to estimate the amount of harm.

Under para 32 of Sch 8A to the CA 1998, documents pertaining to leniency applications are either partially or wholly exempted from the rules for the disclosure of evidence, depending on their precise status. This is to ensure that the threat of damages actions does not deter cartel participants from seeking leniency by blowing the whistle on cartels.

Measure of damages

In most cases, the damages that a UK court will award will be compensatory. The aim of compensatory damages is to compensate the claimant for any loss suffered as a result of the anti-competitive behaviour. They are the most common type of damages awarded by English courts and will often be accompanied by an award of interest.

In principle, the amount of compensatory damages is based on the difference between the price actually paid by the victim of anti-competitive behaviour and the price it would have paid in the absence of an infringement. For example, in overcharge cases involving a cartel, the calculation will be based on the difference between the excess price paid owing to the cartel activity and the price that would have been payable but for the cartel activity. Both sides are likely to instruct expert economists to determine the price that would have been charged had the defendants not engaged in cartel activity. As the amount of overcharge can be significant, the damages payable can be substantial.

Note that exemplary damages may no longer be awarded (CA 1998, Sch 8A, para 36, inserted by the Claims in respect of Loss or Damage arising from Competition Infringements (Competition Act 1998 and Other Enactments (Amendment)) Regulations 2017)).

Umbrella pricing

The amount of damages can also be affected by what is known as 'umbrella pricing', where pricing in the market is inflated across all industry participants. This can occur when cartel participants or a dominant undertaking increase prices, and as a result innocent industry participants find it profitable to increase their prices too. In such cases the infringing undertaking may have to pay damages to a claimant that purchased goods from innocent companies which raised their prices under the 'umbrella' of the higher prices.

Joint and several liability

The Damages Directive provides for the joint and several liability of cartel participants. Accordingly, victims of cartels may sue any member of the cartel and recover from it the whole of the loss suffered as a result of the cartel, although a cartel member who has had to pay damages in this way is entitled to seek a contribution from the other cartel members. UK law already provided for joint and several liability before the Directive was passed. The Damages Directive does, though, provide for an exception for undertakings which have been granted immunity from fines. This was implemented in the UK by para 16 of Sch 8A to the CA 1998. Immunity recipients are only obliged to pay damages for the harm they themselves caused their customers. However, they will remain liable should victims be unable to recover damages from the other cartel participants.

The 'passing-on' defence

One of the major debates relating to damages claims concerns the passing-on defence. This arises when a direct purchaser brings a damages claim after being unlawfully overcharged by a cartel participant or dominant undertaking. The defendant may argue that the direct purchaser has passed on any loss it suffered to its own purchasers ('indirect purchasers') by charging them higher prices, and so has not actually suffered any loss itself. As discussed at **4.7.4** below, the US Supreme Court has rejected this defence, as damages play a key role in deterring cartels (under US antitrust law successful plaintiffs are able to claim treble damages). The UK and EU allow the passing-on defence, since if a claimant has passed on its loss to its own customers, it will not need to be compensated for that same loss, and this will reduce the amount it is able to claim as damages. The burden of proof is on the defendant to prove that the claimant has passed on its loss and is therefore not entitled to the amount of damages claimed (see regs 9–11 of the Claims in respect of Loss or Damage arising from Competition Infringements (Competition Act 1998 and Other Enactments (Amendment)) Regulations 2017)).

The passing-on defence was considered in *Sainsbury's Supermarkets Ltd v MasterCard Inc and Visa Europe Services LLC* [2020] UKSC 24. This confirms that 'passing on' is largely a matter for quantification of damages, rather than a defence as such. It is for the court in each case to decide on the evidence whether an overcharge due to a breach of competition law has caused the claimant to suffer loss, or whether all or part of the overcharge has been passed on by the claimant to its own customers. The court can resort to estimates to decide the amount of damages that have been passed on, in accordance with the Commission's 'Guidelines for national courts on how to estimate the share of overcharge passed on to the indirect purchaser'. This is sometimes referred to as 'the broad axe' to determine the quantum of damage.

Indirect purchasers as well as direct may bring a damages claim against an undertaking that has infringed competition law. Where the claimant is an indirect purchaser, it will benefit from a rebuttable presumption that an overcharge was passed on to it. It can be very difficult to establish by how much indirect purchasers have been overcharged, as it is common for direct purchasers to absorb some costs increases rather than pass on the entirety of costs increases to their customers. As seen above, the courts have the power to estimate the portion of the initial overcharge passed on to indirect purchasers.

4.7.3.5 Collective actions

Private enforcement actions can be brought by a single claimant, a group of claimants, or by way of collective action under the Consumer Rights Act 2015. Where collective action is brought, this may only be before the CAT.

In overcharge cases, in particular, there are often a large number of potential claimants who have suffered a small loss. In the replica football kit case in 2003, the OFT fined several sportswear retailers, Manchester United, the Football Association and Umbro Holdings Ltd for entering into price-fixing agreements relating to replica football kit in breach of the Chapter I prohibition (OFT decision of 1 August 2003 [2004] UKCLR 6). It was estimated that about one million customers were each overcharged about £20 when buying replica kit. In this type of situation it would be completely impractical for each individual customer to bring a claim, so s 47B of the CA 1998 paves the way for collective actions (sometimes termed 'class actions'), enabling a specified consumer body to bring a 'representative' or 'collective' follow-on action before the CAT on behalf of two or more consumers. Currently, only the Consumers Association (now known as Which?) has been specified as a consumer body. In the replica football kit case, Which? negotiated a settlement with one of the retailers involved, whereby the retailer agreed to compensate customers who had been overcharged for replica shirts.

Before the Consumer Rights Act 2015, collective actions could only be brought on an 'opt-in' basis, ie consumers had to give their consent to join in the action. In the replica football kit case, fewer than 1,000 out of an estimated one million consumers decided to opt in. Those consumers who did not opt in remained free to bring their own actions.

The Consumer Rights Act 2015 provides for representative claimants (such as consumer groups, industry bodies and trade associations) to bring collective actions on an 'opt-out' basis. In opt-out actions, all members of a defined claimant class will be included in the claim unless they explicitly opt out of the action, save that non-UK claimants will have to opt in. The proposed class of claimants in the *Merricks Mastercard* collective action was estimated at 46.2 million individuals.

The CAT is required to certify that a proposed collective action is suitable for a collective action and must decide whether it should proceed on an opt-in or opt-out basis. The UK's first opt-out collective action on a standalone basis (ie which did not follow on from a decision of a competition authority) authorised by the CAT was *Justin Le Patourel v BT Group Plc* (CAT 1381/7/7/21) [2022] EWCA Civ 593. This ongoing action is for alleged abuse of a dominant position under s 18 of the CA 1998, with a potential class numbering 2.31 million customers and the average claim between £148 and £333 per affected customer.

Only the representative body would be liable for costs awarded against the claimant class, and not the individual members of the class. Any damages left unclaimed by members of the claimant class will be paid to the Access to Justice Foundation. Claimants who opt out will be able to pursue their own claims.

As a result of action taken at both EU and national levels, the private enforcement of competition law has increased not only in the UK but also in EU Member States. The UK has created a favourable litigation environment with specialist courts and wider disclosure rules, which often result in the UK courts being chosen as the preferred forum in which to litigate competition law claims.

4.7.4 Private enforcement in the US

In the US, private enforcement has always been prevalent. Below is a brief overview. The Clayton Act provides that:

> any person who shall be injured in his business or property by reason of anything forbidden in the antitrust laws may sue therefor ... and shall recover threefold the damages by him sustained, and the costs of suit, including a reasonable attorney's fee. (15 USC §15(a))

This statute provides a strong deterrent against antitrust violations, due not only to the trebling of damages but also to the award of attorney's fees. Normally, civil litigants in the US bear their own attorney's fees, regardless of the outcome of the suit.

To have standing to sue under the Clayton Act, the plaintiff must have incurred a pecuniary loss, the loss must be the type of harm that the antitrust laws seek to prevent, and the causation must be direct not remote (*Brunswick Corp v Pueblo Bowl-O-Mat, Inc*, 429 US 477

(1977)). For example, a monopolist that drives its competitors out of the market can be sued by those competitors, whose damages would be the amount of profit they would have earned but for the predatory pricing. However, creditors and employees of the companies driven out of the market have no standing to sue, because their losses are indirect and are not the type that the antitrust laws are designed to prevent.

In cartel cases, purchasers from the cartel who paid an overcharge due to the illegal agreement have standing to sue, and their damages are measured as the amount overcharged, multiplied by three. Liability is joint and several, meaning that any one defendant is potentially liable for the overcharges of the entire cartel. An exception is made for defendants who received amnesty from the DOJ; their damages are not trebled and are measured on only their own sales.

Private cartel cases usually are brought as class actions, which assert the claims of almost every purchaser from the defendants throughout the nation, or a substantial part of it. In major cartel cases, the damages sought in class actions can be massive. Claims frequently exceed $1 billion.

As discussed at **4.7.3** above, in some markets purchasers from the cartel resell their products, and they may be able to pass on a part of their overcharges to their own customers. The US Supreme Court rejected the passing-on defence and has ruled that only direct purchasers from the cartel have standing to sue under the Sherman Act (*Illinois Brick Co v Illinois*, 431 US 720 (1977)), and these direct purchasers are entitled to claim damages measured by the full amount of the overcharges, without any deductions for the portions passed on to their customers (*Hanover Shoe, Inc v United Shoe Machinery Corp*, 392 US 481 (1968)). These decisions were controversial, and several states responded by amending their antitrust laws to permit indirect purchasers to sue a cartel. Consequently, cartel members can be held liable for damages to both direct and indirect purchasers on the same overcharges. This treatment of indirect purchasers is the largest variance between federal and state antitrust laws that has developed so far.

In any private damages action against an alleged cartel, the most critical issue usually is whether the defendants actually reached an agreement. The testimony of one or more persons who attended a meeting with competitors where an agreement was reached or affirmed usually would suffice, but such testimony seldom is available, unless the witness has already pleaded guilty or has received amnesty, because the witness would be admitting to the commission of a crime.

Consequently, plaintiffs in private actions must often prove agreement with inferences from the market behaviour of the defendants. The US Supreme Court has ruled that parallel conduct by the defendants, for example when all firms in a market follow a price leader and implement the same price increases at approximately the same time, is not sufficient to prove an agreement under Section 1. Proof of an agreement by inference must include 'evidence that tends to exclude the possibility that the alleged conspirators acted independently' (*Matsushita Electric Industrial Co v Zenith Radio Corp*, 475 US 574 (1986)).

The Clayton Act also authorizes private persons and firms to sue for injunctions against the continuation of violations that threaten them with pecuniary loss, provided that the loss is the type of harm that the antitrust laws seek to prevent and the threatened causation is direct, and not remote (15 USC §26).

4.8 COMPLIANCE PROGRAMMES

We have seen in this chapter the enforcement powers that may be used (and the sanctions that may be imposed) against undertakings which engage in anti-competitive behaviour. Given the significant risks involved for companies (and their staff), many companies adopt competition law compliance programmes to reduce their exposure.

An effective competition compliance programme will:

(a) demonstrate a commitment on the part of the company concerned to comply with the competition rules. Such a commitment should be led from the top of the organisation, not just from the company's compliance department;

(b) educate management and employees to ensure they do not participate in infringements of competition laws. It is important that all relevant staff are subject to the programme, not least as breaches of the rules can (and often do) result from the actions of relatively junior employees;

(c) avoid conduct that might give the appearance or raise suspicions of competition law infringements, or that might adversely affect the likelihood of merger clearance for future acquisitions.

Competition compliance programmes should be tailored to the types of competition law risks arising from the particular activities of the company concerned and may contain elements such as:

• a compliance manual;

• training seminars;

• specific reporting and recording requirements concerning contacts with competitors;

• unannounced or announced internal audits of hard copy and electronic files of relevant personnel; and

• a database to track compliance training.

Having an effective compliance programme which is risk-based and led from the top of the organisation may constitute a mitigating factor if the company is ever faced with allegations of competition law violations.

HORIZONTAL AGREEMENTS

AIMS

This chapter provides an introduction to the treatment of horizontal agreements under competition law. It also highlights the firm stance taken by the competition authorities in all relevant jurisdictions in relation to such agreements.

OBJECTIVES

After studying **Chapter 5**, you should be able to:

- recognise a horizontal agreement, and in particular a cartel, whatever its form;

- appreciate the approach of the various competition authorities towards horizontal agreements; and

- understand the circumstances in which a horizontal agreement might nevertheless be permitted.

5.1 INTRODUCTION

Horizontal agreements are those between undertakings which are at the same level of the market, for example, two manufacturers of competing goods. Horizontal agreements are of particular concern under competition law because any arrangement that removes (or reduces) competition between competitors (or potential competitors) is more likely to harm consumers than other types of arrangements. Conversely, some agreements between competitors may actually provide benefits which outweigh competition concerns, or may have a neutral effect on competition. This chapter will start by considering the most harmful types of horizontal agreements – cartels – before turning to other types of horizontal agreements.

5.2 HORIZONTAL AGREEMENTS – CARTELS

Horizontal agreements include arrangements that are generally considered to be the most anti-competitive form of behaviour – cartels. Cartels can come in many forms and include agreements to fix prices, share markets, limit output or exclude potential new competitors from the market (these are considered in greater detail below).

Unsurprisingly, given the seriousness of cartel behaviour, the enforcement powers we considered in **Chapter 4** are used to their greatest extent in this area. As we have seen, penalties include the imposition of significant fines on the companies concerned.

5.2.1   Competition authorities and the fight against cartels

5.2.1.1   The European Commission

A former Commissioner responsible for competition policy, Mario Monti, referred to cartels as 'the most pernicious agreements among competitors'. Some see cartels as a form of theft as they deprive consumers of the benefits of competition.

The Commission has been increasingly zealous in its efforts to uncover and sanction price-fixing, market sharing and bid-rigging cartels. These efforts have been particularly fruitful thanks in part to the Leniency Programme adopted by the Commission (see **Chapter 4**). The Commission has a specific unit within DG Comp (Directorate G) with the remit to find and punish cartel activity ('cartel-busting').

The Commission does not have the power to impose penalties on the individuals involved in a cartel, as these are not usually undertakings covered by Articles 101 and 102. The EU does not consider itself best placed to pursue criminal law penalties on individuals and leaves such matters to the national competition authorities. Many EU Member States, as well as the UK (as seen in **Chapter 4**), have enacted criminal law sanctions that apply to individuals.

5.2.1.2   The CMA

The CMA, which is the competition authority with primary authority to enforce competition law in the UK, is similarly focused on its 'cartel-busting' activities. As we have seen (**Chapter 4**), in addition to the sanctions regime similar to that available to the Commission, the CMA also has the power to pursue individuals who commit the cartel offence or who are directors of a company involved in cartel activity.

5.2.1.3   International organisations

The following are some of the international groups cooperating on competition law policies and enforcement.

(a)   The Organisation for Economic Cooperation and Development ('OECD')

The OECD launched its anti-cartel programme in 1998 with the adoption of a Council recommendation 'concerning *Effective Action Against Hard Core Cartels*' and since then has been at the forefront of the international effort to eliminate cartel conduct. In 2005 the OECD published an update of the 1998 recommendation (*Third Report on the Implementation of the 1998 Recommendation*), in which it acknowledged that much had been achieved in tackling cartel behaviour but that a lot remained to be done, including the imposition of individual criminal sanctions in many more countries.

Since then the OECD has published a raft of recommendations and guidance, including *Improving International Co-operation in Cartel Investigations*, published in November 2012. This document stresses the need for enhanced co-operation between competition authorities, as cartel activity has become increasingly international in scope due to globalisation.

(b)   The International Competition Network ('ICN')

The ICN aims to facilitate cooperation between competition authorities globally. It has a membership of over 100 competition authorities, including the UK's Competition and Markets Authority, the US Department of Justice (Antitrust Division) and the US Federal Trade Commission. It has a Cartel Working Group which addresses anti-cartel enforcement. Working Group members primarily consult each other electronically, eg by e-mail and through holding periodic webinars. The Working Group also arranges discussions at the ICN's annual conference and produces guidance on competition law enforcement.

(c)   EU/US cooperation

The EU cooperates with the US competition authorities (the Department of Justice and the Federal Trade Commission) primarily on the basis of their 1991 Cooperation Agreement and

1998 'Positive Comity Agreement' (see also **1.6**). The authorities hold regular meetings to share information on enforcement, priorities and policies, and to discuss other matters of mutual interest relating to the application of competition laws.

5.2.2 Anti-competitive agreements and concerted practices

In **Chapter 2**, we saw that the concept of 'agreement' in Article 101/Chapter I was wide enough to include less formal expressions of intent, such as a simple understandings between the parties or a mere meeting of minds. There is no need for the agreement to have any enforcement mechanism, or for the agreement to involve reciprocal obligations. For example, sending an e-mail to a competitor with details of a confidential price increase can be sufficient in the circumstances to give rise to an agreement under Article 101 or Chapter I (see the CMA's decision concerning RBS and Barclays, *Loan products to professional service firms: investigation into anti-competitive practices* CE/8950/08, 2011).

Where the competition authority can find evidence of a written or informal agreement between companies to coordinate their pricing, it will, of course, act. However, price-fixing cartels are by their very nature secret, and it is unlikely that a formal agreement will be at the root of such behaviour. Rather, more subtle forms of coordination are likely. For example, parallel conduct of the type that we looked at in **Chapter 2** is a more likely vehicle for price-fixing.

In any event, it will be important to distinguish between collusive cartel activity and innocent parallel strategies on the market. As we saw at **2.1.1.3**, in Case 48/69 *ICI v Commission* [1972] ECR 619 (commonly referred to as *Dyestuffs*) it was stated that the concept of concerted practice will bring within the prohibition:

> a form of coordination between undertakings which, without having reached the stage where an agreement properly so-called has been concluded, knowingly substitutes practical cooperation between them for the risks of competition.

It is not usually necessary that anti-competitive effects are produced on the market; most cartels involve particularly egregious arrangements such as price-fixing, market-sharing and bid-rigging, and so have as their object the restriction, distortion or prevention of competition (see **5.2.3** below).

The onus to prove the alleged conduct falls on the competition authority, and where there is no agreement it may resort to direct or indirect evidence of a concerted practice. Direct evidence may consist of proof of plans, meetings, minutes of meetings or the exchange of confidential information, whereas indirect evidence may amount to showing the existence of and participation in an informal system of exchange of information or joint discussions, or proof of market behaviour which can only be explained by collusion. Where there is evidence of both parallel conduct and contact between the parties (even a single meeting), it is probable that a concerted practice will be held to exist (Case C-8/08 *T-Mobile Netherlands BV v Raad van Bestuur van de Nederlandse Mededingingsautoriteit* [2009] ECR I-4529).

However, where indirect evidence is adduced, it will be open to the parties to rebut the allegations by providing alternative explanations for the conduct. The burden thus shifts to the company implicated where there is uniformity of price which is not supported by the market structure and other factors may point towards collusion. Lastly, it should be noted that simply proving isolated instances of independent behaviour will not be sufficient to rebut an allegation of concerted practice.

5.2.3 Types of horizontal agreements classified as cartels

In this section we consider the types of horizontal agreements which are commonly called cartels and which are analysed under Article 101/Chapter I as restrictions 'by object'. In this regard we shall concentrate on the decisions of the Commission and CJEU under Article 101 (as the behaviour outlined below will also amount to infringements under UK rules which mirror Articles 101 and 102 – see **Chapter 2**). We also consider, at the end of this chapter, the type of horizontal behaviour that will amount to a breach of the US rules.

5.2.3.1 Price-fixing agreements

The competition authorities consider that the object (see **Chapter 2**) of any horizontal price-fixing agreement is the restriction of competition. There is therefore no need to show that a price-fixing agreement has had any anti-competitive effect on the market due to the pernicious effect on competition of such behaviour. Of course, in addition to blatant price-fixing, there is an entire range of restrictive practices which have as their object the stifling of price competition. The competition rules, as well as individuals responsible for monitoring the behaviour of companies for compliance with the competition rules, must be capable of comprehending these more subtle forms of price restriction.

The following is a non-exhaustive list of the types of activity which will fall foul of the prohibition on price-fixing agreements:

- jointly setting prices, price levels, minimum or maximum prices, or jointly observing mutually acceptable price lists;
- jointly agreeing on the amount and date of price increases;
- jointly agreeing on a price list or increase to be announced publicly by one competitor but which others are prepared to follow;
- jointly agreeing on an essential element of the price or, sometimes, the underlying formula for the calculation of the price;
- jointly setting different price levels for different customers/countries;
- direct or indirect setting of prices under revenue sharing agreements;
- jointly agreeing on identical levels of discount or setting a maximum level of trade discount;
- jointly setting recommended prices; and/or
- exchanging commercially sensitive price information.

As a rule, such practices promote an atmosphere in which businesses feel comfortable about raising their prices, confident that their competitors will do the same. This is harmful to the consumer whether or not actual price increases follow, since it creates, at the very least, disincentives for businesses to strive for greater efficiency.

5.2.3.2 Market sharing

In addition to collusion on prices, horizontal agreements relating to market sharing will also be caught by Article 101/Chapter I. Indeed, it may be considered that certain arrangements to divide up markets will be even more anti-competitive than basic price-fixing, since such an arrangement will not only eliminate price competition but will also restrict consumer choice by reducing the number of products available in a territory or to particular customers. Dividing up the market geographically along national lines will be particularly serious in the context of the EU since such an agreement cuts directly across the fundamental objective of a single internal market.

Markets may be divided geographically or by class of consumer, and such arrangements tend to be favoured by companies in that they are much easier to police than price-fixing agreements; the mere presence of someone else's goods on 'your' market betrays a flouting of the agreed divisions. Such arrangements may be embodied in writing, eg by means of reciprocal exclusive distribution agreements, but may also be inferred from other evidence and behaviour on the market. However, in this latter situation, the competition authority must ensure that the circumstantial evidence being relied upon can be interpreted in only one way.

Market-sharing arrangements are considered to have as their object the restriction of competition and therefore actual effects need not be proven.

Due to their nature, market-sharing arrangements will rarely qualify for exemption under Article 101(3)/CA 1998. However, other forms of cooperation such as joint selling and joint production may well generate positive effects, and will be judged on their merits (see the European Commission's Horizontal Cooperation Guidelines and the CMA's Horizontal Guidance discussed at **5.3.2** below).

The Commission decision in *SAS-Maersk* 2001/716/EC illustrates the attitude of the Commission to market-sharing behaviour. SAS and Maersk (two airline operators) entered into a formal cooperation agreement. Under the terms of a block exemption relating to the air transport industry, they were allowed to do this, provided their agreement was notified to the Commission for approval. However, subsequent to the notification, a third airline company complained to the Commission that the cooperation between SAS and Maersk went far beyond that contained in the notification. The Commission investigated and discovered evidence that the airlines had effectively agreed to allow each other to operate exclusively on particular air routes that had previously been operated by both. Such market sharing fell outside the scope of any available exemption.

5.2.3.3   Collective tendering/bid-rigging

This infringement relates to the common commercial practice of putting work out to 'tender'. Under a tender process, a company, instead of approaching a potential supplier in respect of negotiating a contract for works, will ask many suppliers to tender for the contract. In theory, each tender submitted by each supplier should be done confidentially and not in collusion with other suppliers.

Put simply, collusive tendering, or bid-rigging, consists of agreeing or simply consulting in advance with a competitor as to the terms of the bid they intend to make in response to an offer to tender. It will be caught by the prohibitions in Article 101/Chapter I. Indeed, such activity robs the tendering process of its very essence, namely the calculation and submission of bids independently formulated and representing the best offer of that particular company.

Collusive tendering may take many forms and can range from simply agreeing to quote identical prices (although such level tendering is more likely to arouse the suspicions of the competition authorities) to setting up a central administration to deal with all tendering opportunities according to an often elaborate system of pre-determined rules.

If companies get together, either informally or in an extremely organised fashion (see, for example, the Commission decision *Building and Construction Industry in the Netherlands* [1992] OJ L92/1), in order to allocate contracts and fix tenders, not only is the price competition which is at the heart of the tender process eliminated, but a situation may also result in which markets are allocated and customers are shared out along lines other than those which would arise under normal competition (see, for example, the Commission decision in relation to *Pre-Insulated Pipes* [1999] OJ L24/1). Note also that actual agreement on the terms of the tender is not necessary for a finding of anti-competitive activity. Providing prior knowledge of a proposed tender to a competitor will be sufficient to amount to collusive tendering.

Thus, any form of collusive tendering will, in principle, have as its object the restriction, prevention or distortion of competition and will, as such, be illegal. Moreover, it is unlikely that any system of bid-rigging will satisfy the conditions set out in Article 101(3)/CA 1998, s 9 and thereby qualify for an exemption from the prohibitions.

5.2.3.4   Information sharing between competitors

Information exchanges between competitors are in many instances a necessary and legitimate part of business activity (eg, as part of a purchase/supply relationship). Other exchanges of information (eg, in support of a cartel) have an anti-competitive object and are illegal infringements of Article 101/Chapter I. Where information exchange does not have an anti-competitive object, it is necessary to consider whether it has an anti-competitive effect, ie whether the information exchange is capable of providing an *artificial transparency* between the parties which influences their conduct to the detriment of consumers. Whether the sharing of information will fall foul of Article 101/Chapter I will depend in each case on a number of factors.

The structure of the market in question would appear to be of particular significance, and it seems clear from the Commission decisions thus far that a market with oligopolistic tendencies (ie where there are only a few very large operators on the market) is more likely to result in a finding that information sharing will have a negative impact on competition. Essentially, information exchanges which appear only to be capable of marginally affecting the commercial decisions of competitors will take on greater significance if those competitors together control a significant proportion of the market. The nature of the information exchanged is also important, and it would appear that general statistics or historical information will not pose competition concerns whereas specific information on pricing policies or intended conduct in the future (whether it be in relation to pricing, investments, R&D or otherwise) will tend to lead to further and closer investigation (see Case C-238/05 *Asnef-Equifax* [2006] ECR I-11125). The key point to note is that the nature of the information exchanged may raise competition concerns if it is commercially valuable, ie it is commercially sensitive information that can be relied upon to determine strategy/policy and reduce active competition between the parties.

The fact that the information exchanged is available publicly elsewhere on a less convenient basis will reduce but not eliminate the competition risk associated with the information exchange. Essentially, it is a business question as to whether information is commercially valuable. However, information in relation to pricing, costs, capacities, customers and general business strategy may potentially be commercially sensitive. The category of person having access to the information, the frequency of the information exchange and its purpose may also influence the attitude of the competition authorities.

See also the European Commission's Horizontal Cooperation Guidelines and the CMA's Horizontal Guidance discussed at **5.3.2**.

Lastly, it should be noted that while information sharing may constitute an infringement in itself, it is perhaps most often encountered either in conjunction with other infringements (as a means of facilitating either the implementation or the enforcement of the price-fixing cartel) or as evidence of a concerted practice.

5.2.3.5   Other types of cartel behaviour

(a)   Restrictions on production/quotas

Another way in which undertakings can ensure that they control the price of the product is by ensuring that only a pre-agreed amount of the product is released onto the market at any one time (therefore ensuring demand for the limited supply remains high). Agreements relating to restrictions on production are usually one element of a wider scheme. For example, in Case T-117/07 *Re Gas Insulated Switchgear Cartel* [2011] 4 CMLR 26, members of the cartel had entered into an arrangement whereby the global market was divided on geographic lines, and each market also had pre-agreed production restrictions.

(b)   Joint purchasing

Here a number of undertakings may agree to enter into a joint purchasing agreement, whereby they agree to pool their purchases. The competition concerns include that sellers may be excluded from selling into the pool and the undertakings' cooperation may lead to cost alignment, with actual or potential spill-over effects into the markets in which the undertakings compete.

Joint purchasing can, however, have pro-competitive effects if they lead to lower prices or better quality for consumers. See the the Horizontal Cooperation Guidelines and Horizontal Guidance discussed at **5.3.2**.

This is not an exhaustive list and there are many other examples of cartel-like behaviour, such as those dealt with in the US law examples at **5.4**.

5.2.4 Horizontal agreements (cartels) and abuse of dominance (collective dominance)

As seen at **3.3.5**, Article 102/Chapter II may apply where the companies present themselves on the market as a collective entity. Where there is also evidence that the companies have engaged in a concerted practice, depending on the strength of the evidence, it may be more appropriate to pursue the case as one of horizontal collusion under Article 101/Chapter I.

5.3 OTHER TYPES OF HORIZONTAL AGREEMENTS

5.3.1 Overview

Most competition regimes recognise that some cooperation, even horizontal, may in fact bring about substantial economic benefits, or may have neutral effects on competition. Cooperation between competitors can be a means to share risk, save costs, pool know-how and launch innovation faster. To this end, many systems permit many forms of horizontal cooperation.

The European Commission and the CMA have adopted a number of guidelines and legislation relevant to horizontal agreements. These include the following.

5.3.1.1 Appreciable effect on competition (*de minimis*)

The European Commission's Notice on Agreements of Minor Importance, also used by the CMA (see **2.1.1.7**), is the first port of call for legal advisers considering whether a horizontal agreement which does not contain object restrictions might breach competition law. Where parties are competitors (or potential competitors) and their combined market share is no more than 10%, provided that their agreement does not contain 'hardcore' or object restrictions such as price-fixing, their agreement will be considered *de minimis* and outside the scope of Article 101 and/or Chapter I.

5.3.1.2 Horizontal Guidelines

The European Commission's Horizontal Cooperation Guidelines and the CMA's Horizontal Guidance cover a wide field of commercial activity (see **5.3.2**). They also cover two of the most important block exemptions covering horizontal agreements: the Research and Development (R&D) block exemptions and the Specialisation block exemptions.

The European Commission's Horizontal Cooperation Guidelines were updated on 1 June 2023. These *Guidelines on the applicability of Article 101 of the Treaty on the Functioning of the European Union to horizontal cooperation agreements* (C(2023) 3445) are referred to as the 'Horizontal Cooperation Guidelines'.

The CMA produced its own version of the guidelines in August 2023. This *Guidance on the application of the Chapter I prohibition in the Competition Act 1998 to horizontal agreements* (CMA 184) is referred to here as the 'Horizontal Guidance'.

5.3.1.3 R&D and Specialisation Block Exemptions

The European Commission updated its block exemptions on 1 June 2023:

- 'R&D BER': the *Commission Regulation (EU) 2023/1066 of 1 June 2023 on the application of Article 101(3) of the Treaty on the Functioning of the European Union to certain categories of research and development agreements* (OJ L 143, 2.6.2023, p. 9–19).
- 'Specialisation BER': the *Commission Regulation (EU) 2023/1067 of 1 June 2023 on the application of Article 101(3) of the Treaty on the Functioning of the European Union to certain categories of specialisation agreements* (OJ L 143, 2.6.2023, p. 20–26).

The European Commission's previous R&D and Specialisation block exemptions were applied in the UK as 'retained exemptions' (see **2.1.3.3**) until they expired in December 2022.

The UK's own R&D and Specialisation block exemptions took effect on 1 January 2023:

- 'R&D BEO': the Competition Act 1998 (Research & Development Agreements Block Exemption) Order 2022 (SI 2022/1271).
- 'SABEO': the Competition Act 1998 (Specialisation Agreements Block Exemption) Order 2022 (SI 2022/1272).

5.3.1.4   Other block exemptions

There are numerous other block exemptions which cover special types of horizontal relationships, for example, liner shipping consortia agreements. The Technology Block Exemption (covered in **Chapter 8**) is also relevant to some forms of horizontal cooperation.

Notwithstanding the duplication of legislation and guidance, the EU and UK approach to horizontal agreements remains very similar. The CMA's Horizontal Guidance refers to many of the same EU cases as the European Commission's Horizontal Cooperation Guidelines, not just domestic UK cases.

5.3.2   The Horizontal Cooperation Guidelines and Horizontal Guidance

The European Commission's Horizontal Cooperation Guidelines and the CMA's Horizontal Guidance cover many types of arrangements between competitors or potential competitors, including many forms of commercial joint ventures or looser forms of cooperation. These guidelines provide a useful analytical framework for legal advisers. For instance, a legal adviser may turn to the guidelines in order to assess whether competitors pooling their resources to enter a new market would breach Article 101/Chapter I. Some level of cooperation may be necessary to achieve pro-competitive outcomes, but cooperation may decrease the parties' decision-making independence and increase the risk of collusion.

As you will appreciate, horizontal cooperation may involve restrictions 'by object' (such as where the parties coordinate to exchange confidential information), which do not necessitate an effects-based analysis. It is more difficult to analyse arrangements which contain restrictions 'by effect', as they cannot be assumed to infringe Article 101 and/or Chapter I and require significant substantive analysis. This requires an understanding of all the relevant circumstances (such as the parties, their industry, the restrictions and their impact on the structure of the market) and an understanding of how similar circumstances are dealt with under the guidelines and case law.

For purposes of analysis, it is common to divide horizontal cooperation agreements into the following categories:

- *Information exchanges.* Information exchanges between rivals, including benchmarking by competitors to understand how competitive they are in the market, may remove some of the uncertainties of competition and lead to collusive outcomes. Legal advisers may be able to structure an information exchange to avoid falling within Article 101/Chapter I, for instance by ensuring that only anonymised, aggregated and historical data are released to competitors, usually through a neutral third party, and made available on a non-discriminatory basis. Even then, the degree of market transparency that may result could have anti-competitive effects where the market is highly concentrated.

- R&D. Research and development agreements may fall outside Article 101/Chapter I where they do not involve any restrictions of competition, for example when research is undertaken at an early stage of development, without joint exploitation of results. Hence the guidelines deal with agreements that may be structured as falling outside Article 101/Chapter I. The guidelines also deal with agreements that fall within the prohibitions but may benefit from the EU's R&D BER or UK's R&D BEO.

- *Production agreements.* Production agreements, where parties come together to produce jointly rather than independently, can result in the coordination of competitive behaviour with anti-competitive outcomes, particularly where the parties also agree to jointly distribute the products. Specialisation and joint production agreements may benefit from the EU's Specialisation BER or UK's SABEO. The section of the guidelines on production agreements also deals with subcontracting agreements that are horizontal in nature and not covered by a vertical block exemption (considered in **Chapter 6**).

- *Purchasing agreements.* Purchasing agreements, where parties come together to purchase as a single block rather than independently, are capable of giving rise to anti-competitive outcomes and are usually prohibited where the parties have a degree of market power.

- *Commercialisation agreements.* The guidelines also deal with commercialisation agreements, such as distribution agreements which are not covered by a vertical block exemption (considered in **Chapter 6**), for instance distribution agreements between competitors.

- *Standardisation agreements.* Standardisation agreements may be beneficial, as agreeing common manufacturing standards can benefit industries and consumers, as long as the standards are objectively structured so as not to unduly benefit any particular group of competitors to the detriment of others.

- *Sustainability agreements.* Agreements that pursue a sustainability objective (including but not limited to climate change) are covered by the Horizontal Cooperation Guidelines. The CMA published its Green Agreement Guidance on environmental sustainability agreements (CMA 185) on 12 October 2023.

The guidelines also cover the doctrine of ancillary restraints under Article 101/Chapter I (see **7.3.9.1** and **7.4.6.1**). The doctrine excludes from the scope of Article 101/Chapter I restrictions that are objectively necessary to implement a cooperation agreement, as long as they are proportionate to the (legitimate) objectives of the cooperation.

The observations above give only a simplified explanation. More detail is provided in the Horizontal Cooperation Guidelines and Horizontal Guidance. These can be obtained from the European Commission and CMA's websites.

5.4 HORIZONTAL AGREEMENTS UNDER US ANTITRUST LAWS

In the United States, the DOJ has been prosecuting cartels as criminal offences for more than a century. The DOJ's enforcement activities increased dramatically in the mid-1990s, fuelled by the adoption of the Corporate Leniency Program described in **Chapter 4**. The DOJ obtained its first $100 million fine in 1996 from Archer Daniels Midland Corporation for its participation in the lysine and citric acid cartels. The next few years saw even larger fines extracted from participants in cartels involving graphic electrodes, vitamins and dynamic random access memory chips. Criminal enforcement against classic cartel behaviour remains an institutional policy of the DOJ and is expected to continue regardless of changes in the political party of either the President or the majorities in Congress. The DOJ has also expanded its enforcement efforts in recent years, announcing in 2019 the establishment of the

Procurement Collusion Strike Force, a task force comprised of the DOJ and other federal, state and local government agencies focused on detecting and deterring collusion in government procurement, as well as expanding its criminal enforcement activity to the labour sphere, targeting unlawful wage-fixing and no-poach agreements between employers.

The DOJ has made the prosecution of international cartels a high priority. Initially, few other nations imposed criminal penalties for cartel offences on individuals. As a consequence, the DOJ usually could not obtain the extradition of foreign citizens, which diminished the deterrent effect of the criminal penalty. Some deterrence nonetheless remained: foreigners charged with criminal violations of the Sherman Act face a lifetime barrier to travel to the United States, a serious impediment to an international business career, as well as the status of an international fugitive. In an effort to avoid these burdens, several foreigners have travelled to the United States voluntarily to plead guilty to cartel violations and to serve prison sentences. To encourage these pleas, the DOJ will obtain commitments from immigration authorities that foreign citizens who plead guilty and cooperate with the DOJ will retain their ability to enter the United States after their imprisonment.

With more countries now adopting criminal penalties for cartel violations, the DOJ has a greater ability to obtain extradition of individual offenders, and its criminal enforcement efforts can be strengthened. Furthermore, many countries that have not adopted criminal penalties have nonetheless come to regard international cartels as a serious offence and have shown a greater willingness to cooperate with the DOJ.

An important manifestation of this cooperation is the DOJ's cooperation within internationally coordinated dawn raids. Although law enforcement agencies in the US cannot conduct the full equivalent of a dawn raid, the DOJ will, at the same time as the raids are conducted in Europe and elsewhere, execute search warrants and conduct surprise interviews of employees of the targets. In these interviews, the agents cannot compel the employees to answer any questions, but with the surprise of a visit from a law enforcement agent, the isolation (agents usually confront an employee at their home early in the morning) and the fear induced by the employee's sudden realisation that the cartel has been exposed, the interviews often lead to the disclosure of incriminating information.

As discussed in **Chapter 2**, some forms of agreements among competitors are deemed illegal *per se* under Section 1 of the Sherman Act, while others are illegal only when found, under the Rule of Reason, to have an overall negative effect on competition, based on the facts and circumstances of the particular agreement. The following describes how the courts have determined the legality of various types of horizontal agreements.

5.4.1   Cartels

Cartel agreements are *per se* illegal under Section 1 of the Sherman Act. A cartel agreement subject to the *per se* rule is any agreement among actual or potential competitors that has the purpose and effect of directly raising or stabilizing the prices on which they compete with one another (*United States v Trenton Potteries Co*, 273 US 392 (1927)). This category includes agreements among competitors to:

- restrict the volume of their sales or output;
- allocate customers or sales territories;
- restrain competition from spot markets;
- take turns submitting low, winning bids in competitive bidding situations; or
- impose uniform credit or delivery terms.

These agreements cannot be defended on the grounds that they might enhance efficiency in a particular case or on any other grounds.

5.4.2 Group boycotts

A horizontal agreement among two or more competitors is *per se* illegal when it pressures suppliers or customers not to deal with other competitors or otherwise to deny the disadvantaged competitors access to a necessary business relationship (*Northwest Wholesale Stationers, Inc v Pacific Stationery and Printing Co*, 472 US 284 (1985)). This type of agreement is known as a 'group boycott' or a 'concerted refusal to deal'.

A group boycott will not always be *per se* illegal. For example, for a hospital to maintain its standards of medical care, it must have the power to deny staff privileges to incompetent physicians. Therefore, the decision of a hospital's medical staff to deny staff privileges to a physician on grounds of incompetence will not be found illegal *per se*.

The *per se* rule also does not apply to boycotts organised to advance social, political or other non-economic goals, provided that the participants do not stand to profit from the lessening of competition resulting from the boycott. In one case, a group of lawyers contended that the fees paid by the state for representation of criminal defendants were so inadequate that the defendants were being deprived of effective assistance of counsel at their trials, and they refused to accept any new assignments until the fees were raised. The US Supreme Court found this action *per se* illegal, despite the political motivation, because the lawyers would benefit from the higher fees that their boycott was seeking to obtain (*FTC v Superior Court Trial Lawyers Ass'n*, 493 US 411 (1990)).

5.4.3 Industry self-regulation

A trade association is almost always an assembly of competitors. When a trade association adopts rules that directly restrict price competition, for example a schedule of minimum prices that its members must charge, its conduct is indistinguishable from a cartel, and the conduct will be found illegal *per se*. Except for cartel behavior, the collective actions of a trade association will be assessed under the Rule of Reason. For example, the association might facilitate competition by adopting industry standards for testing products or standard forms that are easier for consumers to understand.

Exclusion of a firm from membership in a trade association can lead to competitive disadvantages, in the same manner as a group boycott. However, courts will not apply the *per se* rule. Denial of association membership is legal if it advances a legitimate purpose, such as reasonable membership criteria and disciplinary rules applied generally by the association, and if the decision to deny membership is reasonably designed to advance that legitimate purpose.

5.4.4 Information exchanges

Information exchanges among competitors are not necessarily illegal. However, in some circumstances, they can serve as evidence of a cartel agreement. For example, if competitors have a regular practice of exchanging information on future price increases, a court is likely to infer that the practice serves no legitimate business purpose and is actually a mechanism for collusion on price increases.

In some circumstances, information exchanges among competitors can be illegal in the absence of an agreement on prices. The leading case is *United States v Container Corp of America*, 393 US 333 (1969). A group of sellers who represented 90% of the relevant market adopted a practice of responding to each others' inquiries for the price most recently charged or quoted to a customer. Although the sellers had no agreement to adhere to any prices, the practice had the effect of keeping prices within a fairly narrow ambit. To find this arrangement illegal, the Court considered that the market was highly concentrated, with a few dominant sellers. Given these market conditions, sellers were discouraged from offering competitive bids, because they knew that their lower prices would be discovered and matched promptly by their competitors. More recently, in February 2023, the DOJ withdrew longstanding guidance for the business community containing principles for aggregating and anonymising data to be shared among competitors, and in September 2023, the DOJ brought an enforcement action against a data aggregator, alleging that the aggregator facilitated increased prices and restricted output among competitors that purchased the data: DOJ case re AgriStats, September 2023.

5.4.5   Joint ventures

Competitors often form joint ventures in which they integrate one or more of their functions, such as purchasing, sales, production, or research and development, but otherwise remain separate entities. A joint venture of this type invariably involves some measure of restraint on competition among the participants. For example, if competitors form a joint venture to market their products at a price set by the joint venture, then effectively they will no longer compete with one another on the sale of these products. However, the US Supreme Court has ruled that joint ventures are not *per se* illegal. Rather they are subject to the Rule of Reason, which considers not only the impairment of competition but also the possibility that by integrating some of their functions through the joint venture, the participants might be able to compete more effectively with other competitors (*Texaco, Inc v Dagher*, 547 US 1 (2006)).

To qualify for the Rule of Reason, the joint venture must involve some integration of functions that enables the participants to compete more effectively. For example, joint production might lower costs due to economies of scale. If a joint venture involves no meaningful integration, then the Rule of Reason will not apply. For example, a 'joint venture' that merely assigned exclusive sales territories to its participants will be regarded as a sham and the agreement will be treated as a cartel (*Timken Roller Bearing Co v United States*, 341 US 593 (1951)).

5.4.6   Joint lobbying

Petitioning the government is immune from the antitrust laws. Competitors can join together to petition a government body, including a legislature, an agency or a court, and their actions do not violate the Sherman Act, even if they are seeking government actions that will impair competition (*Eastern Railroad Presidents Conference v Noerr Motor Freight*, 365 US 127 (1961)). This immunity does not apply, however, when the conduct seeks to impair competition, not through the adoption of legislation or the actions of an agency or court, but through the petitioning process itself. For example, if competitors jointly undertake to discourage the entry of new companies into a regulated industry by advancing frivolous objections to applications for essential permits and making the process prohibitively expensive for the applicants, their conduct is not immune from the antitrust laws.

VERTICAL AGREEMENTS

AIMS

This chapter introduces you to types of vertical agreement and to how the competition authorities assess them. Vertical agreements are considered to be less likely to cause harmful anti-competitive effects than horizontal agreements, and there are various techniques available to avoid a breach of the competition rules. In this chapter we examine a number of these techniques.

OBJECTIVES

After studying **Chapter 6**, you should be able to:

- understand the pro- and anti-competitive effects of vertical agreements;
- appreciate the different types of vertical agreements;
- apply the Vertical block exemptions; and
- understand the basic approach taken under the US system.

6.1 INTRODUCTION

A vertical agreement is one between parties that operate at different levels in the production or distribution chain. Examples of vertical relationships are a manufacturer appointing a wholesaler, a wholesaler appointing a distributor, or a supplier appointing a retailer. Vertical agreements include:

- distribution agreements, where the supplier supplies products for resale by a wholesaler, distributor or retailer (such as exclusive distribution agreements, selective distribution agreements, franchise agreements and commercial agency agreements);

- supply agreements, where the supplier supplies products for processing (such as supply agreements for raw materials);

- online intermediation services supplied by online platforms (such as price comparison websites).

As a general rule, vertical agreements are considered to have a broadly positive effect and give rise to fewer competition concerns than horizontal agreements. However, competition law concerns can arise, for example where the supplier seeks to control some of the distributors' business decisions, such as the prices at which products should be sold or to whom they should be sold. Some of these vertical restraints will constitute restrictions by object (see **2.1.1.5**), while others are considered for their effects on competition.

6.1.1 Inter- and intra-brand competition

In order to understand how vertical agreements can impact on competition, it is important to appreciate the difference between *inter-* and *intra*-brand competition, since any adverse effects on competition will be more limited if there is sufficient inter-brand competition.

6.1.1.1 Inter-brand competition

This describes the competitive dynamic relating to the *different* brands of products in the same market. For example, there are many brands of jeans on the market – Levi's, Lee, Wrangler, Diesel, Armani (to name but a few). Inter-brand competition relates to how these brands compete against each other in order to gain greater sales.

Vertical agreements can impact on inter-brand competition. For example, let us assume that there is a very powerful retailer which is known as one of the best places to purchase clothes, including jeans. This retailer enters into an exclusive arrangement where it agrees to purchase only Armani jeans (this is referred to as a single branding agreement). In these circumstances, other jean manufactures (such as Levi's, Lee, etc) will not be able to sell their products at this influential store (see **Figure 6.1** below). In essence, their route to market (and the final consumer) is restricted due to the single branding agreement.

Figure 6.1

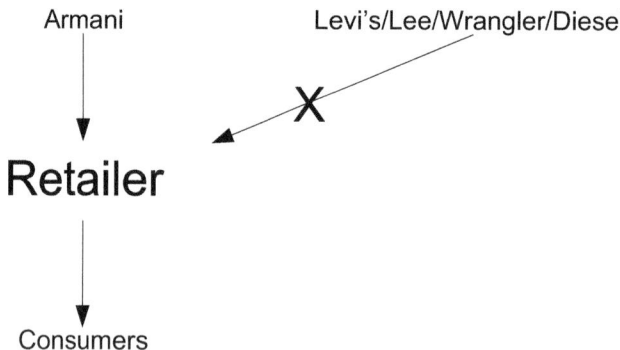

Whether the market is in fact restricted will be dependent on the market power of the retailer. Where it is significant, then competition concerns may arise. However, where it has low market power, a single branding agreement will have very little (or no) impact on the market as other jean manufacturers will have many other available routes to market (Figure **6.2** below demonstrates this).

Figure 6.2

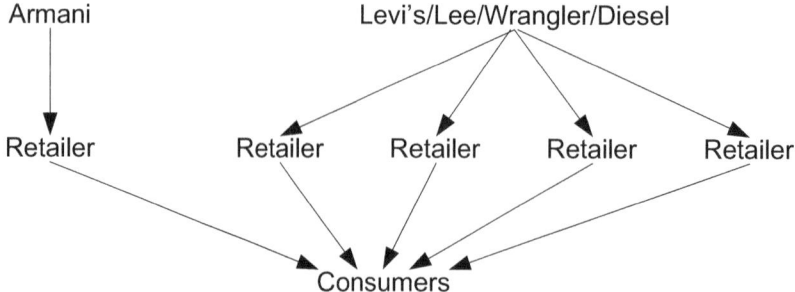

By this simple example it can be seen that, when assessing a vertical agreement (outside an objects infringement), the legal adviser must have some idea of the market share of the parties involved.

6.1.1.2 Intra-brand competition

Intra-brand competition describes the competition dynamic relating to the *same* brand or product. Again, a simple example is the best way to demonstrates this. In this case let us assume that a manufacturer enters into agreements with a limited number of retailers. This in itself is not of concern as the arrangement will not remove or reduce inter-brand competition since other manufacturers will be able to sell their products in the same stores. However, concerns will arise where the manufacturer attempts to prevent or reduce competition between the stores that stock its goods. This will occur where the manufacturer insists that all the stores are required to sell the product at the same price. In these circumstances, there is no opportunity for the stores to attract more consumers by lowering their price for the product. In addition, consumers are forced to buy the product at a fixed price, irrespective of where they attempt to purchase the product.

6.1.2 Pro-competitive effects of vertical agreements

Although vertical agreements can give rise to competition concerns (as demonstrated above), it is important to note that they may increase the competitive dynamic on a market. As we have seen, vertical agreements can aid a manufacturer's ability to get its product to market. Some manufacturers will not have the resources or desire to sell their products directly. This may be particularly relevant where the manufacturer wishes to enter into a new sector or market where it has very little (or no) experience.

Accordingly, a vertical arrangement by which the products pass down the production chain, for example to a specialist distributor, is a useful commercial solution. Without the ability to enter into vertical arrangements, products simply may not get to market. For example, suppose a British manufacturer (X Ltd) of a product wants to break into the French market. X Ltd will probably not have the expertise to market its product successfully in France, so it will appoint a French distributor to do so. The competition rules relating to vertical arrangements must be sufficiently robust in order to prohibit anti-competitive behaviour, but also sufficiently flexible to allow parties to enter into useful commercial arrangements. In the example of X Ltd, the distributor will want a certain degree of protection as it will have to invest time and money in marketing X Ltd's products. It would understandably be upset if, having found new customers for X Ltd's products, X Ltd appointed a second French distributor who could 'free load' off the first distributor's efforts. Similarly, the distributor would be upset if X Ltd cashed in on the distributor's efforts by selling direct to the newly found French customers. Accordingly, many distribution agreements are *exclusive*, ie the supplier of a product agrees to appoint only one distributor for a particular territory and not to sell direct to customers in that territory. However, competition law needs to ensure that the protection granted to distributors goes no further than necessary and does not stifle competition.

We examine below how the EU and UK systems deal with this balancing act.

6.1.3 The ECJ's approach

One of the first cases that the ECJ heard on vertical agreements was Cases 56 and 58/64 *Consten and Grundig v Commission* [1966] ECR 299. As one of the leading cases on the topic, it is worth further consideration.

Grundig was a German manufacturer of consumer electrical goods. It appointed Consten as its distributor in France. Under the terms of the agreement, both parties accepted a number of conditions which restricted their commercial freedom. Grundig would:

(a)   not sell its products directly to customers in France;

(b)   not appoint any other distributors in France;

(c)   assign the trademark it used on its products to Consten (this would enable Consten to take trademark infringement proceedings against any undertaking which imported Grundig products into France);

(d)   prohibit its distributors in other Member States from selling its products to customers in France (this is known as an *export ban*).

The agreement was accordingly an exclusive distribution agreement, but it went further by requiring Grundig to impose an export ban on its distributors in other Member States.

In return the following restrictions were imposed on Consten. It would not sell:

(a)   the products of competing manufacturers;

(b)   Grundig products to customers outside France (also an export ban).

The Commission found that the agreement breached Article 101(1) and the parties appealed to the ECJ. The ECJ rejected the argument that Article 101(1) did not apply to vertical agreements, as its wording did not make any distinction between vertical and horizontal agreements. The ECJ also rejected the argument that the agreement did not affect trade as it in fact resulted in an increase in trade. The export ban on Grundig's distributors in other Member States and on Consten itself meant that patterns of trade were affected and so Article 101 was engaged.

The ECJ then went on to hold that the agreement restricted competition by object. It rejected the argument that the Commission should have taken into account the possibility of inter-brand competition (see **6.1.1** above). The agreement isolated the French market for Grundig products and artificially maintained separate national markets for a very well-known brand, thereby distorting competition within the internal market.

The main objection with the agreement was that it granted Consten *absolute territorial protection*. If a French retailer wanted to stock Grundig's products, it had no choice but to buy them from Consten. It could not buy them direct from Grundig, nor from distributors in other Member States. The agreement therefore precluded the possibility of *parallel imports*. (Parallel imports are imports of non-counterfeit goods that take place outside of an undertaking's official distribution system. Parallel imports typically occur where the price of a given product is high in one Member State and low in another. A parallel importer in the high-cost State would seek to import the product from the low-cost State, thereby obtaining the product at a cheaper price.) A fundamental aim of EU competition law is to ensure that there is always the possibility of parallel imports.

Consten and Grundig should be contrasted with Case 56/65 *Société Technique Minière v Maschinenbau Ulm GmbH* [1966] ECR 235 (also cited at **2.1.1.4** as one of the leading cases on the meaning of 'may affect trade between Member States'). The parties involved, STM and MU, entered into an agreement whereby MU, a German manufacturer, appointed STM as its exclusive distributor in France. The terms of the distribution agreement were similar to the one in *Consten and Grundig*, but there were crucial differences: no export bans were imposed on MU's distributors in other Member States, nor on STM. As the restrictions were less onerous than those in *Consten and Grundig*, the agreement did not have an anti-competitive object, so the ECJ then considered whether the agreement had the effect of restricting competition. The ECJ stated that the following factors should be taken into account when analysing the effect of an agreement:

(a)   the nature and quantity, limited or otherwise, of the products covered by the agreement;

(b)   the position and size of the parties on the market for the products concerned;

(c)   the isolated nature of the agreement or its position in a series of agreements (a network of similar agreements is more likely to distort competition than an isolated agreement);

(d)   the severity of the clauses intended to protect the exclusive distributorship; and

(e)   the opportunities allowed for other commercial competitors in the same products by way of parallel trade.

Applying these factors, the ECJ held that the distribution agreement between MU and STM did not have anti-competitive effects. The parties did not have high market shares, the agreement was not part of a network, nor did it preclude the possibility of parallel imports.

Accordingly, the ECJ's case law recognises that exclusive distribution agreements are a legitimate business practice, provided they do not go too far in partitioning markets along national lines and do not give distributors excessive protection. The UK adopts the same approach.

6.1.4   Legal instruments

The sections below set out the relevant EU and UK competition legislation relating to vertical agreements.

6.1.4.1   EU VBER and Guidelines

On 10 May 2022, the European Commission adopted a new vertical agreements block exemption (Regulation 2022/720, [2022] OJ L134/4) (VBER). The VBER came into force on 1 June 2022 and expires on 31 May 2034. It applies to all EU Member States (and therefore not to the UK). The VBER is reproduced in **Appendix 6**.

The VBER replaces a previous, similar block exemption (Regulation 330/2010, [2010] OJ L102/1), which had been in force since 1 June 2010 and was effective in the UK. Following Brexit and until 1 June 2022, the VBER was part of EU retained law ('the retained EU Vertical Agreements Block Exemption').

On 10 May 2022, the European Commission also published its Guidelines on Vertical Restraints (2022/C 248/01) ('Vertical Guidelines' or 'EU Guidelines'). These replace the 2010 EU Guidelines on Vertical Restraints. They set out the principles for the assessment of vertical agreements under Article 101.

The VBER and the EU's Vertical Guidelines do *not* apply in the UK. The position on vertical restraints in the UK nevertheless remains very similar to the EU's position. UK businesses that operate their agreements both in the UK and in EU Member States will need to comply with both sets of laws.

6.1.4.2   UK VABEO and Guidance

In the UK, the Competition Act 1998 (Vertical Agreements Block Exemption) Order 2022 (SI 2022/516) (VABEO) replaces the retained EU Vertical Agreements Block Exemption. The VABEO came into force on 1 June 2022 and applies until 1 June 2028 (giving the UK a shorter review point of six years rather than 12 under the VBER). The VABEO is reproduced in **Appendix 7**.

On 12 July 2022, the Competition and Markets Authority (CMA) published guidance on vertical agreements ('Vertical Guidance' or 'UK Guidance'). The Vertical Guidance supersedes the 2010 EU Guidelines on Vertical Restraints in the UK and the 2004 OFT Guidance on Vertical Agreements. It sets out the principles for the assessment of vertical agreements under Chapter I.

6.1.4.3   EU and UK position compared

The VBER and VABEO ('the Vertical block exemptions') and the EU and UK Vertical Guidelines/Guidance generally adopt a consistent position in relation to the treatment of vertical restraints. Too much inconsistency would create legal uncertainty for businesses operating across borders and raise compliance costs.

Given the similarity of approach, the EU and UK positions are treated together below. Where there are significant differences, these are specifically highlighted. These include the following:

(i)   *OIS and hybrid platforms.* Both Vertical block exemptions are capable of applying to distribution through online intermediation platforms (OIS). The EU VBER does not apply to OIS with a hybrid function, where the provider of the online intermediation service is itself a competitor on the market intermediated by the platform. The UK has no carve out for hybrid platforms, which may lead to a more generous approach. Hybrid platforms are dealt with at **6.2.4.4**.

(ii)   *Retail parity obligations.* The UK VABEO does not apply to an arrangement containing wide retail parity obligations, a stricter approach than the EU's. The EU VBER merely excludes wide parity obligations from the benefit of the block exemption, while the remainder of the arrangement may benefit from the VBER. Parity clauses are dealt with at **6.2.9**.

(iii) *Number of exclusive distributors.* Under the EU approach, exclusive distributors must be limited to five per territory or customer group. In the UK there must be a 'limited number', which is not specified. See **6.2.6.6**.

(iv)   *Information exchanges.* Information exchanges between competitors are subject to stricter conditions in the text of the VBER, although the UK's Vertical Guidance sets out a similar approach. See **6.2.10**.

(v)   *Rolling contracts.* The previous vertical block exemption treated automatically renewable non-compete clauses as clauses of an indefinite duration. The UK maintains this approach while the EU allows automatic renewal in some circumstances. See **6.2.7.1**.

(vi)   *Market share grace period.* There is slight variance in the grace periods during which the parties may continue to benefit from a Vertical block exemption if they exceed the 30% market share threshold after entering into their agreement. See **6.2.5**.

6.1.4.4   Transition period

For agreements already in force on 31 May 2022, which satisfy the conditions for exemption provided for in Regulation 330/2010, the parties benefit from a one year transition period. This means that for these agreements, the parties may continue to benefit from Regulation 330/2010 until 1 June 2023. After that date, the parties will need to amend their agreements to comply with the VBER and/or VABEO.

6.2   ANALYSIS OF VERTICAL AGREEMENTS IN THE EU AND IN THE UK

6.2.1   Analysis of vertical agreements

Analysing vertical agreements involves a consideration of:

- the broad arrangement between the parties (written or unwritten);
- the nature of the parties' relationship (vertical or with horizontal aspects);
- the types of restrictions (object and/or effect) – 'vertical restraints'.

Where vertical restraints are present or anticipated, the practitioner will need to consider a number of factors, including:

(a)   In Article 101(1) cases only, does the 'no appreciable affectation of trade' (NAAT) rule help? (See **2.1.1.4**.)

(b)   Does the De Minimis Notice on agreements of minor importance (NAOMI) help? (See **2.1.1.7** and **2.1.4.1**.) As a reminder, in a vertical relationship:

(i)   Where the parties' market shares do not exceed 15% of the relevant market, the agreement will fall outside Article 101/Chapter I as it will not have an appreciable effect on competition.

      (ii)   However, even if the shares are within the 15% threshold, NAOMI will not apply where the agreement contains restrictions by object or restrictions that are listed as hardcore restrictions in a block exemption (eg fixed minimum prices or export bans).

(c)   Is the agreement between parties that form a single economic unit?

      (i)   *Parent/subsidiary*: As we have seen at **2.1.1.1**, for an agreement to come within Article 101/Chapter I, it must be made between separate undertakings that are not part of a single economic unit. For example, where a manufacturer owns a subsidiary which retails the manufacturer's products, the agreement is between the parent and a subsidiary which is part of the same economic unit, and will fall outside Article 101/Chapter I.

      (ii)   *Agency*: A genuine agency relationship falls outside the scope of Article 101/Chapter I (see **6.2.2**).

(d)   Does a block exemption apply? (See **2.1.3.3** generally and **6.2.4** for the Vertical block exemptions.) The benefit of falling within a block exemption is that it provides legal certainty to the parties, a so-called 'safe harbour' within which it is assumed that their agreement complies with competition law. Thus, the block exemption is often the starting point of the analysis. If practitioners are able to craft an agreement such that it falls within the safe harbour of a block exemption, this provides a measure of legal certainty.

(e)   If no block exemption is available, does the agreement qualify for an individual exemption? (See **2.1.3**.)

(f)   Are there any other relevant circumstances? For example, under the ancillary restraints doctrine (see **7.3.9** and **7.4.6**), restrictions that are directly related and necessary to achieve a pro-competitive or legitimate objective may fall outside Article 101/Chapter I as 'ancillary restraints'. Certain relationships may fall outside the scope of Article 101/Chapter I, such as sub-contracting agreements (see **6.2.3**) and franchising agreements (**6.2.14**).

Additional considerations apply in the case of dominant undertakings under Article 102/Chapter II.

6.2.2 Agency agreements

Agency agreements are an important way of avoiding the scope of Article 101/Chapter I. If the helpful rules on agency apply, it is not necessary to rely on a Vertical block exemption.

6.2.2.1 Concept of agency agreements

In a 'pure' agency agreement, where the agent undertakes the activity of the principal rather than carrying on an independent economic activity in its own right, the relationship between the principal and the agent will fall outside Article 101(1)/Chapter I. The agent will not be acting as an independent operator but as an agent negotiating contracts for the principal.

Whether or not Article 101(1)/Chapter I applies to an agency relationship is outlined in some detail at paras 29–46 of the EU Vertical Guidelines and paras 4.8–4.33 of the UK Vertical Guidance.

The legal form of the agreement is not relevant: it may be called an 'agency agreement' but as a matter of economic reality the relationship may be one of independent supplier and re-seller.

For an agreement to be treated under the agency rules, the agent must bear no significant financial or commercial risks in relation to the contracts negotiated for the principal (para 30 EU Guidelines; para 4.11 UK Guidance).

Where the 'agent' acts for a large number of principals, it is less likely that the agreement will be treated under agency rules (para 30 EU Guidelines). The UK Guidance is more neutral: it merely lists as a relevant factor to the assessment 'the extent to which the agent acts for a large number of principals, which may indicate that the agent is independent and not an integral part of its principal's undertaking' (para 4.20(c) UK Guidance).

Other factors to take into consideration include the types of financial or commercial risks taken by the parties and whether the agent is paid by commission (paras 31 and 32 EU Guidelines; paras 4.12 and 4.13 UK Guidance).

A number of criteria are listed in the EU Guidelines and UK Guidance, such as whether property in the contract goods vests in the agent, whether the agent pays for sales or promotional material, maintains stock at its own cost and/or offers after-sales services. The more the agent undertakes these activities, the more likely that the agent has assumed financial and commercial risk. Where the agent takes on the commercial or financial risk then the agreement will not qualify as an agency agreement and Article 101(1)/Chapter I may apply.

6.2.2.2   Applying Article 101 and Chapter I to agency agreements

In a pure agency agreement, the principal is able to determine the agent's commercial strategy, for example the prices which the agent may charge for the principal's goods (para 41 EU Guidelines; para 4.29 UK Guidance). Where the agreement is not covered by the agency rules, price restrictions are of course restrictions by object under Article 101/Chapter I.

Article 101(1)/Chapter I may apply to aspects of the agency relationship that are not an inherent part of the agency agreement. For example, a provision requiring the agent not to compete with the principal after termination of the agency agreement (a 'post-term non-compete') may restrict competition and fall within the scope of Article 101/Chapter I (para 43 EU Guidelines; para 4.31 UK Guidance).

An agency agreement may also fall within the scope of Article 101(1)/Chapter I, even if the principal bears all of the commercial and financial risk, where it facilitates collusion. For example, a number of principals using the same agents could exclude other principals from using that agent; or a number of principals could use the agents to collude on marketing strategy or to exchange sensitive market information. In these cases, Article 101(1)/Chapter I would apply (para 44 EU Guidelines; para 4.32 UK Guidance).

6.2.3   Sub-contracting agreements

Agreements under which one firm (the contractor) entrusts another firm (the sub-contractor) to manufacture products or perform works under the contractor's instructions generally fall outside the scope of Article 101(1)/Chapter I. EU guidance is provided in its Subcontracting Notice (OJ C 1, 3.1.1979, p 2) and para 47 of the EU Vertical Guidelines. In the UK, competition authorities have regard to the Subcontracting Notice and further guidance is contained in para 4.34 of the UK Vertical Guidance.

6.2.4   The Vertical block exemptions

The following sections (**6.2.4–6.2.10**) describe the conditions that must be satisfied in order to benefit from the 'safe harbour' of a Vertical block exemption (the VBER and/or VABEO).

For cases where these conditions are not satisfied, the 'safe harbour' is not available. However, it does not necessarily follow that Article 101(1)/Chapter I apply in the first place. As seen above (**6.2.1**), it may be possible to benefit from one of the exclusions available (NAAT, NAOMI). It may also be possible to use the principles of agency in order to fall outside the scope of Article 101/Chapter I altogether (see **6.2.2**). If Article 101(1)/Chapter I do apply, an individual exemption may be available (see **2.1.3.2**).

6.2.4.1 Definition of vertical agreements

The Vertical block exemptions apply to vertical agreements, irrespective of the business model used. To qualify as a vertical agreement, it is necessary to fall within the definitions and requirements set out in the VBER (Article 2) and VABEO (article 3).

Both Article 2(1) VBER and article 3(1) VABEO exempt 'vertical agreements'. The following definition of 'vertical agreements' is taken from Article 1(1)(a) VBER. The definition in article 3(2) VABEO is essentially the same, with some very minor differences in wording. A 'vertical agreement' means:

> an agreement or concerted practice between two or more undertakings, each of which operates, for the purposes of the agreement or the concerted practice, at a different level of the production or distribution chain, and relating to the conditions under which the parties may purchase, sell or resell certain goods or services. (Article 1(1)(a) VBER)

6.2.4.2 Competing undertakings

The Vertical block exemptions do not apply to vertical agreements between competing undertakings, except in cases of dual distribution set out below.

Competing undertakings are defined in Article 1(1)(c) VBER and article 3(7) VABEO to include potential, as well as actual, competitors.

6.2.4.3 Dual distribution

As an exception to the rule that Vertical block exemptions do not apply to agreements between competitors, the Vertical block exemptions do apply where competing undertakings enter into a non-reciprocal vertical agreement, as long as the supplier and the buyer are not operating at the same level of trade for the purposes of the agreement (see Article 2(4)(a) and (b) VBER and article 3(5) VABEO).

For example, a German supplier of raw materials may use a subsidiary for distribution in Germany. If the German supplier appoints a third party to distribute the raw materials in France, the German supplier and its French distributor operate at different levels of trade for the purpose of that agreement. The Vertical block exemptions are capable of applying, as long as the agreement is non-reciprocal. Paragraph 6.17 of the UK Guidance explains that:

> Non-reciprocal means, for instance, that where one manufacturer becomes the distributor of the products of another manufacturer, the latter does not become a distributor of the products of the first manufacturer.

The rationale for this exception is based on the balancing exercise discussed above (**6.1.1**), namely that 'in a dual distribution scenario, the potential negative impact of the vertical agreement on the competitive relationship between the supplier and the buyer at the downstream level is considered to be less important than the potential positive impact of the vertical agreement on competition ...' (para 95 of the EU Guidelines). See also recital 12 VBER.

6.2.4.4 Hybrid platforms

Online Intermediation Services ('OIS') are defined in both Vertical block exemptions by reference to the EU definition of information society services (recital 11 VBER and article 2(1) VABEO). Examples of OIS include e-commerce marketplaces, app stores, price comparison tools and social media services used by undertakings (para 64 of the EU Guidelines).

EU approach to hybrid platforms

According to the VBER, the rationale for exempting vertical agreements in cases of dual distribution does not extend to hybrid online intermediation platforms (OIS), as providers of these platforms may have the ability and incentive to distort competition for the intermediated products. Hybrid OIS are those:

where the provider on the online intermediation services is also a competing undertaking on the relevant market for the sale of the intermediated goods or services. (recital 14 VBER)

Under Article 2(6) VBER, hybrid OIS platforms do not benefit from the VBER. The Guidelines (paras 104–109) explain the Commission's approach to hybrid OIS platforms.

UK approach to hybrid platforms

The UK approach is more generous. All vertical OIS may benefit from the VABEO, and there is no 'carve out' for hybrid OIS where the provider of the OIS competes on the market for the sale of the intermediated product. However, where the UK's competition authorities consider that a particular vertical agreement should not be exempted, the VABEO may be cancelled (article 13(1) VABEO). This is an area which the UK is keeping under review (as noted previously the VABEO is to be reviewed after six years – **6.1.4.2**).

6.2.4.5 Other block exemptions do not apply

The Vertical block exemptions cannot apply where the subject matter of the agreement is dealt with under another block exemption. For example, the distribution of motor vehicles is dealt with in a separate block exemption.

In the case of the sale of products involving the licensing of intellectual property (IP) rights, Article 2(3) VBER and article 3(4) VABEO allow the block exemption to cover vertical agreements under which IP rights are licensed or assigned, as long as the IP provisions of the agreement do not constitute the 'primary object' of the agreement. Where IP licensing is the subject matter of the agreement, the Technology Transfer Block Exemption Regulation may apply instead (see **8.3.4.2**).

6.2.5 Market share thresholds

As seen above (at **6.1.1**), an agreement's effect on competition will, to a large degree, be dependent on the market shares of the parties to the agreement. Article 3 VBER and article 6 VABEO set out the market share thresholds above which the Vertical block exemptions will not apply. There are two thresholds:

(a)   The market share of the supplier must not exceed 30% of the relevant market on which it sells the products. Usually this is the most relevant market share as the supplier tends to be the stronger party.

(b)   The market share of the purchaser must not exceed 30% of the relevant market on which it purchases the products. This threshold is less easy to grasp than the supplier threshold at (a) above. Its purpose is to ensure that where the purchaser of the products is the stronger party, with its market share of purchases exceeding 30%, the Vertical block exemptions will not apply.

Market shares are determined in accordance with the technique set out at **3.3.1**.

In the case of online intermediation services (OIS), the supplier is the provider on the online platform.

Article 8(d) VBER and article 7(2) and 7(3) VABEO contain grace periods during which the relevant Vertical block exemption will continue to apply even if a market share rises above the 30% threshold at some time during the life of the agreement. Under Article 8(d) VBER, the block exemption continues to apply for up to two years following the year in which market share levels exceed 30%. Under article 7(2) and 7(3) VABEO there is a two year grace period as long as market share levels do not exceed 35%, reduced to one year if market share levels exceed 35% (reflecting the position under the old retained EU Vertical Agreements Block Exemption).

6.2.6 Hardcore restrictions

The VRBE and VABEO cannot apply if the arrangement includes any hardcore restrictions. Article 4 VRBE lists the hardcore restrictions under the VRBE and article 8 VABEO lists the hardcore restrictions under the VABEO. The list of hardcore restrictions is similar in both block exemptions; where there are material differences, these are set out below.

If a hardcore restriction is contained within the agreement or operated by the parties, then the *whole* agreement falls outside the relevant Vertical block exemption. Article 9 VABEO is specific in this regard: including a hardcore restriction 'has the effect of cancelling the block exemption in respect of vertical agreements'. This reflects the EU position.

When an arrangement includes a hardcore restriction, it may be possible to 'save' the agreement by individual exemption. An agreement containing hardcore restrictions is generally unlikely to come within the rules relating to individual exemption. Consequently, legal advisers will ensure that no hardcore restrictions remain within the agreement.

Let us look at some of the hardcore restrictions in a little more detail.

6.2.6.1 Pricing restrictions

Article 4(a) VBER and article 8(2) VABEO prevent restrictions on the buyer's ability to set its sale price – in particular the setting of a fixed or minimum price. In the context of a vertical agreement, the supplier cannot dictate to the distributor the price at which it sells the goods to retailers. This activity will clearly restrict price competition, and as such intra-brand competition will be removed as consumers will have to pay the same price for the goods or services regardless of where they attempt to purchase them. This type of infringement is commonly referred to as 'resale price maintenance' (RPM).

Resale price maintenance is an object restriction listed as a hardcore restriction under Article 4(a) VBER and article 8(2)(a) VABEO. As such, not only does its presence in an agreement make the Vertical block exemptions unavailable, but it is unlikely that the agreement would benefit from individual exemption. However, there may be exceptions. Paragraph 195 of the EU's Vertical Guidelines states that resale price maintenance may, in certain circumstances where there are efficiencies, be capable of individual exemption under Article 101(3). This is, however, very rare. The UK's position is also that resale price maintenance may sometimes benefit from an individual exemption under s 9 of the Competition Act 1998, and some examples are provided in the Guidelines (paras 8.19–8.21, such as where a new product is introduced and RPM leads to efficiencies).

Article 4(a) VBER and article 8(2)(a) VABEO permit two kinds of pricing restrictions on the buyer. One is a restriction on the maximum sale price that may be imposed. The other is the ability for the supplier to recommend a price. However, the maximum or recommended price must not amount to a minimum sale price as a result of pressure from the supplier or incentives offered by the supplier. These are important limitations and the authorities will consider all the evidence, including the extent to which dealers actually sell below a recommended price.

6.2.6.2 Territorial and customer restrictions – general position

Another way in which competition can be severely restricted or removed is by the imposition of territorial or customer restrictions. This is particularly sensitive in the context of the EU, as free movement of goods and services is one of the founding principles of the Treaty.

The treatment of territorial and customer restrictions is a good example of how the Vertical block exemptions attempt to balance the pro- and anti-competitive effects of vertical agreements. The general position is that no restriction can be placed on the distributor as regards the customers to which or territories in which it can sell the goods or services subject to the vertical agreement. However, such a wide-ranging restriction could cause as many problems as it attempts to solve.

For example, although prohibiting such a wide-ranging restriction would initially seem a good thing for competition, it would not afford any protection to the distributors (who may have invested significant sums and who are essential to the competitive dynamic – see **6.1.2** above). If distributors could not be protected (to some extent), they simply may not wish to make the necessary investment, and consumers would be denied access to a new product. Accordingly, the Vertical block exemptions attempt to reach a compromise between restrictions on distributors and protection for distributors. In this regard, the Vertical block exemptions make a distinction between active and passive sales. 'Active sales' describes the process where a seller approaches potential buyers. 'Passive sales' describes the process where consumers approach the seller (see paras 211–215 of the EU Guidelines on the distinction between 'active sales' and 'passive sales'). This is outlined in the diagram below (in the context of a distribution agreement).

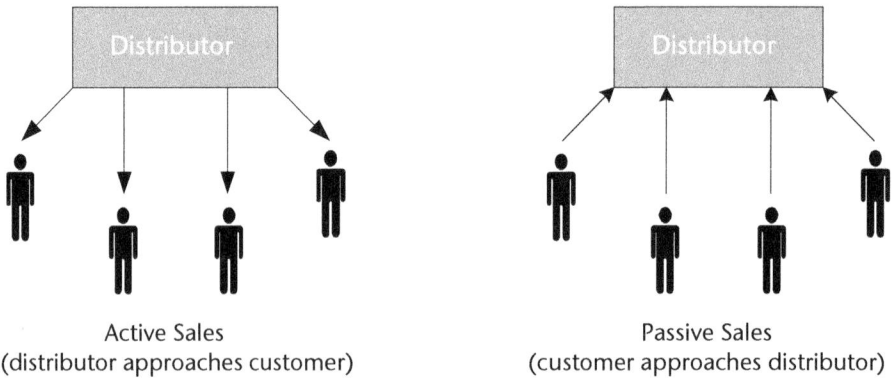

Active Sales
(distributor approaches customer)

Passive Sales
(customer approaches distributor)

The Vertical block exemptions allow restrictions on active sales in territories or customer groups that have been awarded on an exclusive basis (or reserved to the supplier). Accordingly, a supplier can provide protection for a distributor by placing *in other distribution agreements* a restriction which prevents those distributors from actively seeking orders in the exclusive territory allocated to another distributor and/or from actively seeking orders from the exclusive customer group allocated to another distributor. Given this protection, the distributor will be more willing to make the necessary investment (and consumers will get access to the product).

This can be confusing, so let us look at this by way of an example. Assume that a supplier appoints distributors in four territories (A, B, C and D). Only one of these territories has been awarded on an exclusive basis, Territory C. In these circumstances, the supplier can place restrictions in the agreements of the distributors in Territories A, B and D preventing them from actively seeking customers in Territory C (see **Figure 6.3** below).

Figure 6.3   Territory C appointed on an exclusive basis – restriction of active selling

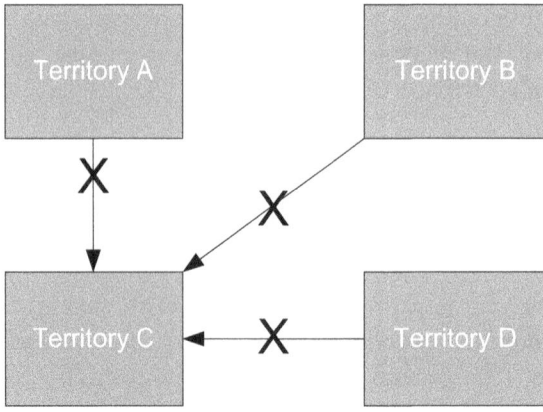

Conversely, the Vertical block exemptions do not generally allow restrictions on passive selling. Accordingly, a customer cannot be prevented from approaching the distributors in

Territories A, B and D to source the product (see **Figure 6.4** below). In theory, the distributor in Territory C, aware that customers are able to source the product elsewhere, will not charge excessive prices.

As there can be no restrictions in the agreements operating in Territories A, B and D preventing them from responding to passive sales requests, things such as total export bans will be prohibited.

Figure 6.4   Passive sales request

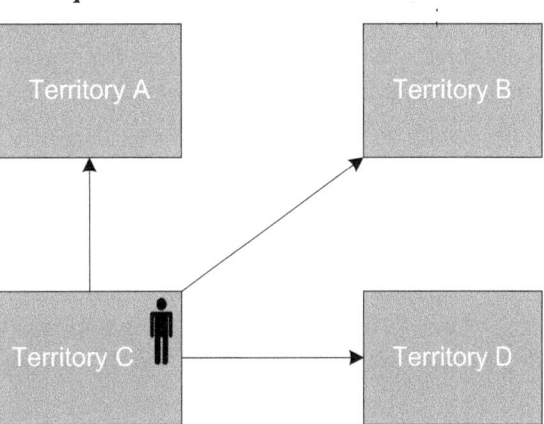

The precise scope of the exemption for territorial and customer restrictions depends on the type of agreement. See **6.2.6.5**.

First let us consider the 'active'/'passive' sale classification, as the line between the sales that are considered 'active' and generally permitted, and sales that are 'passive' and generally prohibited, is often a fine one.

6.2.6.3   Restrictions on use of the internet

The prohibition on restricting passive sales is particularly problematic where sales are predominantly made over the internet rather than in physical stores.

(i)   *Effective use of the internet*

A blanket restriction on making products available over the internet will constitute a restriction on passive sales and will not be permitted: both Article 4(e) VBER ('the prevention of the effective use of the internet by the buyer or its customers') and article 8(6) VABEO ('the prevention of buyers or their customers effectively using the internet') list restrictions on effective use of the internet as hardcore.

(ii)   *Active/passive online sales*

Restrictions on some forms of internet advertising may be considered as forms of active selling (and therefore permitted). Paragraphs 212 to 214 of the EU Guidelines give a number of examples. Thus, 'establishing an online store with a top-level domain corresponding to a territory other than the one in which the seller is established is a form of active selling into that territory, whereas offering an online store with a generic and non-country specific domain name is a form of passive selling' (para 213). Article 8(7) VABEO also contains some examples of active and passive sales, including online sales.

6.2.6.4   Restrictions on suppliers and unjustified geo-blocking exception

(i)   *Restrictions on suppliers*

Under the Vertical block exemptions, restrictions on suppliers (as opposed to buyers) are not generally hardcore restrictions (Article 4(b) VBER and article 8(2) VABEO only apply to territorial and customer restrictions imposed on the buyer and not on the seller). (It is helpful in this regard that OIS platforms are classified as 'suppliers'.)

Consequently, the supplier may generally be restricted from actively and passively selling into an exclusive territory or to an exclusive customer group allocated to a buyer.

(ii)   Unjustified geo-blocking exception

Geo-blocking takes place when traders block or limit online access to customers situated in a different geographical area. This may limit parallel imports, contrary to Article 101. For instance, in *Valve v EC Videogames* (Case T-172/21) (27 September 2023), the General Court found that blocking players of video games from accessing (potentially cheaper) games outside an authorised territory constituted restrictions by object under Article 101.

Regulation (EU) 2018/302 of 28 February 2018 on addressing unjustified geo-blocking (the 'Unjustified Geo-blocking Regulation') provides that, in certain circumstances, restrictions of passive sales *by the supplier* to end-users are void (Article 6(2) of the Geo-blocking Regulation, para 222 of the EU's Vertical Guidelines).

Although the Unjustified Geo-blocking Regulation no longer applies in the UK (see the Geo-Blocking Regulation (Revocation) (EU Exit) Regulations 2019 (SI 2019/880)), the Unjustified Geo-blocking Regulation continues to apply to UK businesses that trade in the EU.

6.2.6.5   Types of distribution system

The list of hardcore restrictions and exceptions depend on the type of distribution system in question. Broadly speaking, three types of distribution systems are covered by Article 4(b), (c) and (d) VBER and article 8(2)–(5) VABEO: exclusive, selective and free distribution systems.

Exclusive distribution systems are defined in Article 1(1)(h) VBER and article 8(7) VABEO. In exclusive distribution systems, the supplier allocates territories or groups of customers exclusively to itself and to some distributors, and restricts the other distributors from actively selling into another exclusive territory or exclusive customer group. Case 56/65 *Société Technique Minière v Maschinenbau Ulm GmbH* [1966] ECR 235, mentioned at **6.1.3**, is an example of an exclusive distribution system. To benefit from a Vertical block exemption, the number of exclusive distributors must be limited (that number is specified as no more than five under the EU system: see **6.2.6.6**).

Selective distribution systems are defined in Article 1(1)(g) VBER and article 2(1) VABEO. In selective distribution systems, the supplier only sells to distributors selected on the basis of specified criteria, and distributors undertake not to sell goods or services to unauthorised distributors in the area where the supplier operates the selective distribution system. Not all restrictions contained in selective distribution systems fall foul of Article 101(1)/Chapter I: see **6.2.13**.

Mixed agreements, namely distribution systems that contain both exclusive and selective features, are covered by the Vertical block exemptions. Under the EU system, exclusive and selective distribution may not co-exist within the same territory (para 236 EU Guidelines). This is not a feature of the UK system, where exclusive distribution at the wholesale level and selective distribution at the retail level may be combined (para 8.71 UK Guidance).

The main difference between exclusive and selective distribution systems:

> lies in the nature of the protection granted to the distributor. In an exclusive distribution system, the distributor is protected against active selling from outside its exclusive territory, whereas in a selective distribution system, the distributor is protected against active and passive sales by unauthorised distributors. (para 145 EU Guidelines, similarly worded in para 10.85 UK Guidance)

Franchising agreements may contain features that are either exclusive or selective. For example, franchising agreements may prohibit franchisees from selling to non-franchisees and are assessed under the principles applicable to selective distribution; whereas franchise agreements that do not create a closed network but which grant protection from active sales into the franchisee's territory are assessed under the principles applicable to exclusive distribution (para 167 EU Guidelines, similarly worded in para 10.106 UK Guidance). Not all restrictions in franchise agreements fall foul of Article 101(1)/Chapter I: see **6.2.14**.

So-called 'free distribution systems' are neither exclusive nor selective but contain territorial or customer restrictions (Article 4(d) VBER and article 8(2)(d) VABEO).

The Vertical block exemptions methodically list the hardcore restrictions and their exceptions in relation to these three different types of distribution structures (exclusive, selective and free). A common element, as seen in **6.2.6.2**, is that, generally, restrictions on active sales are permitted while restrictions on passive sales are hardcore.

Only the restrictions relating to exclusive distributions systems are fully covered here. These are contained in Article 4(b) VBER and article 8(2) and 8(3) VABEO.

6.2.6.6   Restrictions in exclusive distribution agreements

The VBER only applies if the number of exclusive distributors is limited to *five*; whereas the VABEO does not dictate an exact number, specifying that the VABEO only applies if there is a '*limited number*' of exclusive distributors, determined in such a way as to preserve their investment efforts.

In the VBER, 'exclusive distribution system' means:

> a distribution system where the supplier allocates a territory or group of customers exclusively to itself or to a maximum of five buyers and restricts all its other buyers from actively selling into the exclusive territory or to the exclusive customer group. (Article 1(1)(h) VBER)

In the VABEO, 'exclusive distribution system' means:

> a distribution system where the supplier allocates a geographical area or customer group exclusively to itself or to one or a limited number of buyers, determined in proportion to the allocated geographical area or customer group in such a way as to secure certain volumes of business that preserves their investment efforts, and restricts other buyers from actively selling into the exclusive geographical area or to the exclusive customer group. (article 8(7) VABEO)

Article 4(b) VBER and article 8(2) VABEO start with stating that restrictions in an exclusive distribution system as to the territory into which, or the customer group to whom, the exclusive distributor may actively or passively sell the contract goods or services are hardcore. However, five exceptions are then listed, in Article 4(b) itself under VBER and in a separate sub-article 8(3) in VABEO.

The following restrictions are *permitted*:

(a)   Restrictions on *active* sales by the exclusive distributor into a *territory* or to a *customer group* reserved to the *supplier* or exclusively allocated to:

(i)   in the EU, a maximum of *five* buyers;

(ii)   in the UK, a *limited number* of buyers.

These active sales restrictions may only be imposed on the *exclusive distributor and on the exclusive distributor's direct customers*. They may not be passed on to those buying from the exclusive distributor.

(b)   Restrictions in *mixed exclusive and selective distribution systems*. Where a supplier appoints exclusive distributors in one territory and selective distributors in another, the supplier can restrict *active and passive sales* by the exclusive distributor and its customers to *unauthorised distributors in territories where the supplier operates a selective distribution system*.

(c)   A supplier may restrict the *place of establishment* of the buyer to which it has allocated an exclusive territory or customer group. For example, the supplier may require the distributor to restrict its distribution outlets to a particular address, place or territory (known as a location clause).

(d)   Restrictions on an exclusive *wholesaler* from making active or passive sales to the retail trade are permitted. This enables the supplier to keep the wholesale and retail levels of trade separate.

(e)   Restrictions on active and passive sale of components – see **6.2.6.8**.

6.2.6.7   Restrictions in selective and free distribution agreements

The types of restrictions that are listed as hardcore in selective and free distribution agreements are not specifically covered in this textbook.

6.2.6.8   Restrictions on the sale of spare parts and components

The general position is that the supplier may impose some restrictions on the buyer regarding the sale (both active and passive) of components to prevent their incorporation by the buyer into competing products (Article 4(b)(v) VBER and article 8(3)(e) VABEO for exclusive distribution agreements; Article 4(c)(i)(5) VBER and article 8(4)(e) VABEO for selective distribution agreements; and Article 4(d)(v) VBER and article 8(5)(e) VABEO) for free distribution).

However, any restriction on the supplier's ability to sell components as spare parts to end users or independent providers is hardcore (Article 4(f) VBER and article 8(2)(e) VABEO) for all types of agreements.

6.2.7   Excluded restrictions

Excluded restrictions are those which are excluded from the benefit of the Vertical block exemptions. There is, however, no presumption that Article 101/Chapter I apply to excluded restrictions, and they may benefit from an individual exemption.

6.2.7.1   Non-compete obligations

The first type of excluded restrictions concern 'non-compete' obligations (Article 5 VBER and article 10 VABEO). These are defined in Article 1(1)(f) VBER and article 10(5) VABEO. Broadly speaking, a 'non-compete' in this context is an obligation on the buyer not to deal with competing goods. It includes an obligation on the buyer to purchase more than 80% of its requirements for the products from the supplier, since that is very close to an exclusive purchase obligation. A non-compete obligation will have an impact on inter-brand competition. However, the Vertical block exemptions recognise that a supplier will want some reassurance that a distributor will not start to procure or otherwise deal in competing products. Without this reassurance, the supplier may not want to appoint distributors at all.

Accordingly, the Vertical block exemptions again arrive at a compromise, allowing non-compete obligations but only for a limited time, namely no more than the duration of the agreement and in any event not exceeding five years (Article 5(1)(a) VBER and article 10(2)(a) VABEO).

Article 10(2)(a) VABEO covers rolling contracts. Where a non-compete obligation is automatically renewable beyond a period of five years, the contract is deemed to have been concluded for an indefinite duration. The VBER does not specifically mention rolling contracts, and the EU's Vertical Guidelines adopt a more flexible approach. Paragraph 248 explains that non-compete obligations that are tacitly renewable beyond a period of five years may benefit from the block exemption, provided that the buyer can effectively renegotiate or terminate the contract.

In the case of certain leases of land, the five-year limitation does not apply (Article 5(2) VBER and article 10(3) VABEO).

6.2.7.2   Post-term non-compete obligations

Non-compete obligations that endure beyond the life of the contract (post-term bans) are excluded restrictions that do not generally benefit from the Vertical block exemptions (Article 5(1)(b) VBER and article 10(2)(b) VABEO).

Post-termination non-compete obligations that are limited to one year from termination are, however, permitted in limited circumstances, usually applicable in cases of franchising (Article 5(3)(d) VBER and article 10(4)(a)(iv) VABEO). For franchising, see **6.2.14**.

6.2.7.3   Non-compete obligations in selective distribution systems

Article 5(1)(c) VBER and article 10(2)(c) VABEO specify, in the case of selective distribution systems, that an obligation not to deal in brands of particular competing suppliers is an excluded restriction. Thus a non-compete which targets specific competing suppliers, rather than competing brands in general, is excluded from the benefit of the Vertical block exemptions.

6.2.8   Effect of including hardcore/excluded restrictions

There is an important difference between hardcore and excluded restrictions in terms of whether the contract containing such restrictions is enforceable in a court of law.

6.2.8.1   Effect of including hardcore restrictions

If an agreement contains any of the hardcore restrictions contained in Article 4 VBER/article 8 VABEO, the effect is that the Vertical block exemptions do not apply. Article 9 VABEO specifies that the effect of including a hardcore restriction is to cancel the block exemption in respect of the vertical agreement.

The hardcore restrictions will likely be void and unenforceable, but this does not mean that the whole contract is void and unenforceable. To assess whether any of the contract survives, it will be necessary to consider whether the hardcore restrictions are severable from the 'legitimate' parts of the agreement as a matter of the governing law of the contract (see **2.1.2**).

6.2.8.2   Effect of including excluded restrictions

If an agreement contains any of the excluded restrictions contained in Article 5 VBER/article 10 VABEO, the effect is that the excluded restrictions do not benefit from the block exemption. The excluded restrictions may be void and unenforceable, but the remainder of the agreement may still benefit from the block exemption. It will be necessary to consider whether the excluded restrictions are severable from the 'legitimate' parts of the agreement as a matter of the governing law of the contract (see **2.1.2**).

Article 11 VABEO specifies that where the excluded restriction is severable from the agreement, the block exemption is cancelled in respect of the excluded restriction only. Where the restriction is not severable from the agreement, the block exemption is cancelled in respect of the entire agreement.

6.2.9   Wide retail parity clauses

The EU and UK adopt a slightly different approach to retail parity obligations (also known as Most Favoured Nation or MFN clauses).

6.2.9.1   EU: wide retail parity obligations on OIS are excluded

Article 5(1)(d) VBER excludes from the benefit of the VBER retail parity obligations imposed by OIS suppliers and causing buyers of OIS not to supply products to end-users under more favourable conditions via competing OIS ('across-platform retail parity obligations') (para 253 EU Guidelines). These are known as 'wide' retail parity obligations because the product supplier, who is the buyer of the intermediation service, offers parity not just over its own retail channel (narrow) but also over competing intermediaries (wide).

Other types of parity clauses can benefit from the VBER, including (para 254 EU Guidelines):

- 'narrow' retail parity obligations which impose an obligation on buyers of OIS to offer no more favourable terms on their direct sales channels;
- parity obligations relating to the conditions under which products are offered to businesses rather than end-users;
- 'most favoured customer' obligations where products are purchased by manufacturers, wholesalers or retailers as inputs.

6.2.9.2   UK: wide retail parity obligations are hardcore

The UK system is more restrictive, erring on the side of caution in order to achieve greater protection for the consumer. Wide retail parity obligations are listed as hardcore, whether on OIS or offline.

The CMA's Guidance explains that *parity clauses* require one party to an agreement to offer to the other party goods or services on terms that are no worse than those offered to its own customers; and *retail parity clauses* describe restrictions that apply in the retail context and involve sales to end-users (para 8.79 UK Guidance).

Wide parity clauses at the end-user or retail level are hardcore restrictions. A wide retail party obligation means 'a restriction by reference to any of the supplier's indirect sales channels (whether online or offline, for instance online platforms or other intermediaries), which ensures that the prices or other terms and conditions at which the supplier's goods or services are offered *to end users* on a sales channel are *no worse* than those offered by the supplier on another sales channel' (article 8(7) VABEO and para 8.81 UK Guidance) (*emphasis added*).

The CMA's concern is that wide retail parity obligations restrict competition at all levels, including between suppliers of the products being intermediated on the online platform (paras 8.84–8.88 UK Guidance).

Only an agreement setting the terms of supply to end-users at the retail level (consumers) are hardcore. Other types of parity clauses can benefit from the VABEO, including:

- a wide parity obligation imposed in upstream business-to-business markets (para 8.89 UK Guidance);
- narrow retail parity obligations, where the product supplier agrees not to offer products to end-users on its direct sales channels (for example, the product supplier's own website) on better terms than those offered on an indirect sales channel by which it reaches end-users (para 10.164 UK Guidance).

Narrow retail parity obligations which are not exempted (for example if the market share thresholds are exceeded) may benefit from an individual exemption (para 10.163 UK Guidance).

6.2.9.3   Implications for agreements containing wide retail parity clauses

As a consequence of the difference in approach between the EU and UK:

- In the EU, the VBER is available to an arrangement even if it contains a wide retail parity obligation. A wide retail parity obligation on OIS, as an excluded restriction, will not benefit from the VBER but may benefit from an individual exemption (section 8.2.5 EU Guidelines). Conversely, where a wide retail parity obligation causes concerns, the benefit of the VBER may be withdrawn from the arrangement in individual circumstances under Article 6 VBER.

- In the UK, if the arrangement contains a wide retail parity obligation, the VABEO is unavailable to any part of the arrangement. An individual exemption may be available to exempt the restrictions contained in the arrangement in the particular circumstances.

As a practical matter, the EU and UK systems may lead to a consistent result in most cases, but under the UK system if the criteria for individual exemption are not met the consequence is the complete loss of the VABEO for the arrangement as a whole.

6.2.10 Information exchanges

Vertical agreements often contain provisions requiring the buyer to provide information to the supplier, for example in relation to market conditions in the territory allocated to the buyer. These information exchange provisions, to the extent that they amount to vertical restraints, are normally exempted as part of the general Article 2(1) VBER and/or article 3(1) VABEO exemption.

However, in cases of dual distribution, where the supplier sells products not only at the upstream level but also at the downstream level, thereby competing with its independent distributor, the information exchange may take on horizontal aspects and be detrimental to competition.

The VBER and VABEO take a different approach in relation to information exchanges in a dual distribution scenario.

EU position on information exchanges in dual distribution

The VBER only applies where the exchange of information (whether formalised in the written agreement or not) satisfies both the following conditions (recital 13, Article 2(5) VBER):

- the information exchange must be directly related to the implementation of the vertical agreement; and
- the information exchange must be necessary to improve the production or distribution of the contract goods or services.

If these conditions cannot be satisfied, the VBER does not apply to the dual distribution agreement, although an individual exemption may be available (para 102 EU Guidelines).

UK position

The UK's VABEO does not specifically mention information exchanges. These are covered in the UK's Vertical Guidance, which achieves a similar (but more generous) position to that in the VBER.

Paragraph 6.25 of the UK Guidance sets out the types of information exchanges that can be exempted in a dual distribution scenario, such as information relating to the supplier's recommended resale prices or maximum resale prices, provided that such information exchange is not used to restrict the buyer's ability to determine its sale price (para 6.25(e) UK Guidance).

Paragraph 6.26 of the UK Guidance sets out the types of information exchanges that constitute restrictions by object and do not benefit from the VABEO, such as information as to the future prices at which the parties will sell the products to their customers.

Paragraph 6.27 of the UK Guidance explains that exchanges of information between the parties to a dual distribution agreement that do not benefit from the VABEO must be assessed individually under Chapter I. The other provisions of the vertical agreement may benefit from the exemption provided by article 3(1) VABEO, provided that the agreement otherwise complies with the conditions set out in the block exemption.

6.2.11   Withdrawing the benefit/cancelling a Vertical block exemption

The competition authorities may withdraw (EU) or cancel (UK) the benefit of a Vertical block exemption:

- where the agreement is not considered to meet the criteria for exemption in any particular case (Article 6 VBER; article 13 VABEO). Thus, the strict conditions of the Vertical block exemptions may well be satisfied on the letter of the law, but in the specific circumstances the competition authorities are of the view that the agreement is such that it does not meet the four criteria for exemption (see **2.1.3**). Article 6 VBER give an example in the case of the supply of OIS where the market is highly concentrated and competition is restricted by the cumulative effect of parallel networks of similar agreements;

- where parallel networks of vertical agreements are extensive and may lead to anti-competitive effects, because they cover more than 50% of a given market (Article 7 VBER; not specifically mentioned in article 13 VABEO but dealt with in paras 13.7–13.9 UK Guidance).

6.2.12   A block exemption checklist

The following checklist may be useful in applying the Vertical block exemptions:

(1)   Does the agreement contain restrictions on competition which fall within Article 101(1)/Chapter I?

(2)   Are you dealing with a 'vertical agreement' as defined in the Vertical block exemptions (eg, a distribution agreement, an exclusive purchasing agreement, a franchising agreement, a selective distribution agreement)?

(3)   If so, is the agreement between non-competitors; or between competitors but non-reciprocal, with the parties competing at different levels of the supply chain for the purpose of the agreement (dual distribution)?

(4)   In a dual distribution scenario, does the agreement involve the exchange of information?

(5)   Are the parties' market shares below the 30% thresholds?

(6)   Does the agreement contain any hardcore restrictions (eg price-fixing, export ban)?

(7)   If so, these must be removed or amended.

(8)   Does the agreement contain any excluded restrictions?

(9)   If so, these must be amended, or the client should be aware that they could be unenforceable if they exceed the limits.

6.2.13   Selective distribution systems outside Article 101/Chapter I

Selective distribution systems enable the supplier to specify the retail outlets to whom its distributors can supply the goods on the basis of certain criteria. This is often considered to be essential by manufacturers of specialist and luxury goods (eg cameras, perfume) in order to maintain the brand image and reputation of the goods, ensuring that the goods are only sold through outlets which the manufacturer deems suitable. Similarly, suppliers of technical goods such as computer hardware may wish to require that their resellers have suitable technical knowledge so as to be able properly to explain, market and provide after-sales service for their goods.

A classic selective distribution arrangement would operate as follows. A manufacturer enters into distribution agreements with a number of different wholesalers (in other words, there is usually a 'network' of agreements), appointing them as distributors for its products. In each agreement, the manufacturer specifies the retail outlets which the wholesalers can supply; this is usually done by the manufacturer laying down conditions which the retail outlets must satisfy before the wholesaler is permitted to sell to them. Depending on how these conditions are expressed, competition law problems may result, especially if the manufacturer is using the agreement simply to stop certain outlets selling its products (restricting intra-brand competition). An extensive network of similar selective distribution agreements can effectively close off a particular market to potential resellers.

Purely *qualitative* selective distribution selects dealers only on the basis of objective criteria required by the nature of the product, such as training of sales personnel, the service provided at the point of sale, a certain range of the products being sold, etc. Purely *qualitative* selective distribution is in general considered to fall outside Article 101(1)/Chapter I for lack of anti-competitive effects, provided that three conditions are satisfied, known as the '*Metro* criteria' (Case 26/76 *Metro v Commission* EU:C:1977:167, paras 20 and 21) and set out in para 148 EU Guidelines/para 10.88 UK Guidance:

(a)   the nature of the product in question must necessitate a selective distribution system, in the sense that such a system must constitute a legitimate requirement, having regard to the nature of the product concerned, to preserve its quality and ensure its proper use;

(b)   resellers must be chosen on the basis of objective criteria of a qualitative nature which are laid down uniformly for all potential resellers and are not applied in a discriminatory manner; and

(c)   the criteria laid down must not go beyond what is necessary.

The *Metro* criteria will not be met where restrictions are imposed that are not proportionate to their objective or go beyond what is necessary. It will not be proportionate to include hardcore restrictions.

It may be proportionate to include restrictions on distributors using online marketplaces, as long as this does not prevent the effective use of the internet (para 150 EU Guidelines; para 10.89 UK Guidance). For example, a restriction on selling via a specific online portal in the context of a selective distribution system may be permitted, as long as the restriction does not amount to a blanket restriction on internet sales, is necessary to maintain objective qualitative criteria and is applied without discrimination (Case C-230/16 *Coty Germany GmbH v Parfümerie Akzente GmbH*, 6 December 2017 concerning a restriction on selling via Amazon.de).

Irrespective of whether the *Metro* criteria are satisfied, restrictions may benefit from the VBER and VABEO. This is true not only of *qualitative* restrictions, but also *quantitative* restrictions (para 151 EU Guidelines; para 10.90 UK Guidance). *Quantitative* selective distribution adds further criteria for selection that more directly limit the potential number of dealers, for instance by fixing the number of dealers.

The EU Guidelines and UK Guidance provide further guidance on selective distribution systems that are not covered by the VBER or VABEO, or in the case of cumulative effects resulting from parallel networks of selective distribution.

6.2.14   Franchise agreements outside Article 101/Chapter I

A franchise agreement enables the franchisor to establish, with limited investments, a uniform network for the distribution of its products. These agreements usually contain licences of intellectual property rights, such as know-how for the use and distribution of goods or services. In addition, the franchisor usually provides the franchisee with commercial and technical assistance during the life of the agreement. The licence and the assistance are integral components of the business method being franchised.

Case 161/84 *Pronuptia* [1986] ECR 353, [1986] 1 CMLR 414 establishes that restrictions on competition that are essential to the franchising relationship do not fall within Article 101(1). For example, a non-compete obligation, requiring the franchisee to purchase products exclusively from the franchisor, falls outside Article 101(1)/Chapter I when the obligation is necessary to maintain the common identity and reputation of the franchised network.

Although many franchising agreements will not fall within the scope of Article 101(1)/Chapter I, they may contain restrictions on competition that are not essential to franchising. These may fall within Article 101(1)/Chapter I and are capable of being exempted by the VBER and VABEO. Generally, if the relationship is vertical, the parties meet the market share thresholds, and there are no restrictions on competition that are hardcore, the VBER and VABEO will operate to exempt all restrictions on competition, except those that are excluded (Article 5 VBER; article 10 VABEO).

As seen at **6.2.7.1**, Article 5(1)(a) VBER and article 10(2)(a) VABEO exempt non-compete restrictions during the term of the agreement up to five years. However, in franchising agreements, non-compete restrictions during the term of the franchise will not generally fall within Article 101(1)/Chapter I. Therefore, a non-compete restriction which operates during the term of, say, a six-year franchising agreement may be outside the scope of Article 101(1)/Chapter I and not need to obey the strictures of Article 5(1)(a) VBER and article 10(2)(a) VABEO (see para 166 EU Guidelines; para 10.105 UK Guidance).

Post-termination, Article 5(3) VBER and article 10(4) VABEO exempt post-term non-compete obligations in franchising agreements where the relevant conditions are satisfied, including that the duration of the restriction is limited to one year (see **6.2.7.2**).

6.3 SUMMARY

The questions at **6.2.1** and block exemption checklist at **6.2.12** set out a step-by-step approach to assessing vertical agreements under EU and UK competition law. The following summary may also be helpful:

- Is the agreement between undertakings?
- Is the agreement vertical, horizontal, or a combination of both?
- Is the agreement excluded from the operation of Article 101/Chapter I by the rules relating to no appreciable effect on trade (EU only), *de minimis* (NAOMI) or agency? In some cases, the ancillary restraints doctrine may also assist.
- Does the agreement benefit from a Vertical block exemption:
  — Does it fall within the definition of a vertical agreement?
  — Do the parties meet the market share thresholds?
  — Are there any object restrictions?
  — Are there any effects restrictions, including excluded restrictions?
  — Are there any horizontal aspects? (if so, comply with rules on OIS and information exchanges, if relevant)
- If no Vertical block exemption applies, does the agreement benefit from an individual exemption?
- If no exemption applies (block or individual), and the prohibitions in Article 101(1)/Chapter I are engaged, is the entire agreement void or only the restrictions it contains?
- What are the other consequences of breach?

6.4 US ANTITRUST LAWS AND VERTICAL AGREEMENTS

6.4.1 Restraints on distribution

As we have previously seen, US courts applying Section 1 of the Sherman Act have found some forms of agreement to be *per se* violations while finding others illegal, under the Rule of Reason, only if the evidence shows that the overall effect of the particular agreement is to impair competition. Historically, the courts applied the *per se* rule to several forms of restraint that a manufacturer imposes on the wholesalers or retailers of its products. This approach began to change with *Continental TV, Inc v GTE Sylvania Inc*, 433 US 36 (1977), where the Supreme Court held that territorial restrictions on distribution were subject to the Rule of

Reason. The trend was completed in *Leegin Creative Leather Products, Inc v PSKS, Inc*, 551 US 277 (2007), which held that minimum resale price agreements are subject to the Rule of Reason. After *Leegin*, the Rule of Reason essentially applies to all Sherman Act, Section 1 challenges to the restraints that a manufacturer imposes on the resale of its products.

Under the Rule of Reason, restraints on distribution are usually upheld if the evidence shows them to be reasonably designed to promote inter-brand competition. For example, a manufacturer might wish that retailers maintain floor displays and train their sales force to promote its products, but retailers might be reluctant to invest in these promotional activities if nearby discounters who do not make similar investments are able to capture a significant portion of sales. Restraints such as exclusive territories or minimum resale prices can protect the retailer making investments.

Proof of the manufacturer's market power is critical. If the retail price of the manufacturer's product cannot be increased above the prevailing market price, then restraints that the manufacturer imposes on the resale of its products are not likely to harm the consumer and the agreement will probably not be found to violate antitrust laws, even if evidence is sparse that the agreement will promote inter-brand competition.

Although the *Leegin* decision was initially somewhat controversial, it has generally been accepted as a recent development in federal antitrust case law. However, a number of state legislatures enacted *Leegin* 'repealer' laws shortly after the decision was rendered, effectively retaining *per se* unlawful status for minimum resale price maintenance on a state-by-state basis; other states retained *per se* status because their antitrust statutes do not automatically follow federal case law.

As a result, in order to avoid the need for state-by-state policies, many manufacturers are continuing their prior practices of influencing the retail prices of their products without violating the *per se* rule. These methods include:

(a) *consignment agreements*, in which the retailer does not take title or risk of loss of the manufacturer's products and functions as the manufacturer's sales agent;

(b) *suggested resale prices*, so long as the reseller is not compelled to follow the suggested prices;

(c) *minimum advertised pricing programs*, in which the manufacturer refuses to contribute cooperative advertising funds to advertisements that display a price below the manufacturer's suggested resale price.

An important means of avoiding the old *per se* rule against resale price maintenance was for the manufacturer not to enter an agreement with its resellers. In *United States v Colgate & Co*, 250 US 300 (1919), the US Supreme Court held that no agreement will be found when a company merely exercises its right to choose with whom it does business. Subsequent decisions interpreted *Colgate* to mean that a manufacturer could announce that it would refuse to sell to a retailer that failed to honour its schedule of suggested resale prices and then terminate those retailers which charged prices below the schedule. Even if the manufacturer took these actions with the intention of pressuring retailers to follow the resale price schedule, no agreement and hence no Sherman Act, Section 1 violation would be found, so long as the manufacturer never extracted a pricing commitment from a reseller.

6.4.2 Tying arrangements

A vertical arrangement that often leads to antitrust claims is tying, which is an agreement to sell or lease a product, or service, on the condition that the buyer also purchases or leases a second product or service. A tying agreement is a restraint of trade and a *per se* violation of Section 1 of the Sherman Act (*Jefferson Parish Hospital District No 2 v Hyde*, 466 US 2 (1984)), provided that four elements are established:

(a)   *Two products.* Tying will not be illegal when it involves only separate components of a single product, such as tyres on an automobile or laces on shoes. Two separate products must be involved. Products will be deemed separate if demand for each product is sufficient to make selling both of them separately efficient.

(b)   *Conditional sale.* Tying occurs when the seller makes the purchase of one product (the 'tying product') a condition for the purchase of the other product (the 'tied product'). Coercion is essential. No tying will be found if the buyer has the practical ability to purchase the tied product alone, or if the buyer voluntarily agrees to purchase a package of two or more products.

(c)   *Market power.* The seller must have market power in the tying product, the product that the buyer wants. As in a Rule of Reason case, market power is the ability to charge a price above competitive levels and depends upon proof of high market shares, barriers to market entry and other factors.

(d)   *Substantial amount of commerce.* Tying is illegal only if it affects a substantial amount of inter-state commerce in the tied product, the product that buyers are forced to purchase. No definition of 'substantial' has been adopted. Courts have found as little as $10,000 to be sufficient to find a violation.

6.4.3   Price discrimination

The Robinson-Patman Act, adopted by Congress in 1936 as an amendment to Section 2 of the Clayton Act, contains a specific prohibition of price discrimination (15 USC §13(a)). The Robinson-Patman Act is a complicated statute. To establish a violation, several facts must be established:

(a)   *Commodities.* The Act applies only to sales of commodities, meaning goods and not services.

(b)   *Of like grade and quality.* Price discrimination only occurs on sales of essentially the same product. Charging a higher price for a premium grade or a higher quality version of a product is not illegal.

(c)   *Sold to two or more purchasers.* A violation requires sales to different purchasers. Thus, offering a product to a second customer at a different price does not violate the Act unless the offer results in a sale. Similarly, sales to the same purchaser at different prices are not a violation.

(d)   *In commerce.* The Act applies only if the goods in one of the discriminatory sales cross a state line. Discrimination on sales to customers in the same state as the seller is not subject to the Act. Furthermore, both sales must be made for use or resale within the United States. Sales for export are not subject to the Act.

(e)   At *different prices.* Discrimination requires that the different purchasers pay different prices, after accounting for all discounts, rebates and other factors that affect the price paid. The price difference must be found in reasonably contemporaneous sales. Price differences due to seasonal changes in demand or changes in market conditions over time are not illegal.

(f)   *Causing competitive injury.* To violate the Act, the price discrimination must cause injury of one of the following forms:

   (i)   *Primary line injury is injury to a competitor of the seller.* For example, if the seller faces a competitor in only one segment of the market, the seller might discriminate by lowering its prices only to customers in that segment. The courts treat primary line injury claims essentially the same as predatory pricing under Section 2 of the Sherman Act. To prove primary line injury, the evidence must show that the lower price was below the seller's cost and that the seller is likely to recoup its losses in the future after driving competitors out of the market.

(ii) *Secondary line injury is injury to a competitor of the favoured purchaser.* The price discrimination might enable the favoured purchaser to lower its resale prices and take business away from the disfavoured purchaser. A secondary line injury claim can be established only with discrimination between customers who compete with each other. If the purchasers operate in separate markets or at different levels of distribution, or if they are consumers who do not compete at all, no secondary line injury will be found. Where purchasers do compete, evidence of a substantial difference in the prices charged to them over a substantial period of time will create a presumption of injury. The defendant can rebut that presumption with evidence that the price discrimination did not cause the disfavoured purchaser to lose sales or profits.

(iii) *Tertiary line injury is injury to a competitor of a customer of the favoured purchaser.* For example, a manufacturer might discriminate in price between wholesale distributors, enabling a retailer supplied by the favoured wholesaler to take business from a retailer supplied by the disfavoured wholesaler. The courts treat tertiary line claims the same as secondary line claims.

6.4.3.1 Defences

A defendant can avoid liability under the Robinson-Patman Act by establishing one of the following defences:

(a) *Meeting competition.* A seller may offer a discriminatory price to meet the price of a competitor on a particular sale. The essential requirement of this defence is good faith; the seller must honestly and reasonably believe that a competitor has offered a lower price to the customer and that it must meet that price to make the sale. The defence does not allow the seller to underbid the competitor, only to meet or approach the competitor's price.

(b) *Cost justification.* Price discrimination is legal to the extent that price differences reflect only lower costs to the seller resulting from selling or delivering higher quantities to the favoured purchaser. The actual cost savings must be proven to establish this defence.

(c) *Functional availability.* If the unfavoured purchaser had a real opportunity to obtain the lower price, on the same terms and conditions as the favoured purchaser, its decision not to take the lower price will not result in a violation of the Act.

MERGER CONTROL

AIMS

Chapter 7 provides an introduction to merger control in the EU and in the UK, and an overview of the US system.

OBJECTIVES

After studying **Chapter 7**, you should be able to:

- identify mergers that should be notified to the European Commission and/or to the CMA;

- understand the review procedures that take place;

- identify factors likely to raise competition law concerns regarding proposed mergers; and

- understand that mergers may be reviewed in other jurisdictions.

7.1 INTRODUCTION

Merger control is concerned with the maintenance of a competitive market structure. In this sense, it differs from the rules preventing anti-competitive behaviour that we have already looked at in this textbook (see in particular **Chapters 2** and **3**). The process of merging is not, in itself, anti-competitive. It is the effect that such mergers can have on the competitive dynamic of a market which is the subject of merger control. Broadly speaking, 'merger' in this sense means any transaction whereby a previously independent entity becomes controlled by another. However, note that the concept of 'control' covers not only the acquisition of a controlling interest but also lesser forms of control, including some forms of joint venture.

If such a transaction were to lead to the creation of, or an increase in, market power such that consumers' interests are harmed, merger control rules may operate to prevent or modify the transaction.

7.2 MERGER NOTIFICATION AND REVIEW

The most widely adopted means of controlling mergers is by way of notification and review. In general, parties to a proposed merger must notify their plans (where the arrangement exceeds designated thresholds) to the relevant competition agency (or agencies) before the merger is implemented. The relevant agency will then examine the proposed transaction according to its own rules and will decide whether or not the merger can go ahead, or if it can take place only subject to conditions. The review procedure is generally subject to strict time limits so as to minimise the delay in implementing an acceptable merger.

The following sections deal with EU Merger Control under the EU Merger Regulation, and UK Merger Control under the Enterprise Act 2002. They do not deal with special regimes, such as the notification requirements for 'gatekeepers' (including Alphabet, Meta and Amazon) under the Digital Markets Act.

7.3 EU MERGER CONTROL

7.3.1 Historical background

Until the adoption of Council Regulation 4064/89, the EU lacked a specifically designed regulation dealing with merger control. Before this time the ECJ had acknowledged the possibility that, in appropriate circumstances, a merger might breach what is now Article 101 (relating to anti-competitive agreements) and/or Article 102 (relating to abuse of a dominant position). However, these provisions were not specifically designed to deal with merger control. Article 101 and 102 apply *ex post* to control undertakings' behaviour after it has happened, rather than allowing for the pre-emptive review of mergers on an *ex ante* basis. The merger regulation introduced a system of pre-emptive control, allowing for the assessment of mergers before they were implemented.

The current merger regulation is Council Regulation 139/2004/EC ([2004] OJ L24/1) (the 'Merger Regulation'), extracts from which are reproduced in **Appendix 8**. The Merger Regulation is based largely on Regulation 4064/89, but incorporates a number of changes. The principal amendment was to lower the turnover thresholds used to establish whether the Commission had jurisdiction. The substantive test was also amended (see **7.3.7.1**) and there were a number of other changes.

As with many of the EU rules on competition, the Commission has produced guidelines to assist in application and interpretation. With regard to the Merger Regulation, these include the Commission's Consolidated Jurisdictional Notice ([2008] OJ C95/1) (the 'Jurisdictional Notice') (extracts from which are reproduced in **Appendix 9**). There are many other useful guidelines, including best practice guidelines; some of the most important ones are covered below.

7.3.2 Jurisdictional issues

Mergers must be notified to the Commission where there is a 'concentration' with a Community dimension' (Merger Regulation, Article 1(1)). Put simply, this means that notification is required where the arrangement is of a type (concentration) and size (a Community, or 'EU dimension') which should be examined by the Commission before it can go ahead. Where the Commission has jurisdiction, notification of the arrangement is compulsory. Failure to notify can result in penalties. There are also severe penalties for implementing a merger prior to clearance, and for implementing a merger that has been prohibited by the Commission.

The Merger Regulation provides a 'one-stop shop' in the EU for transactions which fall within its scope. As such, the competition authorities of the EU Member States will not generally have jurisdiction to examine a concentration. There are exceptions, such as where the Commission specifically decides to refer a concentration with a Community (or EU) dimension, in whole or in part, to such authorities (see **7.3.6**). Accordingly, coming within the scope of the Merger Regulation can be of benefit to the parties, as it removes the need to make separate (and possibly numerous) merger notifications to the authorities of the different EU Member States.

Since the end of the Brexit transition period, the UK is no longer part of the 'one-stop shop' for mergers. This means that a merger caught by the Merger Regulation may also be reviewed by the UK's Competition and Markets Authority (see **7.4**).

'EU dimension' does not mean that mergers between companies outside the EU fall outside the EU notification regime. Many sizeable UK mergers will continue to fall within the Merger

Regulation, even after Brexit. Under its qualified effects doctrine, the Commission is able to review many foreign mergers that meet its jurisdictional thresholds, on the basis that these have effects in the EU (see **1.6**).

The Merger Regulation uses the term 'Community' rather than 'EU' (it was adopted before the 'European Union' terminology was applied). References in the Merger Regulation to 'Community' should now be construed as references to 'EU'.

7.3.3 Definition of 'concentration'

The purpose of the Merger Regulation is to allow the Commission to assess whether the transaction results on a lasting basis in a change in the structure of the market. Accordingly, it is concerned with establishing the *economic potential* of the transaction, and therefore the *economic unit* (or concentration) that is being created.

7.3.3.1 Mergers and acquisitions

Under Article 3(1) of the Merger Regulation, a concentration exists where:

(a) two or more previously independent undertakings merge; or

(b) one or more undertakings acquire 'whether by purchase of securities or assets, by contract or any other means, direct or indirect control of the whole or parts of one or more other undertakings'.

Article 3(1)(a) is fairly narrow. It covers a full or 'legal' merger, such as the merger of building societies. Article 3(1)(b) is more common and can apply to many types of transactions, for example a public takeover, a sale of a business or a significant transfer of assets conferring control on a lasting basis.

7.3.3.2 Meaning of 'control'

When considering whether there is an acquisition of 'control' under Article 3(1)(b), one must turn to Article 3(2). 'Control' means more than just voting control, and is assessed by reference to the 'possibility of exercising *decisive influence* on the undertaking' (emphasis added). 'Decisive influence' means the power to determine the strategic commercial behaviour of an undertaking (Jurisdictional Notice, para 62).

7.3.3.3 Minority shareholdings

The acquisition by an undertaking of a substantial minority stake can give rise to the acquisition of 'control' within the meaning of Article 3(2), for example:

•   The minority stake is sufficient for the acquiror to achieve a majority of votes cast at general meetings (which usually happens where other shareholdings are fragmented). It may be necessary to consider evidence of past voting patterns before deciding whether the minority shareholding that is being acquired (be it 49% or 20%) would be sufficient to carry a majority of the votes on a lasting basis.

•   A shareholders' agreement may confer 'negative' control through blocking rights, for example if the acquiror has the right to veto strategic business plans (see **7.3.3.4**).

•   A shareholders' agreement could give a minority shareholder the right to appoint a majority of the directors on the board and therefore control the company's strategic commercial behaviour.

7.3.3.4 Sole or joint control

The acquisition of control can be either 'sole control', or it can be 'joint control'. In the case of sole control, only one company will acquire control or decisive influence. 'Joint control' is acquired when several undertakings (usually acting through a joint venture company) acquire control and must agree operations between them.

Joint control usually involves the parent companies having blocking rights, such that because of the possibility of deadlock the shareholders have to agree major strategy decisions on a lasting basis (also known as 'negative' control). The blocking rights must be over key strategic decisions, in particular in relation to the budget, the business plan and the appointment of senior management. For example, where the acquiring vehicle is a joint venture company and its parent companies have entered into a shareholders' agreement, the parent companies may each have the right to appoint half the directors, or the right to block the company's budget which is crucial to the ability to run a company. In such cases, the joint venture company cannot run without each parent agreeing operations with the other, and the parents have 'joint control'.

The nature of control matters because changes in the nature of control (for example from joint control to sole control) result in a new concentration.

Moreover, for the purpose of assessing whether the concentration has an EU dimension (see **7.3.4**), the turnover of the whole group must be included (see para 175 of the Jurisdictional Notice). The group includes 'parents' who have sole or joint control over the undertaking concerned. It also includes subsidiaries and other entities 'controlled' (solely or jointly) by the undertaking concerned.

7.3.3.5 Full function joint ventures

Joint ventures are a common form of business vehicle, commonly used where parties pool their respective resources into a specific company (a joint venture company). Not all joint ventures will give rise to a concentration. For there to be a concentration:

(a)   there must be the formation of a joint venture (for example the formation of a new jointly controlled company, or the acquisition of rights conferring joint control in an existing undertaking); and

(b)   the joint venture must be a 'full function' entity, which generally means that the joint venture company must have sufficient financial, human and other resources to carry on, on a lasting basis, independently from its parent companies.

It should be noted that non-full functional joint ventures may fall to be considered under Article 101(1) rather than under the Merger Regulation.

Where a full function joint venture (therefore concentration) involves coordinated aspects, the European Commission will assess the concentrative aspects under the SIEC test (see **7.3.7**) and in addition it will consider the coordinated aspects under Article 101 (see **7.3.8**).

7.3.4 Definition of 'EU dimension'

As we have seen, the Merger Regulation is only concerned with transactions that can result in a change in the structure of the market. Not all transactions, even if of a *type* that could give rise to concerns, will be of a sufficient *size* to cause a change to the structure of the market.

7.3.4.1 Turnover thresholds

The size (or EU dimension) is assessed under the Merger Regulation by reference to the turnover of the parties. The turnover thresholds are contained in Article 1 of the Merger Regulation (see **Appendix 8**). It is important to note that there are two sets of alternative thresholds contained in Article 1. Article 1(2) contains the higher set of thresholds; Article 1(3) the lower set. In applying the thresholds, a legal adviser must take care to ensure that the test is followed carefully, for example whether the test relates to worldwide, EU or Member State turnover. In addition, care should be taken to assess whether the test relates to combined or individual turnover. The Commission has explained the two thresholds in the following terms:

> The first alternative requires:

    (i)   a combined worldwide turnover of all the merging firms over €5 000 million, and

    (ii)   an EU-wide turnover for each of at least two of the firms over €250 million.

The second alternative requires:

    (i)   a worldwide turnover of all the merging firms over €2 500 million, and

    (ii)   a combined turnover of all the merging firms over €100 million in each of at least three Member States,

    (iii)   a turnover of over €25 million for each of at least two of the firms in each of the three Member States included under ii, and

    (iv)   EU-wide turnover of each of at least two firms of more than €100 million.

In both alternatives, an EU dimension is not met if each of the firms archives more than two thirds of its EU-wide turnover within one and the same Member State.

7.3.4.2 Turnover of the undertakings concerned

It is important to remember that the *two-thirds rule* described above applies to both sets of thresholds. If each of the undertakings concerned achieves more than two-thirds of its EU-wide turnover in one and the same Member State, the Merger Regulation does not apply (as it is usually appropriate for the national competition authority of that State to have jurisdiction).

In addition, it is important to identify the correct turnover that should be used when applying the tests. In this regard, the Jurisdictional Notice outlines specific rules relating to turnover. Below is an outline of the main issues relating to turnover, and where in the Jurisdictional Notice more guidance can be found:

- identifying the 'undertaking concerned' for the purpose of turnover (para 129 onwards);
- group turnover (para 175 onwards);
- joint venture turnover (para 186);
- the correct accounts (para 169 onwards);
- where the turnover is generated (para 196 onwards).

These paragraphs are reproduced at **Appendix 9**.

7.3.4.3 Sale of parts

When the acquisition is one of parts only of a business, only the turnover relating to those parts is taken into account (Article 5(2)). This means that when considering the seller's turnover, only the turnover that relates to the business being sold is taken into account.

7.3.4.4 EEA dimension

The Commission's review may include not just the EU, but also the EEA. The one-stop shop extends to EEA Member States, and a merger with an EEA dimension that also has an EU dimension will be reviewed by the Commission.

In practice, therefore, the Commission's substantive review will usually include an assessment of markets throughout the EEA, not just the EU, and relevant geographic markets are often described as 'EEA-wide' (rather than just EU-wide).

7.3.5 Notification to the Commission

Under the Merger Regulation, a concentration with an EU dimension must be notified to the Commission prior to implementation and after the conclusion of the agreement, the announcement of the public bid, or the acquisition of a controlling interest. Notifications may also be made under the Merger Regulation where the parties 'demonstrate to the Commission a good faith intention to conclude an agreement or, in the case of a public bid, where they have publicly announced an intention to make such a bid' (Article 4(1)). This enables parties to notify in advance of an agreement provided they can demonstrate sufficient certainty that the agreement is going ahead, for example because they have made a public announcement.

7.3.6 Referrals between EU Member States and the Commission

Jurisdiction can be reallocated between the Commission and EU Member States following notification (Article 9 and Article 22) or prior to notification (Article 4). A Member State may also act in addition to the Commission where legitimate interests are involved (Article 21). These situations are considered in turn below. They no longer apply to the UK, since the end of the Brexit transition period.

Article 9 of the Merger Regulation allows the Commission to refer a merger to a Member State authority where a market within that Member State 'presents all the characteristics of a distinct market' (there are other criteria: see Article 9(2)(a) and (b)). The Member State concerned will make a request to the Commission for an Article 9 referral back, and may be encouraged to do so either by the Commission or by interested third parties.

Under Article 22 of the Merger Regulation, the reverse process is outlined, whereby Member States may request the Commission to deal with a concentration even if it does not have an EU dimension. Member States may make such a request provided the concentration affects trade between Member States and threatens to have a significant effect on competition within the Member State or States making the request. The Commission may 'invite' Member States to hand over jurisdiction.

It is also possible for the parties to a proposed concentration with an EU dimension to find out before making a formal notification whether the merger should more advantageously be considered at Member State level. Article 4(4) of the Merger Regulation permits the parties, prior to notification, to inform the Commission by way of reasoned submission that the concentration may significantly affect competition in a market within a Member State which presents all the characteristics of a distinct market; accordingly, it should be examined, in whole or in part, by that Member State. The Commission must forward the submission to the relevant NCA, and if the NCA agrees, the Commission must then decide whether to make a referral to the NCA.

Conversely, under Article 4(5) of the Merger Regulation, the parties to a proposed concentration which does not have an EU dimension may by way of reasoned submission inform the Commission that the Commission should examine the concentration. This would be appropriate if a concentration falls below the thresholds for an EU dimension but still covers several Member States and so would be subject to notification to and review by several NCAs. The Commission must forward the submission to the NCAs of the Member States concerned. If at least one Member State that is competent to examine the concentration disagrees then the Commission cannot accept the reference. If no NCA objects, the concentration is deemed to have an EU dimension and must be notified to the Commission.

Lastly, although Member States generally have no jurisdiction over concentrations with an EU dimension (subject to what we have learnt about Articles 4 and 9 of the Merger Regulation), Article 21(4) of the Merger Regulation does allow Member States to protect legitimate interests. The circumstances in which a legitimate interest may be invoked are limited. Public security, maintaining the plurality of the media and prudential rules are regarded as legitimate interests.

7.3.7 Substantive issues

7.3.7.1 The SIEC test

The notification procedure will allow the Commission to assess the transaction's impact on the market. When making this assessment, the Commission will apply the test outlined in Article 2(2) and (3), and whether the concentration will or will not 'significantly impede effective competition in the common market or in a substantial part of it, in particular as a result of the strengthening of a dominant position'. This is known as the 'SIEC' test, and it is substantially similar in effect to the merger control tests applicable in the UK and in the US.

It should be noted that the majority of notified transactions do not give rise to competition law concerns; however, in assessing whether or not a merger threatens to significantly impede effective competition, the Commission is required to take into account a number of issues. These include the need to maintain and develop competition, the structure of the markets and any actual or potential competition (Article 2(1)(a)). Specifically, under Article 2(1)(b) of the Merger Regulation, the Commission is required to consider:

(a)   the market position of the undertakings concerned and their economic and financial power;

(b)   the alternatives available to suppliers and users;

(c)   their access to supplies and markets;

(d)   any legal or other barriers to entry;

(e)   supply and demand trends for the relevant goods and services;

(f)   the interests of intermediate and ultimate consumers; and

(g)   the development of technical and economic progress, provided that it is to consumers' advantage and does not form an obstacle to competition.

The SIEC test was introduced in 2004. It incorporates the previous 'strengthening of a dominant position' test, but is wider than simply considering dominance. It fills a perceived gap left by cases such as *Airtours* (see **3.3.5**), where the Commission's finding of collective dominance was overturned because there was insufficient evidence that the companies on the market held a common position. The SIEC test now makes it possible to block mergers that harm consumers in oligopolistic markets, even where evidence of links or commonality between industry participants cannot be established and there is no collective dominance.

7.3.7.2 The Commission's assessment

Guidance on how the Commission will assess mergers can be found in the *Guidelines on the assessment of horizontal mergers* ([2004] OJ C31/03) ('the Horizontal Merger Guidelines') and the *Guidelines on the assessment of non-horizontal mergers* ([2008] OJ C265/07) ('the Non-horizontal Merger Guidelines'). 'Horizontal' mergers are those between actual or potential competitors. 'Non-horizontal' mergers are of two types: between parties at different levels of the supply chain ('vertical mergers' – for example where a manufacturer merges with one of its distributors); or between parties in different markets ('conglomerate mergers' – the parties have neither a horizontal nor vertical relationship).

The Commission focuses on whether the merger will lead to an increase in market power that will have a detrimental effect on customers, for example through increased prices, lower quality or reduced innovation. A number of analytical tools are at the Commission's disposal and it has a wide discretion as to how these may be used. Often the Commission will consider the parties' ability to increase prices after the merger, as an indicator as to how competition may be harmed.

Theory of harm

The Commission will usually build a 'theory of harm', which is an analysis of how the merger would lead to a significant impediment to effective competition. There are two main theories of harm (which may apply to both horizontal and non-horizontal mergers):

(a)   *Non-coordinated (or unilateral) effects*: These consider whether firms would have increased market power, without resorting to coordinated behaviour (see (b) below). In broad economic terms, this means considering whether the merged firms could unilaterally increase prices without a sufficient number of customers switching to competitors.

This could occur for example if the merged firms increased their market shares to become the largest competitor in the market ('single firm dominance'). This may enable the merging firms to sustain a price increase; whereas before the merger, if a party had raised prices, they would have lost some sales to the other merging party.

Unilateral effects could also occur where the market is oligopolistic and the merger could result in higher prices without the creation or strengthening of a dominant position, by eliminating important competitive constraints on the parties or even on a third party. For example, if the second and third largest manufacturers merged but their combined market share was still slightly less than that of the largest manufacturer, the merger would not create or strengthen a dominant position. Nonetheless the merger might significantly impede effective competition by removing the rivalry between the merging manufacturers and the competitive pressure that they had exerted both on each other and the largest manufacturer.

In vertical mergers the concern is often foreclosure, that is, where rivals' access to the market is hampered due to the merger. For example an upstream supplier may have the incentive to increase prices of an upstream input, to place a newly acquired downstream subsidiary at an advantage compared to its rivals.

(b) *Coordinated effects*: In oligopolistic markets the merger may increase the possibility that firms engage in tacit collusion falling short of an agreement caught by Article 101(1) (see **2.1.1.3**). This could occur where the merger alters the market structure in such a way that the merger will facilitate coordination between the firms operating in that market, enabling them to increase prices even without entering into an agreement or concerted practice that would be caught by Article 101(1).

The Horizontal Merger Guidelines explain the Commission's approach in assessing whether coordinated effects are likely to occur, very much following the ECJ's judgment in Case C-413/06 P *Bertelsmann AG and Sony Corporation of America v Impala* [2008] ECR I-04951. In this case the ECJ stated that coordination is more likely to arise if competitors can easily arrive at a common perception of how the coordination should work without having to resort to active collusion that would be prohibited by Article 101. The ECJ set out three conditions for determining whether coordination was sustainable:

(i)   *Transparency.* The coordinating firms must be able to monitor to a sufficient degree whether the terms of coordination are being adhered to. For example, there must be sufficient market transparency for each of the firms involved to be aware of how the other participants in the coordination were conducting themselves.

(ii) *Deterrent.* There must be some form of credible deterrent mechanism that could come into play if deviation were detected.

(iii) *Absence of other competitive constraints.* The reaction of outsiders, such as current and potential competitors and customers, should not be such as to jeopardise the results expected from the coordination.

The Commission will assess whether these three conditions are present, although the ECJ stressed that they should not be applied over-rigidly, but should be applied having regard to 'the overall economic mechanism of a hypothetical tacit coordination'.

Horizontal mergers

The Horizontal Merger Guidelines explain in detail factors that the Commission will consider in determining the likely effect of horizontal mergers. These include the parties' market shares; the degree of market concentration (including the strength and number of competitors); the countervailing buyer power of customers (eg the possibility that buyers could credibly switch to alternative sources of supply should the merged firms increase prices); and the likelihood of new entrants to the market.

With regard to market shares and concentration levels, the Guidelines (para 17) set out the Commission's approach:

- Combined market share of 50%: This may be evidence of a dominant position (see **3.3.2**), though the Commission will take into account the possibility of smaller competitors acting as a constraining influence if they have the capacity to increase supplies.

- Combined market of between 40–50%: Whether there are competition concerns depends on other factors such as the number and strength of competitors and capacity constraints. The Commission has accordingly decided in several cases that mergers resulting in firms holding market shares between 40%–50%, and in some cases even below 40%, would to lead to the creation or the strengthening of a dominant position.

- Combined market share not exceeding 25%: The concentration will be presumed to be compatible with the internal market.

- The Commission will also consider evidence of market concentration by reference to a test developed in the US, the HHI (see **7.5.1**).

Non-horizontal mergers

The Non-horizontal Guidelines focus on vertical and conglomerate mergers. The Non-horizontal Guidelines recognise that these types of mergers do not raise the same competition concerns as horizontal mergers as they may provide substantial scope for efficiencies through the integration of the different stages of production. Accordingly, these pro-competitive effects should be weighed against potential anti-competitive aspects of the mergers.

The Commission examines vertical links between the parties to ensure that the merger will not have serious anti-competitive effects in any relevant upstream or downstream market, for example by hampering actual or potential competitors' access to supplies or markets, thereby reducing those companies' ability to compete (*anti-competitive foreclosure*). A merger can lead to the foreclosure of an important input to the market ('input foreclosure'); or to the foreclosure of access to a base of customers needed to sell into in the market ('customer foreclosure').

The Non-horizontal Guidelines provide that there are unlikely to be competition concerns where the market share of the new entity post-merger is below 30% in the affected relevant markets. The post-merger HHI is also relevant.

Conglomerate mergers do not usually raise competition concerns but may do so where the parties' products are complementary or give them 'portfolio power'. For example, the merged parties may be able to offer discounted product bundles that cannot be matched by competitors.

Often, mergers will have both horizontal and vertical aspects (and sometimes also conglomerate aspects). These will all need to be assessed by the Commission.

Counterfactual

In both horizontal and non-horizontal mergers, the Commission will usually identify what would be the situation in the market absent the merger, namely what is called the 'counterfactual'. There may be adverse market developments which are unrelated to the merger, and where any SIEC identified cannot be shown to arise from the merger.

The Commission will also consider any efficiencies arising from the merger (see **7.3.7.4**) and any other relevant factors, such as what is known as the 'failing firm defence'.

7.3.7.3   Relevant markets and 'affected markets'

Relevant markets

As seen above, the Commission's substantive assessment involves identifying relevant markets, the parties' shares in these relevant markets and other parties' (including competitors') market shares in the relevant markets.

In respect to defining the relevant market, the Commission will apply the principles contained in the *Commission's Notice on the definition of relevant market for the purposes of Community competition law* ([1997] OJ C372/03). For further information, please refer to **3.3.1**.

Affected markets

Many large mergers will affect a number of relevant markets. As it is often difficult to define the relevant markets, the process of notification to the Commission requires the parties to identify the 'affected markets'. These include not just the relevant markets, but also 'all plausible alternative relevant product and geographic markets'. Requiring the parties to provide information on plausible relevant markets avoids the need to define the relevant markets too early, before a full assessment has been made by the Commission.

Affected markets should be identified at an early stage. They have a bearing on the correct process to follow when notifying the Commission.

Where there are no affected markets, or where there are affected markets but certain conditions are met, the simplified procedure may be available. This enables the parties to notify their transaction to the Commission under the Short Form CO. The conditions for qualifying under the simplified procedure reflect circumstances in which a merger or joint venture is unlikely to raise competition concerns. These include where the parties' combined market shares are below 20% in horizontal mergers; or where the parties' market shares are below 30% in vertically related markets; or where the combined market shares of the parties are below 50% and the HHI concentration levels are low (for HHI see **7.5.1**).

Where the simplified procedure does not apply, a full notification is required on Form CO. Form CO requires the parties to provide extensive information about the affected markets that have been identified.

On the notification process, see **7.3.10.1**.

7.3.7.4   Appraising the concentration – role of efficiencies

The Commission may consider that the negative effects of a concentration are outweighed if the efficiencies generated by a concentration are likely to motivate the merged entity to act pro-competitively for the benefit of consumers. However, it is for the parties to prove that the strict conditions for the 'efficiency defence' are met. The grounds for such a defence are that any such efficiencies must be 'merger-specific, substantial, timely and verifiable'. In addition, the efficiencies must be likely to be passed on to consumers. Efficiencies are usually considered in Phase II rather than Phase I (see **7.3.10**).

7.3.7.5   Remedies

If a concentration would have a materially detrimental effect on consumer welfare, despite any efficiency gains, the Commission may still authorise it on the basis of modifications or conditions and obligations designed to remove the competitive concerns raised by the concentration. Such 'remedies' are normally of a structural nature and typically involve the merged entity divesting (selling) part of its combined activities so that effective competition is maintained. Behavioural remedies (for example, a commitment to grant a licence to a third party) may also be acceptable in conjunction with structural remedies or in cases where structural remedies are not feasible. In general, however, the Commission prefers structural remedies, particularly divestiture, because they deal with problems arising from market structure and do not require medium- or long-term monitoring.

7.3.8 Appraising joint ventures

If a joint venture is not full function (see **7.3.3** above), and does not therefore fall within the Merger Regulation, it may have to be analysed for compliance with Article 101(1) (see **Chapter 2**). The situation becomes potentially more complex where a joint venture falls within the Merger Regulation but also has aspects which involve the coordination of the competitive behaviour of its parents as the direct consequence of the joint venture.

Under Article 2(4) of the Merger Regulation, this type of joint venture will be subject to a dual analysis, conducted under both the Merger Regulation and Article 101. As regards the structural aspects of the joint venture, the normal Merger Regulation test will apply; that is, the joint venture will be prohibited if it will significantly impede effective competition in the common market or a substantial part of the common market. To the extent that the creation of the joint venture will result in coordination of the competitive behaviour of the parent companies (which are often competitors), this will be assessed in accordance with the criteria of Article 101(1) and (3).

Article 2(5) of the Merger Regulation sets out the factors relevant to the assessment of the cooperative aspects of joint ventures. This includes:

* whether two or more parent companies retain, to a significant extent, activities in the same market as the joint venture or in a market which is downstream or upstream from that of the joint venture or in a neighbouring market;
* whether the coordination which is the direct consequence of the creation of the joint venture affords the undertakings concerned the possibility of eliminating competition in respect of a substantial part of the products or services in question.

For example, in *Telia/Telenor/Schibsted* (Case No IV JV.1) [1999] 4 CMLR 216, the European Commission assessed the transaction not only for its concentrative aspects, but also for its 'spill-over' effects arising as a consequence of the creation of the joint venture. Since the parents remained active in markets closely related to the markets in which the joint venture was to operate, the Commission assessed whether creating the joint venture had as its object or effect the coordination of the parties' competitive behaviour. In view of the characteristics of the markets (including the parents' limited market shares), the Commission found that the market structure was not such as to be conducive to anti-competitive behaviour.

The Commission will only assess coordination that arises directly from the creation of the joint venture. If the joint venture agreement contains restrictions which cannot be said to arise from the creation of the joint venture, these must be self-assessed by the parties and will not be considered by the Commission as part of its decision-making process under the EU Merger Regulation.

7.3.9 Ancillary restraints

7.3.9.1 Generally

The doctrine of ancillary restraints was developed in early decisions of the European Court under Article 101. The doctrine holds that restrictions on competition may fall outside the scope of Article 101 when they are directly related and necessary to the implementation of a main (legitimate) operation. This doctrine has been applied, for example, to protect intellectual property rights and to protect the value of the business transferred in acquisitions. The following restraints have been held to be ancillary and hence outside the scope of Article 101:

- In the *Maize Seeds* case (Case 258/78 *LC Nungesser KG v Commission* EU:C:1982:211), an exclusive licence of plant breeders' rights without which there would have been no investment in the production of maize seeds.

- In *Remia/Nutricia* (Case 42/84 *Remia BV and Verenigde Bedrijven and Nutricia v Commission* EU:C:1985:327), a non-compete covenant in the disposal of a business involving the transfer of goodwill, as it would not have been possible to sell the business if the seller were able to undermine the goodwill transferred by competing with the business being sold.

- In Case 161/84 *Pronuptia de Paris v Schillgalis* EU:C:1986:41, restrictions in a franchise agreement to protect the franchisor's intellectual property and maintain a common identity (see **6.2.14**).

7.3.9.2   Ancillary restraints in concentrations under the EU Merger Regulation

When ancillary restraints are directly related to an operation that amounts to a concentration (including mergers, acquisitions and concentrative joint ventures – see **7.3.3**), the EU Merger Regulation's regime applies, to the exclusion of Article 101:

- The EU Merger Regulation provides that 'restrictions that are directly related and necessary to the implementation of the concentration' automatically benefit from a clearance decision (recital 1 and Articles 6.1(b), 8(1) and 8(2)).

- Regulation 1 (the EU's main implementing regulation for Article 101 and 102) does not apply to these restrictions.

The advantage for merging parties is that ancillary restraints automatically benefit from a clearance decision under the EU Merger Regulation.

The European Commission's Notice on restrictions directly related and necessary to concentrations ([2005] OJ C56/24) (the 'Ancillary Restraints Notice') provides guidance on the meaning of 'restrictions that are directly related and necessary to the implementation of the concentration'. These include non-compete covenants (including non-solicitation clauses), restrictions in intellectual property agreements and restrictions in purchasing and supply agreements. The Ancillary Restraints Notice has a separate section dealing with ancillary restrictions in concentrative joint ventures.

Non-compete covenants

Ancillary restraints in mergers commonly include covenants by the sellers not to compete with the business they have just sold, as permitting competition would undermine the value of the business transferred. Such restrictions should be no longer in duration or wider in geographic scope or subject matter than objectively necessary. They are justified for up to three years when the transfer includes both know-how and goodwill, and two years when only goodwill is included (Ancillary Restraints Notice, para 20). Restrictions in joint venture agreements are dealt under similar principles: they should only cover products and geographical areas covered by the joint venture and are permissible over the life of the joint venture (Ancillary Restraints Notice, para 36).

Licences, purchase and supply agreements

The Ancillary Restraints Notice also covers exclusive licences, purchase or supply agreements for fixed quantities, and non-solicitation agreements. Again, their scope and duration must be no greater than objectively necessary to the implementation of the transaction.

7.3.9.3   Ancillary restraints in concentrations without a community dimension

Many concentrations do not have a community dimension, as they fall below the turnover thresholds of the EU Merger Regulation. For these concentrations, Article 101 may apply and the guidance in the Ancillary Notice is useful by analogy. The general position is that ancillary restrictions, such as non-compete covenants, may fall outside the scope of Article 101 altogether, provided that they are directly related and necessary to the concentration, and no wider in scope and duration than objectively necessary.

7.3.10 Process

Where a concentration has an EU dimension and notification is required, the parties will be unable to complete their transaction without clearance from the Commission. The parties' legal advisers will be working to secure that clearance, which has timing implications for the transaction. The legal advisers drafting the transaction documents will be inserting provisions which deal with eventualities such as the merger being blocked or cleared only subject to conditions, known as 'conditions precedent' (see **7.3.10.3**). The legal work involved is often complex and undertaken within tight timetables.

7.3.10.1 Application procedure

Parties are required to provide all relevant information to the Commission in a prescribed manner, as required by Form CO. This can be a complex document, outlining all aspects of the transaction, and it will take a considerable amount of time and effort for the parties and their legal advisers to complete.

Given the administrative burden involved in notifying the Commission under Form CO, a simplified procedure is available. Its scope was increased by the 2023 Merger Simplification Package. For the mergers that qualify (see **7.3.7.3**), using the simplified procedure or the super-simplified procedure results in a reduction of the amount of information provided to the Commission and possible timetable advantages. Notification may be on a Short Form CO instead of the full Form CO.

In practice, the filing of the forms will be the last element of the application procedure. Where a transaction is likely to require notification to the Commission, the parties will normally have initial discussions with the Commission to identify issues and possible solutions prior to a notification being made. The parties can better calibrate the information to be provided to the Commission once they have engaged in pre-merger discussions, and the Commission prefers to resolve any issues (such as market definition) prior to notification. Pre-notification contact is voluntary, not mandatory.

Figure 7.1   Timeline for merger assessments under the Merger Regulation

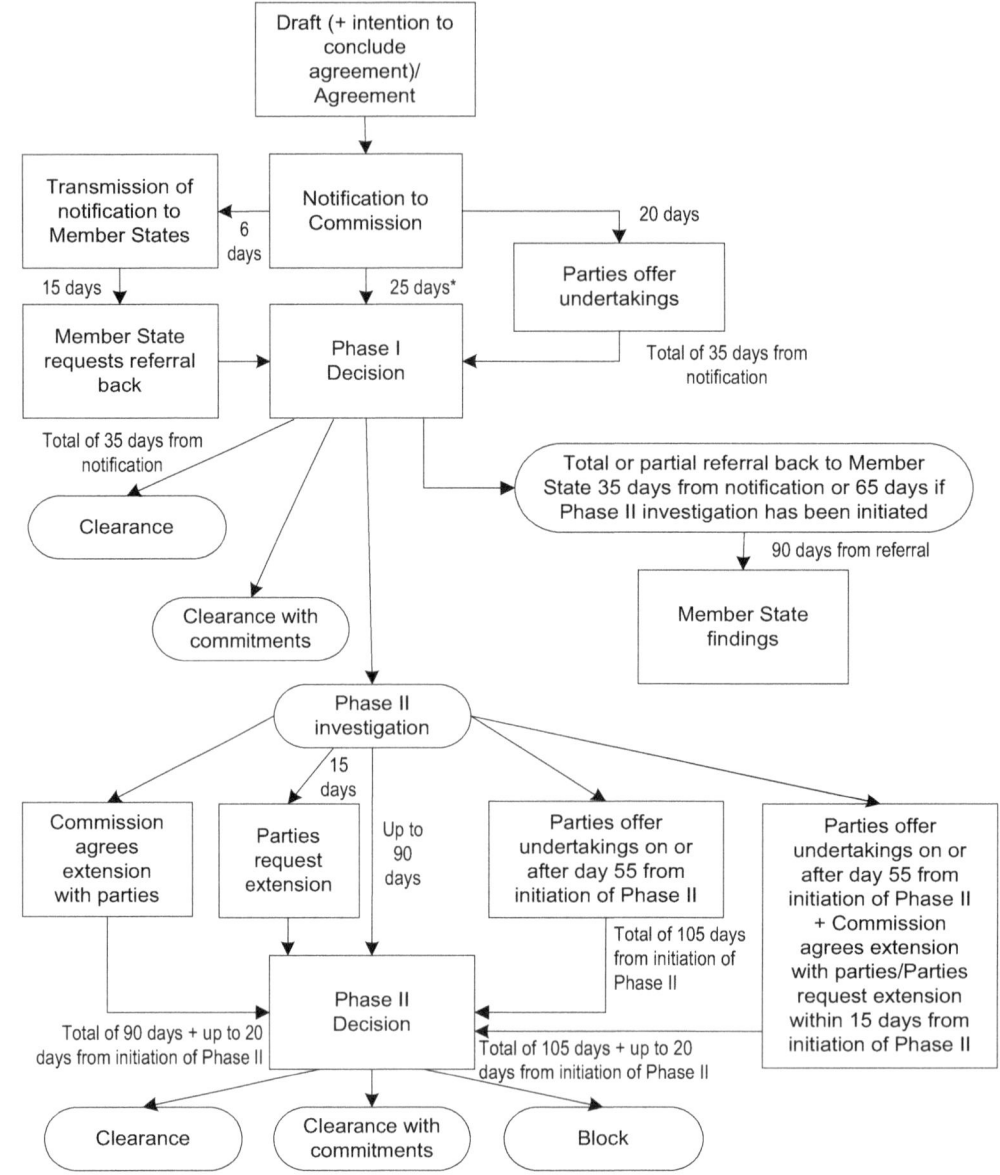

*In this chart, 'days' are working days. One week having five working days, except if it includes official Commission holidays.

7.3.10.2   Timing issues

Timing considerations are crucial to any notification procedure. Parties to a transaction will need to know with precision the time the Commission will likely need to review the notification. Clearly, an open-ended procedure will impact on commercial certainty. Consequently, the Merger Regulation (and associated guidance) sets specific time limits for the examination of the transaction (see Article 10). In essence there are two separate (but related) parts of the timetable for review. The first relates to the 'Phase I' examination of the transaction. At this stage of the process, the Commission will assess whether the transaction gives rise to serious doubt about its compatibility with the common market. It should be noted that the vast majority of assessments will be completed at the Phase I stage. At the end of Phase I there are three main conclusions that the Commission can reach, namely that the concentration:

(a)   is compatible with the common market, ie the Commission clears the merger unconditionally; or

(b)   as modified by the parties, no longer raises serious concerns (eg where the parties have offered effective remedies such as commitments to sell or divest certain assets) and so is compatible with the common market, ie the Commission clears the merger subject to conditions; or

(c)   raises serious doubts as to its compatibility with the common market.

The Commission may also conclude that the transaction does not amount to a concentration with an EU dimension.

If the Commission believes that the transaction does give rise to serious doubts, it will open a full, or 'Phase II', investigation.

At the end of Phase II there are three main conclusions that the Commission can reach. The first two are essentially the same as for Phase I, namely that the concentration is compatible with the common market or, following modification by the parties (eg through offering effective remedies), it is compatible with the common market. The third possible conclusion is that the concentration is incompatible with the common market; ie the Commission prohibits the merger.

The time limits for Phase I and Phase II are outlined in **Figure 7.1** above. Where a Short Form CO is filed, the Commission will endeavour to give a short form decision as soon as possible after the expiry of 15 working days, rather than the standard 25 working days to give a Phase I decision.

7.3.10.3   Conditions precedent

Since the Merger Regulation prohibits parties from implementing a concentration with an EU dimension until it is cleared by the Commission, it is usual for the parties' agreement (share purchase agreement or sale of business agreement) to contain a 'condition precedent'. Such a condition ensures that the transaction is conditional on the transaction being cleared by the Commission. Special rules apply to public bids, which cannot in practice be suspended since they involve the acquisition of shares in the market, to ensure that shares are not voted on prior to clearance (Article 7(2)).

7.4   THE UK SYSTEM OF MERGER CONTROL

This section provides an outline of the UK merger control rules. As an initial point, it should be noted that the UK merger rules ante-date and do not follow the same format as the EU rules discussed above. Therefore, unlike rules relating to anti-competitive behaviour (as outlined in **Chapters 2** and **3**), UK merger rules differ from the EU system. The jurisdictional thresholds, including the situations in which control is acquired, differ from the EU system. However, the substantive assessment of mergers is very similar in the UK and in the EU, since both jurisdictions are concerned with ensuring that the merger does not have an adverse effect on the competitive process.

Lastly, in terms of introduction, the UK merger control rules are one set of rules that could apply to a transaction. A transaction may also require notification to the European Commission and in other jurisdictions outside the UK (see **7.6**).

7.4.1   Legislative and institutional background

The main provisions in the UK system of merger control are contained in Part 3 of the EA 2002, as amended. The National Security and Investment Act (NSIA) 2021 adds a new layer of merger scrutiny for investments that may threaten national security.

Prior to 1 April 2014 the Office of Fair Trading (OFT) and Competition Commission (CC) dealt with mergers in the UK that did not have an EU dimension. The OFT was responsible for investigating mergers (Phase 1) and referred mergers which raised competition concerns to the CC for an in-depth investigation (Phase 2).

Following the abolition of the OFT and CC, a single authority, the CMA, now deals with mergers. However, the two phases have been retained. Accordingly, the CMA is responsible for Phase 1 and an Inquiry Group within the CMA is responsible for Phase 2. The Inquiry Group panel is composed of independent experts. A group of at least three will be selected from a pool to examine each merger. When carrying out its investigations, the Inquiry Group will be under a duty to act independently.

Most mergers that come within the UK rules are approved at the Phase 1 stage.

The CMA has a statutory duty to refer a merger to the Inquiry Group for further investigation where it believes that the merger has resulted in or may result in a substantial lessening of competition in a UK market (EA 2002, ss 22 and 33). Note that there are several specific exceptions to the duty to refer.

The CMA and UK Government also have a role in the scrutiny and review of mergers affecting certain sectors. 'Media' mergers have special rules to ensure that media plurality in the UK is preserved. Investments that may affect the UK's national security are scrutinised by the UK Government's Department for Business, Energy and Industrial Strategy (BEIS) under the NSIA 2021. (The EA 2002 contained special provisions enabling the review of 'public interest' and 'special public interest' mergers; these have now been replaced by the NSIA 2021.)

Media mergers and the NSIA 2021 are not further considered in this textbook.

7.4.2 Jurisdictional issues

The CMA Mergers: Guidance on the CMA's jurisdiction and procedure (CMA2 revised) contains guidance on the CMA's procedures for operating the UK's merger control regime.

For UK merger control to apply, there must be a referable merger. In order to assess whether a merger is referable, it is necessary to ascertain the nature of the transaction and whether it amounts to a 'relevant merger situation' as defined in s 23 of the EA 2002. A relevant merger situation arises where:

- enterprises cease to be distinct; and
- the jurisdictional thresholds (either the turnover test or the share of supply test) are satisfied.

These two points are considered in (a) ('Enterprises ceasing to be distinct') and (b) ('Turnover and share of supply tests') below.

In addition, for a merger to be referable, less than four months must have elapsed since the merger was made public, if it has been completed. In most cases the CMA intervenes when mergers are still in contemplation, well within the four-month time limit. The timing constraints on the CMA are considered at (c) below.

(a) Enterprises ceasing to be distinct

Two or more 'enterprises' must cease to be distinct, or arrangements must be in progress or contemplation which, if completed, will result in the enterprises ceasing to be distinct.

Enterprises will cease to be distinct where they are brought under 'common ownership or common control'. They also cease to be distinct where one of the enterprises ceases to carry on a business as a consequence of the arrangements between the parties.

Enterprise

'Enterprise' is defined widely as 'the activities, or part of the activities, of a business'. An 'enterprise' must be more than just a collection of assets. For example, the acquisition of ferry boats would be sufficient to come within merger control rules if, as well as the actual physical assets, there is a transfer of know-how and goodwill. In *SeaFrance SA v CMA* [2015] UKSC 75, the Supreme Court agreed with the CMA that Eurotunnel's acquisition of three ferries and related assets formerly owned by SeaFrance came within merger control rules.

Common control

There are three alternative levels of control under the EA 2002:

- Full control (or legal control): these are acquisitions of a controlling interest, for example acquiring more than 50% of the shares in a company.
- Ability to control (or de facto control): this is control that falls short of a controlling interest, but gives an enterprise the ability to control another, for example the ability to exercise blocking rights.
- Material influence: this is a level of control that falls short of legal or de facto control, but confers on the acquirer the ability to materially influence the policy or strategic direction of a business in the market. A shareholding of more than 25% of the shares is likely to confer material influence as it confers the ability to block special resolutions. The CMA will examine any shareholding above 15%, although it may consider lower levels in exceptional circumstances. The CMA will consider factors such as voting patterns, blocking rights, the status and expertise of the acquirer, the right to appoint influential directors on the board, and whether the acquirer will supply important services to the target company.

Minority interests

The threshold of 'material influence' ensures that even acquisitions of minority interests are capable of triggering the merger control provisions of the EA 2002. To illustrate the CMA's approach to 'material influence', see *Anticipated acquisition by Amazon of a minority shareholding and certain rights in Deliveroo* (final report dated 4 August 2020). The CMA considered that a 16% shareholding combined with certain rights constituted material influence. The CMA examined the voting patterns in shareholders' resolutions over three years and determined that the 16% shareholding was below the level that would enable Amazon to block special resolutions; however, Amazon would benefit from certain rights not enjoyed by other shareholders. In addition, although not controlling the board, Amazon had the right to appoint one board director (out of seven) and one board observer. These individuals would carry weight among Deliveroo's voting directors. Looking at the cumulative impact of the sources of influence, including Amazon's status and expertise, the CMA determined that Amazon could influence Deliveroo's commercial policy.

Note that 'material influence' is a lower level of control than 'decisive influence' under the Merger Regulation (see **7.3.3**). For example, in 2015, the CMA considered that the acquisition by Ryanair of a 29.8% stake in Aer Lingus constituted control, and Ryanair was ordered by the CMA to reduce its stake to 5%. The acquisition did not, however, fall within the jurisdiction of the Commission under the Merger Regulation (a previous attempt by Ryanair to acquire Aer Lingus had been blocked by the Commission).

A change in the level of control, for example from material influence to an ability to control, will constitute a new merger situation.

Joint ventures

Joint ventures may involve the acquisition of control of an enterprise, although the UK merger control rules are ill-suited to the formation of 'greenfield' joint ventures where there is no enterprise being contributed (unlike EU rules which apply to the creation of full function joint ventures).

Where enterprises are being contributed, the UK merger control rules must be considered. In a 50:50 joint venture, each party typically acquires control over the business being contributed to the joint venture, a business that was previously independent. For example, the joint venture between Warner Bros Discovery, Inc and BT Group plc (28 September 2022, ME/6989/2) involved the acquisition by each party of material influence over the other's audio-visual sports content business in the UK and Ireland. The combined turnover of the businesses contributed to the joint venture exceeded £70 million. Hence there was a relevant merger situation and the CMA had jurisdiction. The joint venture was cleared by the CMA on the basis that it did not lead to a substantial lessening of competition in view of the parties' position in the market, with Sky as the market leader.

(b)   Jurisdictional thresholds

A relevant merger situation will only arise if either:

(i)   the UK turnover of the enterprise being acquired exceeds £70 million (the 'turnover test'); or

(ii)   as a result of the merger, the merged enterprises supply or acquire 25% or more of the relevant products or services within the UK or a substantial part of it (the 'share of supply test').

It should be noted that there has to be an *increase* in share for this test to apply. Accordingly, if an enterprise which has, for example, 30% share of a particular market purchases another enterprise which operates in a totally unrelated market, there is no increase in a share of supply and this element of the test will not be satisfied.

Note also that the share of supply test is not a market share test, and there is no need to apply the market definition analysis required in Article 101/Chapter I and Article 102/Chapter II cases. This avoids the uncertainty of market definition analysis and provides greater legal certainty when assessing jurisdiction, although market definition becomes relevant at the substantive stage of analysis.

Exceptions

By way of exception, the Health and Care Act 2022 provides that the merger of NHS enterprises will not constitute a relevant merger situation under the EA 2002.

There was a further exception under s 23A of the EA 2002, which has now been repealed. Where there was a change of control over a 'relevant enterprise', the turnover test was reduced to £1 million and the share of supply test was modified so as not to require an increase in share for the supply test to apply. 'Relevant enterprises' were those active in areas of specified activity considered essential to the UK's national security. Section 23A of the EA 2002 became redundant when the NSIA 2021 introduced wide-ranging regulation of investments that may affect the UK's national security.

(c)   Time limits

For there to be a referable merger, the relevant merger situation must be either:

(i)   in progress or contemplation (ie it has not yet taken place); or

(ii)   where the merger has taken place, the time limit for a Phase 2 reference has not expired.

The general rule is that a merger no longer qualifies for a Phase 2 reference after the expiry of four months from the merger being made public or, if has been made public but not completed, the later of completion or four months from being made public. There are some limited exceptions.

(d)   Summary

In summary, where a transaction constitutes a 'relevant merger situation', meets the jurisdictional thresholds and the four-month time limit has not expired, it qualifies for investigation by the CMA in Phase 1. If there may be a substantial lessening of competition, it must be referred by the CMA to a Phase 2 investigation.

There are special rules that apply to certain sectors, such as media mergers and investments involving national security interests.

7.4.3 Notification to the CMA and timing

Why notify?

There is no obligation on parties to a merger that comes within the UK regime to pre-notify their arrangement (this is one the most significant differences from the EU system). In practice many parties do pre-notify to the CMA (usually after a period of informal discussion). Notification is by way of 'Merger Notice' to the CMA.

Merging parties will often be concerned that notification should not hold up their transaction, particularly in cases where several companies are competing to acquire the same target. However, there can be significant risks for parties which do not notify the CMA.

First of all, the CMA may take the initiative in opening an investigation, often at the behest of third party complainants. The CMA has the power to make interim orders requiring the enterprises to hold themselves separate pending investigation (Initial Enforcement Order or IEO). The CMA would normally expect to impose an IEO in completed mergers. If there has already been substantial integration, this may be unwound. The purpose of the IEO is to ensure that harm to competition is forestalled by holding the businesses separate, in case the merger is blocked following a Phase 2 inquiry.

Secondly, where the CMA refers the merger to a Phase 2 inquiry, the IEO imposed in Phase 1 remains in place unless replaced by interim undertakings or by another interim order. The EA 2002 also prevents the acquiror from buying shares in the target during the inquiry, irrespective of whether an interim order has been made or interim undertakings have been given.

Thirdly, at the conclusion of a Phase 2 inquiry, the CMA may order the sale (or divestment) of assets to address competition concerns. If the acquiror has made an unconditional purchase and completed the transaction, it may have to sell the business it acquired and find a willing purchaser, which may only be willing to buy on unfavourable terms. The seller is not obliged to take the business back.

In practice, therefore, the operation of the merger is suspended by the parties until clearance from the CMA has been obtained. However, there may be circumstances in which the parties take the risk of not notifying, as assessed by the parties' legal advisers.

Timing

The merging parties will want to know how long the process will take and when they will be able to safely complete their merger transaction. The timing can be complex, particularly where undertakings are offered by the parties to address any concerns raised by the CMA, and legal advisers will usually draw up a detailed timetable to cover the steps between agreeing, signing and completing a transaction. In broad terms:

- Pre-notification: the CMA strongly encourages parties to hold pre-merger discussions with the CMA. It is in everyone's interests to submit a Merger Notice in a form that provides the CMA with all the information it considers necessary, not least because notification triggers a statutory timetable which puts all involved under a great deal of timing pressure. It also makes it less likely that the CMA will 'stop the clock' (see below).

- Phase 1: the CMA has 40 working days to decide whether to refer the merger to a Phase 2 inquiry. The period starts to run from the day after the CMA accepts a complete

Merger Notice (or where the merger has not been notified, where the CMA has informed the merging parties that it is has sufficient information to start an investigation). However, the CMA can 'stop the clock' if the parties have provided incomplete information.

- Where the parties offer undertakings in lieu of a reference ('UIL's) in Phase 1, which they must do within five working days of the CMA outlining its case for a reference, the CMA must then decide whether to accept the UILs (possibly with modifications) within 50 days of the date of the Phase 1 decision. This period can be extended by up to 40 working days if special reasons exist. If the CMA accepts the UILs, it is no longer under a duty to make a Phase 2 reference.

- Phase 2: the Inquiry Group has 24 weeks to complete its Phase 2 investigation, extendable to 32 weeks in certain circumstances.

7.4.4   Assessment procedure

Once a notification has been received, the CMA may need additional information (including evidence from third parties affected by the merger) before an assessment can take place. The CMA will usually issue an invitation to comment, requesting comments within a certain time period. The CMA will generally also hold meetings with all affected parties and their legal advisers. Once all relevant information is obtained, the CMA will establish if the merger may give rise to a substantial lessening of competition.

If the CMA decides in Phase 1 that the substantial lessening of competition test is not met, it will clear the merger. In more complex cases, there may be a case review meeting of the CMA (which may include other government departments). Where the CMA has concerns, the parties will be invited to an 'issues meeting', which effectively enables them to be heard before a decision is taken to make a reference. If the CMA believes there may be a substantial lessening of competition, it has a duty (with exceptions) to make a Phase 2 reference.

In a Phase 2 reference the CMA's Inquiry Group must consider whether the merger would lead to a substantial lessening of competition, applying the same test as in Phase 1 but this time considering on a balance of probabilities whether a substantial lessening of competition would take place (rather than whether it 'may' take place). The Inquiry Group will carry out a thorough investigation (which will entail more information being required and further hearings).

If the CMA clears the merger, the parties can complete the transaction. On the other hand, if the CMA decides that there is a substantial lessening of competition, it will take steps to remedy the adverse effects it has identified. The CMA has wide-ranging powers to impose remedies aimed at addressing competition concerns (these can be both structural and/or behavioural – see **7.3.7.5** above in the context of the Merger Regulation). For an anticipated merger, this may mean that the CMA prohibits the merger. Alternatively, it could allow the merger to proceed subject to suitable undertakings, eg whereby the parties agree to sell part of the business to be acquired. For a merger that has already been completed, the CMA will normally require the sale of part (or even all) of the acquired business to a suitable purchaser, ie one that is able to provide effective competition. The CMA may also accept undertakings as to future behaviour along with, or instead of, divestiture.

7.4.5   The substantive test

In assessing whether there is a substantial lessening of competition, the CMA adopts a similar approach to the European Commission when it assesses whether there is a significant impediment to effective competition, and the two tests are very similar.

The CMA's Merger Assessment Guidelines (CMA129) ('Merger Assessment Guidelines') set out the CMA's substantive approach when investigating mergers. The CMA's particular analytical method will vary depending on the circumstances of the case. Broadly, the CMA will be concerned to preserve the rivalry between firms that enables markets to be competitive, for the benefit of consumers. The CMA does not apply any pre-determined market share thresholds when deciding whether a loss to competition is substantial. The CMA assesses the competitive effects of the merger by reference to a 'theory of harm', which is a hypothesis as to how the process of rivalry could be harmed as a result of the merger.

Theories of harm are often classified according to whether the merger is a *horizontal* merger between competitors or potential competitors; or a *non-horizontal* merger between parties at a different level in the supply chain (vertical mergers) or between parties whose products do not overlap (conglomerate mergers). The theory of harm is one of the many analytical tools at the CMA's disposal when developing or testing a theory of harm. Some of these are set out below.

(a)   *Unilateral effects.* These may arise where the merger involves competitors or potential competitors and removes the rivalry (or potential rivalry) between them; with the result that the merged firm finds it profitable to raise prices or reduce quality or output. Most mergers that give rise to a significant lessening of competition are within this category.

(b)   *Coordinated effects.* These may arise in oligopolistic markets (markets with a few large firms) where the post-merger market structure is such that firms in the market (including the merged firm) are likely jointly to increase prices because the merger creates or strengthens the conditions under which they can tacitly or expressly coordinate their behaviour. Coordinated effects will arise relatively infrequently. As under the EU merger system, they may be found: (i) in conditions of transparency where firms can reach a common level of understanding of the terms of coordination; (ii) where coordination is internally sustainable and the firms adhere to the expected outcome; and (iii) coordination is externally sustainable and not undermined by firms outside the group.

(c)   *Vertical or conglomerate effects.* These arise principally where the merger creates or strengthens the ability of the merged firm to use its market power in at least one of the markets affected by the merger, thereby reducing rivalry between firms. In vertical mergers, a supplier may, for example, have reduced incentives to supply the competitors of its new subsidiary, which may result in a substantial lessening of competition if these competitors have no other reliable supplier. In conglomerate mergers, the firms may have complementary products which do not overlap but which together give the firms 'portfolio power'.

The CMA will also compare the competitive structure if the merger goes ahead with the 'counterfactual'. The counterfactual is not a detailed description of the competitive structure without the merger but focuses on significant changes, such as whether the merged firms would have entered the market in competition with each other, or would have significantly expanded. For example, one of the firms might be a start-up which might have expanded on the market were it not for the merger.

The Merger Assessment Guidelines give examples of scenarios in which it is more likely to find a substantial lessening of competition ('SLC') (at para 2.18). These include the following situations:

*   a merger which involves the market leader and the number of significant competitors is reduced from four to three;
*   a merger in which the merged firms are close competitors (ie their products are close substitutes) and where products are undifferentiated, ie products that have no unique physical characteristics or perceived attributes and can be easily substituted by products from other suppliers (for example raw materials or mass commodities);
*   a merger in which one of the merged firms would otherwise have entered or expanded, and could be expected to become a strong competitor or threat to the other firm (for

example in dynamic digital markets, firms that do not compete head to head may do so in the future);

- a merger in which the pace of innovation or product development, which are a key aspect of competition, is threatened;
- the merger increases the features of the market that give rise to co-ordination;
- in vertical or conglomerate markets, the merger can be expected to lead to the foreclosure of an important rival.

7.4.6 Ancillary restraints

7.4.6.1 Generally

The ancillary restraints doctrine (see **7.3.9.1**) applies in the UK as retained EU law. Restrictions on competition that are directly related and necessary to the main operation of an agreement may fall outside the scope of Article 101/Chapter I altogether. Restrictions must be no wider in scope and duration than necessary to protect the operation.

7.4.6.2 Merger situations

In the case of UK mergers, there is a specific statutory provision which generally excludes mergers and ancillary restraints from the prohibitions in Chapters I and II of the Competition Act 1998. Under Sch 1 of the CA 1998, an operation under which 'enterprises cease to be distinct' (within the meaning of s 26 of the Enterprise Act 2002) is not caught by Chapters I or II and neither are restrictions that are 'directly related and necessary to the implementation of the merger provisions'. Consequently, ancillary restraints such as non-compete covenants that are objectively necessary in their scope and operation fall outside Chapter I.

Helpfully, the Sch 1 exclusion is not limited to referrable mergers that meet the turnover and/ or share of supply tests of the Enterprise Act 2002 but applies more generally to mergers (enterprises ceasing to be distinct) and to restraints that are ancillary to mergers (directly related and necessary to the implementation of the merger provisions).

As a safeguard, the CMA has some limited claw-back powers.

CMA2 Annex C sets out common forms of ancillary restraints, such as non-compete covenants, restrictions in intellectual property licences and restrictions in purchase and supply agreements. CMA2 broadly follows the approach in the European Commission's Ancillary Restraints Notice (see **7.3.9.2**). Restrictions must be no wider in geographic scope, subject matter or duration than objectively necessary (Annex C.12). Non-compete clauses are justified for up to three years when the transfer includes both know-how and goodwill, and two years when only goodwill is included (Annex C.13).

7.5 MERGER CONTROL IN THE UNITED STATES

7.5.1 Clayton Act, Section 7

Section 7 of the Clayton Act prohibits the acquisition of the voting shares or assets of any business 'where the effect of such acquisition ... may be to substantially lessen competition, or to tend to create a monopoly' (15 USC §18). Transactions that raise serious issues under Section 7 of the Clayton Act typically involve a combination of existing competitors in the same market, that is, horizontal mergers. Courts consider certain relevant factors to determine whether a horizontal merger raises a Section 7 violation, including:

(a)   *Concentration.* Courts will consider the shares of the firms in a properly defined product and geographic market, before and after the acquisition, by application of the Hirfindahl-Hirschman Index (HHI), which is the sum of the squares of the market shares of each firm in the market. For example, in a market with two firms with equal shares, the HHI is $50^2 + 50^2 = 2,500 + 2,500 = 5,000$. An absolute monopoly has an HHI of 10,000 (100^2).

(b)   *Ease of market access.* Courts always consider concentration in the context of the ability of new competitors to enter the market. If significant barriers to entry exist, such as the need to make large capital investments or to obtain regulatory approval, existing firms with large market shares may be able to raise their prices without fear of attracting new competitors.

(c)   *Competitive harm.* The courts will also consider whether the transaction threatens competitive harm in the circumstances of the particular market. Two forms are considered:

(i)   *Facilitating coordinated behaviour.* A transaction can be found anti-competitive if it eases the ability of leading firms to coordinate their actions, meaning to observe and react to each other in a manner that results in higher prices and lower output. A transaction might have this effect, for example, if it enables one firm to dominate the market and to act as a market leader on price moves, or if it removes a firm that had previously undermined the coordinated behaviour of other firms.

(ii)   *Enhancing unilateral market power.* If the merger significantly increases the ability of the merged firm to raise its prices unilaterally, the transaction can be found anti-competitive. An example is a merger creating a dominant firm facing only small fringe competitors and protected by significant barriers to entry.

(d)   *Efficiencies.* In assessing a transaction's potential for competitive harm, courts will also consider whether the transaction will create efficiencies, such as lower costs through elimination of duplicative functions, economies of scale and improved products or services. However, there is some question as to the extent to which courts can or should consider the offsetting effects of efficiencies in an otherwise competitively harmful transaction.

(e)   *Failing company.* A possible defence to a Section 7 claim is that the acquired company is about to fail and cease operations. To establish this defence, three facts must be established: (i) the company is in imminent danger of failing; (ii) reorganization of the company is not possible; and (iii) the company cannot find another buyer that could acquire it with less harm to competition.

Other forms of mergers that have been challenged in court in recent years involve:

(a)   *Potential competition.* A potential competitor is a firm that currently operates not in the same market as its proposed merger partner but in either a related product market or a nearby geographic market. A merger with a potential competitor can be seen as anti-competitive if it has the effect of either (i) removing a firm whose potential entry had discouraged firms in the market from raising prices (a 'perceived potential competitor'), or (ii) pre-empting the target firm's entry into the market by more competitive means, such as merger with a smaller existing firm (an 'actual potential competitor').

(b)   *Vertical mergers.* Mergers between suppliers and customers can be anti-competitive when they foreclose competitors of one of the merging firms either from a critical source of inputs or access to a substantial portion of the market.

(see eg *FTC v Steris Corp & Synergy Health plc* (challenge involving potential competition issue) and *US v AT&T Inc, DIRECTTV Group Holdings, LLC, and Time Warner Inc* (challenge to vertical merger)). The state attorneys general recently have become more active with merger enforcement, bringing challenges when the federal agency has cleared a transaction (see eg *State of NY v Deutsche Telekom AG, et al*, Case No 1:19-cv-05434 (SDNY) (state enforcement action against Sprint/T-Mobile merger, notwithstanding DOJ settlement of the same)). Private parties also have become active enforcers of merger control laws (see eg *Daniel Grace, et al, v Alaska Air Group, et al*, Case No 3:16-cv-05165 (ND Cal) (plaintiffs' lawsuit against the acquisition of Virgin America by Alaska Air Group)).

7.5.2 Enforcement of the Clayton Act, Section 7

Actions to enforce Section 7 of the Clayton Act can be brought by the Department of Justice (DOJ), the Federal Trade Commission (FTC), state attorneys general or private parties, while the DOJ and the FTC are responsible for almost all enforcement actions. The two agencies have issued Horizontal Merger Guidelines and Vertical Merger Guidelines (rescinded by the FTC), which set forth principles for how the agencies will analyze mergers or acquisitions. In January 2022, the agencies announced an initiative to evaluate and revise the Horizontal Merger Guidelines and the Vertical Merger Guidelines, resulting in the draft Merger Guidelines, which cover a wide range of mergers and are not limited to horizontal and vertical mergers. The draft Merger Guidelines were published for comment in July 2023 and are subject to a 60-day notice and comment period. It is anticipated that the final Merger Guidelines will be published in early 2024.

The draft Merger Guidelines provide a framework and guidance for parties to analyze whether a transaction may implicate antitrust laws, centred around the following 13 principles:

1. Mergers should not significantly increase competition in highly concentrated markets.

2. Mergers should not eliminate substantial competition between firms.

3. Mergers should not increase the risk of coordination.

4. Mergers should not eliminate a potential entrant in a concentrated market.

5. Mergers should not substantially lessen competition by creating [an entity] that controls products or services that its rivals may use to compete.

6. Vertical mergers should not create market structures that foreclose competition.

7. Mergers should not entrench or extend a dominant position.

8. Mergers should not further a trend toward concentration.

9. When a merger is part of a series of multiple acquisitions, the agencies may examine the whole series.

10. When a merger involves multi-sided platforms, the agencies may examine competition between platforms, on a platform, or to displace a platform.

11. When a merger involves competing buyers, the agencies examine whether it may substantially lessen competition for workers or other sellers.

12. When an acquisition involves partial ownership or minority interests, the agencies examine its impact on competition.

13. Mergers should not otherwise substantially lessen competition or tend to create a monopoly.

Pre-merger notification

To facilitate enforcement of Section 7 of the Clayton Act, parties to transactions that meet certain financial thresholds are required to give prior notice to both agencies and to delay closing their transactions for specified periods. The notification requirements are set out in a statute known as the Hart-Scott-Rodino Antitrust Improvements Act of 1976 (the 'HSR Act') (15 USC §18a). While the notification is submitted to both agencies, in practice, only one reviews the transaction.

The HSR Act requires parties to delay closing for 30 days after filing their notice. If either agency wishes to investigate the transaction further, it will issue a request for more information and documents, known as a 'second request'. The parties are then barred from closing until 30 days after they make a substantially complete response to the second request (which may be extended by mutual agreement between the parties and the relevant agency). If the agency issuing the second request concludes that the proposed transaction will violate Section 7 of the Clayton Act, it will file an action in federal court for a preliminary injunction against the transaction during this extended waiting period. Alternatively, the parties and the agency will reach an agreement that avoids litigation, such as a commitment by the acquiring party to divest certain assets or operations.

Most HSR Act filings involve transactions that do not trigger second requests for information. If no serious issue is raised by the transaction then the FTC will advise the parties that they are free to proceed with their transaction in less than 30 days, ie grant early termination, often as soon as two weeks after the filing. While technically, parties can still seek early termination, in February 2021, the FTC, supported by the DOJ, stopped granting early termination absent highly limited circumstances (ie, when parties have received a second request, the agency has dropped its investigation, but the parties have not complied – therefore the additional 30-day waiting period has not triggered). The agencies have been clear that they do not intend to reinstate the grant of early termination, and parties should anticipate having to wait at least 30 days prior to be able to consummate their transaction.

Additionally, in the summer of 2021, the FTC began issuing so-called 'Warning Letters' to parties. These parties would receive a letter from the FTC, often on the last day of the HSR waiting period, informing them that the FTC has not completed its investigation and that the parties were free to close at their own risk. Effectively, the FTC was issuing a warning that it still may challenge the deal if it found any antitrust concerns (even post-consummation). At some point in 2022, it also became clear that the DOJ was sending similar letters. But the warning letters amounted to no more than that – just warnings. At no point was there ever any evidence that either the FTC or DOJ actually investigated and took action against a transaction that had received a warning letter. Additionally, the warning letters did not actually change the regulatory state of play – both agencies always retained the right to investigate transactions post-HSR waiting period and post-consummation if they felt that there was an antitrust concern.

The HSR Act filing is required if the transaction meets the following financial thresholds:

- *Size of Transaction*. The acquiring company will hold, in the aggregate, more than $445.5 million of the assets, voting shares or non-corporate interests of the acquired company; or
- *Size of Transaction*. The acquiring company will hold, in the aggregate, more than $111.4 million of the assets, voting securities or non-corporate interests of the acquired company; and
- *Size of Persons*. The acquiring and the acquired companies have annual net sales or total assets in excess of:
  — $227.7 million for one company; and
  — $22.3 million for the other company.

The dollar amounts of these 2023 financial thresholds are adjusted every year to reflect the change in the size of the US economy.

In applying these thresholds, the 'acquiring' and the 'acquired' companies are not necessarily the corporate entities directly engaged in the transaction. Instead, the tests must be applied to the 'ultimate parent entity' of each party to the transaction, consolidating all other entities controlled by that parent.

Furthermore, the thresholds call for consideration of the assets and sales of the parties worldwide, not just assets or sales in the United States. However, exemptions may apply to preclude the value from the Size of Transaction test of assets held outside of the United States and the value of voting shares of issuers organized under the laws of foreign jurisdictions where such issuers do not have a required amount of assets or sales in or into the US.

In transactions that fall short of these thresholds, the parties are not required to file a notification or to delay their transaction for the waiting periods. However, the lack of a filing requirement under the HSR Act is not immunity from the antitrust laws. If one of the agencies determines that a transaction violates Section 7 of the Clayton Act, the agency can file suit to block or unwind the transaction, whether or not an HSR filing was required.

7.6 MULTI-JURISDICTIONAL MERGER REVIEW

International cooperation between merger enforcement authorities is common, as they are frequently required to examine the competition implications of the same case. The presence of large companies, often with overlapping activities in many different jurisdictions, can mean that competition issues raised by a merger become more complex and difficult to resolve, leading to potential problems of timing and the tactical issue of how to reconcile clearance in one jurisdiction with prohibition in another.

Many transactions trigger filing obligations in multiple jurisdictions, which can substantially increase transactional costs. As we have seen, where the arrangement does not fall within the EU merger regime, national merger regimes of the EU Member States may still apply. Conversely, just because the EU merger rules will apply to a transaction does not prevent notification being required outside the EU. Very large mergers will (and often do) require notification to the European Commission and the authorities within the United States (and indeed many others, such as the UK authorities). As implementation of transactions is generally prohibited before merger clearance has been received, careful planning is required to ensure that the notification processes in several jurisdictions are coordinated so as not to delay completion.

COMPETITION LAW AND INTELLECTUAL PROPERTY

AIMS

In this chapter we introduce you to the consideration that must be given to competition law when advising clients of ways in which they might exploit their intellectual property (IP) rights. In particular, we shall be looking at patent licensing.

OBJECTIVES

After studying **Chapter 8**, you should be able to:

- appreciate the relationship between competition law and IP rights;

- consider the operation of Article 101/Chapter I within the context of the exploitation of IP rights, and in particular the operation of the Technology Transfer Block Exemption Regulation an equivalent UK block exemption;

- consider how the use of IP rights can amount to an abuse for the purposes of Article 102/Chapter II; and

- understand how the US system of competition law deals with IP rights.

8.1 INTRODUCTION

This chapter looks at the relationship between competition law and IP rights. It concentrates on the competition law problems which may arise in relation to the exploitation of IP rights (with particular reference to the licensing of patents). The beginning of this chapter deals with the EU system (as the UK system is essentially identical). At the end of the chapter, we consider briefly the system that applies in the US.

Before we look at these systems, let us ensure we understand what we mean by IP rights and how they interact with competition law.

8.2 OVERVIEW OF IP RIGHTS AND RELATIONSHIP WITH COMPETITION LAW

8.2.1 Overview of IP rights

The term 'intellectual property' covers a wide range of rights protecting the product of human intellect. Although the specifics of IP will differ within each jurisdiction, there are some basic categories of IP rights which will be common in most. Accordingly, although the following brief overview of the main IP rights relates to UK law, the categories mentioned will be relevant to most systems.

(a)   *Trade marks.* This IP right relates to branded products or services, and as such will normally consist of an image (eg, the McDonald's golden arches) or wording (such as Coca-Cola). The UK system of trade mark protection requires the mark to be registered before protection will be granted.

(b)   *Copyright.* This is a right which prevents copying; it is most used in publishing and other artistic works. Copyright arises automatically under the UK system, and consequently registration is not required.

(c)   *Design rights.* Under UK law, designs that relate to the appearance of an object may be registered (registered design rights). Functional objects can also be protected by unregistered design right.

(d)   *Patents.* The patents system provides protections for inventions. The right requires registration and will provide a monopoly for the patent holder for 20 years under UK law. Given the length of the monopoly right provided by this IP right, it will form the basis of the discussion in this chapter.

8.2.2   The relationship between IP rights and competition law

The traditional view of the relationship between competition law and IP rights claimed that the two systems of law were diametrically opposed: IP rights dealing with the grant of monopoly powers; competition law dealing with the break-up or regulation of these powers. However, this traditional view has changed. This change has occurred due to a combination of factors. First, the basic assumptions outlined above have been challenged. Secondly, there has been an increasing recognition that the two areas of law are underpinned by the same basic rationale.

8.2.2.1   Challenging the basic assumptions

It is often claimed that IP rights confer a monopoly on the successful applicant (under the UK patent system, the protection lasts for 20 years). However, although the grant of a patent will prevent anyone using (without permission) the *patented technology*, it does not prevent *competing products* being sold or developed. In this regard, the grant of a patent does not provide a monopoly in the economic sense of the word. For example, competing vacuum cleaner manufacturers cannot use each others' patents but they nevertheless compete. Further, some of the main categories of IP rights do not in fact grant so-called 'monopoly' rights in the first place – such as copyright.

Regarding competition law's rationale of the break-up or regulation of monopoly power, this again is open to challenge. Although some aspects of competition law can (and do) address monopoly power (for example, in the UK, the market investigation powers under the EA 2002, which are beyond the scope of this textbook), most competition is not concerned with monopolies or dominance as such. What competition law is particularly concerned with is the behaviour of dominant undertakings. We saw in **Chapter 3** that both dominance and abuse have to be present before the prohibition on abuse of a dominant position is triggered.

8.2.2.2   Similarities between IP law and competition law

The re-evaluation of the relationship is not just due to the lack of conflict, but also due to the common ground between these two areas of law. In particular, both are concerned with the promotion of consumer welfare and with the efficient allocation of resources. Clearly, if inventors cannot be awarded some degree of protection for the things they invent then they may not undertake specific research in order to create new products in the first place. In some areas, for example pharmaceuticals, the cost of research and development is so high that, without patent protection, research would simply be abandoned, with the obvious implications for public health.

This revised view of the two areas can be seen in both Europe and the US. The Technology Transfer Block Exemption Regulation 316/2014 (the 'TTBER') ([2014] OJ L93/17) (a copy of which can be found at **Appendix 10**) and the *Commission's Guidelines on the application of Article 101 of the Treaty on the Functioning of the European Union to technology transfer agreements* (the 'TTBER Guidelines') ([2014] OJ C89/03) both make this point. In particular, the TTBER Guidelines state at para 7:

> [I]t [does not] imply that there is an inherent conflict between intellectual property rights and the Union competition rules. Indeed, both bodies of law share the same basic objective of promoting consumer welfare and efficient allocation of resources. Innovation constitutes an essential and dynamic component of an open and competitive market economy.

Although there may not be any inherent conflict between IP rights and competition law, it does not mean that either area can be ignored. Certain arrangements, particularly licences, will need to be considered by reference to both IP and competition rules.

8.3 ARTICLE 101/CHAPTER I AND IP RIGHTS

8.3.1 Introduction

In this section we consider the position under Article 101/Chapter I, focusing on the TTBER and the TTBER Guidelines. Although these are EU instruments, they are also relevant to UK competition law: as a reminder, EU block exemptions (including the TTBER) apply in the UK as retained exemptions. The TTBER Guidelines also continue to represent the UK's approach.

8.3.2 Article 101/Chapter I and the licence of IP rights

A holder of an IP right may wish to license its rights to a third party (a licensee), rather than exploiting the rights itself. There are many reasons why such an owner may decide to license out its IP rights. One common reason is that the holder may simply not have the capacity to exploit the IP rights in full, for example it does not have the requisite engineering facilities to produce the product. Clearly, in these circumstances, it is more efficient for a specialist third party to undertake the production process (this underlines the point regarding allocation of resources and efficiencies discussed above).

Where an IP right is licensed to a third party, there will be an agreement between the holder and the licensee (for example, a patent licensing agreement, sometimes simply called a 'patent licence'). As there is an agreement between undertakings, Article 101/Chapter I may apply (depending, of course, on the terms of the agreement).

In the next section we shall concentrate on the licensing of patent rights. However, it should be remembered that Article 101/Chapter I may also apply to the licensing of other IP rights, such as copyright (see Case 262/81 *Coditel v Cine Vog Films* [1982] ECR 3381) and trade marks (see *Moosehead/Whitbread* [1991] 4 CMLR 391).

8.3.3 Article 101/Chapter I and patent licensing agreements

Patent licensing agreements can give rise to many of the competition law problems associated with other vertical agreements (see **Chapter 6**), in particular the grant of territorial protection to the licensee. However, other issues, such as the duration of the agreement, non-compete clauses, field of use and pricing restrictions, can also be found within a typical patent licence, and may also give rise to concerns.

Where parties wish to enter into a patent licence, they have two available options through which to ensure that it complies with Article 101/Chapter I. The first option is to ensure that it falls within the TTBER (and the relevant UK block exemption after the end of the Brexit transition period). The second option, used where the TTBER is not available (for example the parties' market shares are too high or the TTBER conditions are too restrictive for the commercial deal), is to assess the agreement by reference to the individual exemption criteria outlined in Article 101(3)/the equivalent Chapter I provision. Here we consider the first of these options; as mentioned above, this will apply to the vast majority of cases. For convenience, when we refer below to the TTBER and the TTBER Guidelines, this also covers the relevant UK provisions.

8.3.4   The Technology Transfer Block Exemption

The current TTBER (see **Appendix 10**) came into force on 1 May 2014 and expires on 30 April 2026. It replaces a previous, similar block exemption and is likely itself to be replaced by a similar version. Although there have been changes in approach over the years, for parties entering into a patent licence expiring after 2026 there is no reason to believe that a similar exemption will not be available.

As with other vertical agreements, the presumption under the TTBER is that agreements do not necessarily give rise to competition concerns, and therefore as long as certain terms do not appear, and the parties' market shares are below certain thresholds, the agreement will be allowed. More technically, the Commission accepts the pro-competitive effects of IP licensing, but this is dependent on the market power of the parties and the extent to which there is competition from parties owning or producing substitutable technology. In particular, the Commission is concerned that an IP licence may be used by competing businesses to divide markets. This can occur where competitors license technologies to each other and in return agree not to compete with one another in other areas. In these circumstances, what looks like a licence designed to make technology more widely available is in fact little more than a cover for a non-compete agreement. Because of this fear, the TTBER applies different rules to competing and non-competing undertakings, including different market share thresholds and lists of hardcore restrictions. Further distinctions are made between 'reciprocal' agreements (ie two-way agreements) and 'non-reciprocal' arrangements (one-way agreements), the former being treated more restrictively.

8.3.4.1   Structure of the TTBER

As with other EU block exemptions, the TTBER begins with the recitals and then, in Article 1, provides a list of definitions. The exemption itself is contained in Article 2. Article 3 sets the market share thresholds.

Article 4 contains the hardcore restrictions. The exemption provided by Article 2 will not apply to *agreements* which contain a hardcore restriction. As indicated at **8.3.4** above, there are two lists. Article 4(1) deals with competing undertakings, whilst Article 4(2) deals with non-competing undertakings.

Article 5 outlines the non-hardcore restrictions, or excluded restrictions. The exemption provided in Article 2 will not apply to an *obligation* outlined in Article 5; however, the rest of the agreement may still benefit from the TTBER.

Article 6 allows the Commission and the NCAs of the EU Member States (or, in the UK's retained exemption, the CMA) to withdraw the TTBER from any given agreement if they find that the agreement is anti-competitive and so does not qualify for the exemption under Article 101(3). One of the situations in which they can do this is where the parties do not exploit the licensed technology; this may be a sham licence agreement of the type mentioned above.

Article 7 allows the Commission to disapply the TTBER from entire markets which are dominated by parallel networks of similar technology transfer agreements.

Article 8 sets out details rules for the calculation of market share for the purposes of Article 3 (further information on calculation of market share can be found in para 3 of the TTBER Guidelines).

8.3.4.2   Applying the TTBER

The following discussion examines how to approach an assessment of an agreement by reference to the TTBER. However, a few introductory points should be made. First, although it may seem obvious, the legal adviser should ensure that the agreement under consideration comes within the TTBER. This will be considered below (under 'entrance requirements'), but it should be noted that some agreements will not neatly fall within the entrance requirements of a particular block exemption, or could indeed apply to more than one block exemption. For example, an exclusive distribution agreement may involve a licence of IP rights. As a general point, the Vertical agreements block exemptions govern where IP rights are only ancillary to (and not the primary object of) the agreement (for further guidance, see section 4.4.2 of the EU Vertical Guidelines and paras 6.39–6.47 of the UK Vertical Guidance).

Secondly, the approach below is made within the context of the TTBER; however, the broad approach can be adapted to other block exemptions.

(a)   What are the 'entrance requirements'?

In order to benefit from the exemption contained in Article 2, the agreement must:

(i)   be a 'technology transfer agreement'. Article 1(1)(c) defines a technology transfer agreement as a 'technology rights licensing agreement' or as 'an assignment of technology rights'. The main focus of this chapter is on licensing agreements, so the ensuing discussion concentrates on them. 'Technology rights' means know-how as well as a number of IP rights, or a combination of them, namely patents, utility models, design rights, topographies of semiconductor products, supplementary protection certificates for medicinal and other products, plant breeder's certificates and software copyright (Article 1(1)(b));

(ii)   allow the IP rights to be exploited by the production of goods or services (recital 7 and Article 1(1)(c) and 1(1)(g) (contract products)). Accordingly, a pure technology licensing agreement which does not contemplate the manufacture of goods or services will not qualify. Conversely, Article 2(3) makes it clear that the definition of technology transfer agreement extends to agreements which contain provisions relating to the purchase of products by the licensee or to the licensing or assignment of other IP rights or know-how to the licensee, if these provisions are directly and exclusively related to the production of the contract products. For example, the TTBER will cover a licence which licenses a patent but also gives the licensee the right to use the licensor's trade mark, provided that the licence of the trade mark enables the licensee to better exploit the patent; and

(iii)   be between two undertakings (Article 1(1)(c)(i)) (agreement between more than two undertakings will not fall under the TTBER, although it could still benefit from individual exemption under Article 101(3)).

(b)   What are the market shares of the parties?

The market shares of the parties will be of importance as the TTBER will only apply to agreements where the parties' share of the market is below certain thresholds. In regard to agreements between competitors, the parties' combined market share must not exceed 20% (Article 3(1)). For non-competing undertakings, the market share of each undertaking must not exceed 30% (Article 3(2)).

When calculating the parties' market shares, it is important to bear in mind the definitions used in the TTBER to define the relevant markets. Its definitions of the 'relevant product market' and 'relevant geographic market' (Article 1(1)(j) and (l) respectively) are very much based on general market definition principles (see **3.3.1.1**). The TTBER also introduces the concept of the 'relevant technology market'; this comprises the licensed technology and its substitutes, ie technologies that are interchangeable and substitutable technologies by reason of the technologies' characteristics, their royalties or intended use (Article 1(1)(k)). It then goes on to define the 'relevant market' as the combination of the relevant product or technology market with the relevant geographic market (Article 1(1)(m)).

For new products, the calculation of market share will be difficult. In this regard, the TTBER Guidelines (para 90) provide that for new markets the technology market share figure will be calculated at zero.

As different market share thresholds are applicable depending on whether the parties are competitors or non-competitors, it is necessary to determine whether the parties to the agreement are competitors. The TTBER provides that the parties are competitors where they compete *either* in the technology market *or* in the market (product and geographic) where the contract products are sold. The contract products are those produced by the licensee with the licensed technology. These two situations are explained further below:

(a)   Competitors in the technology market. The parties must be actual competitors on the market where the technology rights are licensed. That is to say, the undertakings license out competing technology; or the licensee is already licensing out its technology rights and the licensor enters the technology market by granting the licensee a licence for competing technology rights (Article 1(1)(n)(i)) and TTBER Guidelines (para 35)).

(b)   Competitors on the market where the contract products are sold. The parties must be actual or potential competitors on that market.

       According to the TTBER Guidelines (para 30), the parties will be presumed to be actual competitors if prior to the agreement they were active on the same relevant product market.

       The parties are *potential* competitors on the relevant market (product and geographic) if it is likely that, in the absence of the agreement and without infringing the IP rights of the other party, they would have undertaken within a short period of time (one to two years) the necessary additional investment to enter the relevant market in response to a small but permanent increase in product prices (Article 1(1)(n)(ii)).

       The parties to an agreement will not normally be actual or potential competitors if one or both of them is in a 'blocking position', ie where they are unable to compete with each other without one or both parties infringing each other's technology rights (TTBER Guidelines (para 29)).

(c)   Reciprocal/non-reciprocal agreements?

The TTBER makes a distinction between reciprocal agreements (in basic terms, a two-way licensing agreement) and non-reciprocal agreements (where there is only a one-way licence) (see Article 1(1)(d) and (e)). Reciprocal agreements are dealt with more strictly under the terms of the TTBER.

(d)   Does the agreement contain any hardcore restrictions?

As we have seen above, agreements that contain hardcore restrictions will fall outside the TTBER. Accordingly, legal advisers will ensure that agreements do not contain hardcore restrictions so as to benefit from the TTBER. The position is, however, complicated in respect to the TTBER as the list of hardcore restrictions differs for agreements which are between competitors and those between non-competitors.

Below are a few points worthy of note relating to hardcore restrictions:

(i)   *Pricing restrictions.* These are prohibited for agreements between both competitors (Article 4(1)(a)) and non-competitors (Article 4(2)(a)); however in regard to the latter, the TTBER recognises that a setting of a maximum or recommended resale price is acceptable as long as this does not amount to a fixed or minimum sale price as a result of pressure or incentives.

(ii)   *Limitations on output.* These are prohibited where the agreement is between competitors (Article 4(1)(b)).

(iii) *Territorial restrictions.* The main point to note here is that the TTBER allows (in limited circumstances) restrictions on passive selling (if you need a reminder of the difference between active and passive sales, see **6.2.6.4**). The rules relating to territorial restrictions under the TTBER are complex, but a few examples follow:

(1) *Competing undertakings.* The TTBER treats reciprocal agreements between competitors much more strictly than non-reciprocal agreements between competitors, as the former are potentially much more damaging to competition. The key points are:

- *Reciprocal agreements.* Territorial restrictions, including restrictions on active sales, are hardcore restrictions and so are generally not permitted (Article 4(1)(c)).

- *Non-reciprocal agreements.* While territorial restrictions are hardcore restrictions, there are some exceptions, in particular:
  - the licensor may ban active and passive sales into territories that the licensor has exclusively reserved for itself (Article 4(1)(c)(i));
  - the licensor may ban active (but not passive) sales by the licensee into an exclusive territory allocated to another licensee, on condition that the protected licensee was not a competitor of the licensor at the time its own licence was concluded (Article 4(1)(c)(ii)).

(2) *Non-competing undertakings.* The TTBER does not contain any restrictions on active sales where the parties are non-competitors. Accordingly, the licensor may impose a wide-ranging ban on active sales, and not just on active sales into exclusive territories reserved to itself or allocated exclusively to other licensees.

The licensor may also ban passive sales into territories it has exclusively reserved for itself (Article 4(2)(b)(i)).

Additionally, under the previous block exemption, a licensor could ban a licensee from passively selling into the exclusive territory allocated to another licensee, although only for two years from the date on which the protected licensee first marketed the licensed products within its exclusive territory. This exception has been removed from the current TTBER, and so such a restriction on passive sales is now a hardcore restriction if it falls within Article 101(1). Nonetheless, para 126 of the TTBER Guidelines does state that such a restriction may fall outside Article 101(1) for a certain duration (up to a maximum of two years) where it is 'objectively necessary' to enable a protected licensee to penetrate a new market, eg where the licensee has to incur significant upfront costs before it can begin marketing the product.

(e) Does the agreement contain any excluded restrictions?

These are listed under Article 5. If a clause listed under Article 5 remains within the licence then the term itself will fall foul of the TTBER, but the rest of the licence can still benefit from the TTBER if the offending term can be severed. Whether or not the term can be severed is a matter of national law which governs the agreement (see **2.1.2**). In the event it cannot be severed, the whole of the agreement will fall outside the TTBER.

The excluded restrictions contained in Article 5 will generally apply to agreements between both competitors and non-competitors. Below is an outline of the main provisions:

(i) An obligation on the licensee exclusively to grant back to the licensor (or third party designated by the licensor) any improvements made to the licensed technology (Article 5(1)(a)).

(ii) An obligation on the licensee to assign to the licensor (or third party designated by the licensor) any improvements made to the licensed technology (Article 5(1)(a)).

(iii) Any obligation on the licensee in respect to challenging the validity of the licensor's IP rights (Article 5(1)(b)).

In addition, where the parties are non-competitors, there can be no restriction on the licensee's ability to exploit its own technology, nor any limit on either party's ability to carry out research and development (unless necessary to protect know-how) (Article 5(2)).

8.4 ARTICLE 102/CHAPTER II AND IP RIGHTS

This section will consider the extent to which the exercise of IP rights can amount to an abuse for the purposes of Article 102/Chapter II. Of course, it should be remembered that Article 102/Chapter II will apply only where the undertaking is dominant (as discussed in **Chapter 3**).

In terms of the basic position, it has been a long-established principle of the CJEU that there is a distinction between the existence of an IP right (which is acceptable) and its exercise (which may be challenged) (see Case 24/67 *Parke, Davis & Co v Probel* [1968] ECR 55). In relation to free movement within the EU, the doctrine of exhaustion of rights is not covered in this textbook. In relation to competition law, many areas are affected, including one discussed below: refusal to supply under Article 102. Other affected areas include standards setting, referred to in the context of US law where the debate originated (see **8.5.4**; the EU/UK position is not the same but is not discussed further here).

Refusal to supply and IP rights

The general principle is that an undertaking is entitled to refuse to license its proprietary intellectual property. However where that undertaking is dominant, it may be taking a risk. In certain circumstances, the refusal to license (or supply) may amount to an abuse under Article 102/Chapter II (see **3.4.2(c)**).

There may be obvious anti-competitive reasons for the refusal to supply (for example, if a licence is terminated because the licensee independently develops competing technology). In some cases, the intellectual property may constitute an 'essential facility'. In these situations, refusal to supply IP rights is likely to breach Article 102/Chapter II. Outside these circumstances, the CJEU traditionally has been reluctant to hold that a refusal to license IP rights could amount to an abuse. In Case 238/87 *Volvo v Erik Veng* [1988] ECR 6211, the ECJ held that a refusal by Volvo to license its IP rights in order for spare parts to be manufactured 'cannot in itself constitute an abuse of a dominant position'.

This traditional approach was not followed in *Magill* (Cases C-241/91 P and C-242/91 P *RTE and Independent Television Publications Ltd v Commission*) [1995] ECR I-743. This concerned the licensing of weekly TV listing information subject to copyright and owned respectively by the BBC, ITV (both British broadcasters) and RTE (the Irish broadcaster). Magill wished to produce a combined weekly listing magazine, which was not at that time available in the UK or Ireland but was very popular throughout mainland Europe. The broadcasters refused to license the information to Magill, a practice which the Commission held to amount to an abuse, as customers were deprived of the benefit of a weekly listing magazine. This decision was upheld by the CFI (now the General Court) and the ECJ. The case raised a number of issues, not least the extent to which (and the circumstances when) an IP owner with market power can be compelled to license its rights.

Subsequent CJEU cases have provided greater guidance in this regard. In Case C-7/97 *Bronner v Mediaprint* [1998] ECR I-7791, [1999] 4 CMLR 112, the ECJ stressed that compulsory licensing will be required only in exceptional cases and outlined some of the factors that would need to be considered. This was repeated and refined in Case C-418/01 *IMS Health GmbH & Co v NDC Health GmbH & Co* [2004] ECR I-5039. The CFI (now General Court) decision in Case T-201/04 *Microsoft v Commission* summarises the law:

- first, the refusal would have to relate to a product or service indispensable to the exercise of a particular activity on a neighbouring market;

- second, the refusal excludes any effective competition on that neighbouring market; and

- third, the refusal prevents the appearance of a new product for which there is potential consumer demand.

8.5 US ANTITRUST LAWS AND IP RIGHTS

Intellectual property laws in the United States provide the same basic types of rights as in Europe: patents, trade marks and copyrights. United States IP laws differ, however, in many details regarding the scope of the IP rights granted and the requirements for obtaining and preserving those rights.

The exercise of these IP rights has the potential of impairing competition. A patent holder can prevent a competitor from using a particular device, material or process. A trade mark holder can prevent a competitor from using a phrase, a symbol or a design to identify its goods or services. In the absence of the IP rights, such conduct might be a restraint of trade in violation of Section 1 of the Sherman Act or exclusionary conduct in violation of Section 2 of the Sherman Act, but if the conduct is nothing more than the exercise of rights conferred by the patent, trade mark or copyright laws, no antitrust violation will be found. The IP right is effectively a legal right to restrict competition. Antitrust issues arise when holders of IP rights attempt to restriction competition beyond the scope of the rights conferred by the IP laws.

8.5.1 Enforcement of IP rights

In some cases, efforts to enforce patents fail because the court finds that the patent is invalid, or the defendant's product or process did not infringe the patent, but the attempt at enforcement nonetheless discourages competition. The same is true for other types of IP rights. Although the finding of invalidity or non-infringement suggests the plaintiff had no IP rights to enforce, the attempt at enforcement generally does not violate the antitrust laws, because the outcome of infringement litigation is often uncertain, and IP rights would be worth much less if enforcement efforts carried a risk of antitrust liability. Courts have recognised a few exceptions to this general rule:

(a)   Procurement of a patent through fraud on the US Patent and Trademark Office, for example by a knowing failure to disclose prior art, is not immune from the antitrust laws (*Walker Process Equipment Inc v Food Machinery & Chemical Corp*, 382 US 172 (1965)).

(b)   The threat or filing of a sham enforcement proceeding is not immune from antitrust liability. A proceeding will be found a sham when (i) no reasonable litigant would expect to succeed on the merits, and (ii) the plaintiff is seeking to impair competitors with the process, rather than the outcome, of the litigation, for example by imposing costs or discouraging other companies from dealing with the defendant (*Professional Real Estate Investors, Inc v Columbia Pictures Industries*, 508 US 49 (1993)).

Settlements of patent infringement claims can raise antitrust issues. If the result of the settlement is that the defendant agrees to refrain from competitive activity that is broader than the scope of the patent at issue, the settlement can be found a horizontal restraint of trade and a Section 1 violation.

A subject of much controversy is the 'reverse settlement'. The defendant responds to a patent infringement claim by pleading either that the patent is invalid, or that its product or process does not infringe it. The parties then settle, with the patent holder paying the defendant in return for the defendant's agreement to refrain from the allegedly infringing conduct. This scenario arises frequently in the pharmaceutical industry, in disputes between brand-name and generic drug manufacturers. Several of these agreements have been challenged, characterising them as a sharing of monopoly profits to preserve an arguably invalid patent claim (*FTC v Actavis*, 570 US 136 (2013)). Some appellate courts have found reverse settlements legal, provided that the enforcement action was not a sham, reasoning that the patent rights must include the ability to settle infringement claims (*In re Tamoxifen Antitrust Citrate Litigation*, 466 F.3d 187 (2d Cir 2006)).

8.5.2 Patent licensing

Patent licenses can include terms that restrict competition by the licensee, but these terms are not antitrust violations if they impose no more of a restraint on competition than if the patent holder had issued no licences and had exercised the patent entirely on its own. On that basis, courts have held that no antitrust violation occurs in licenses that impose the following restrictions:

- minimum sale prices of patented products;
- exclusive territories or customers;
- discriminatory royalty and other terms; and
- unreasonably high royalties.

However, when a patent license restrains competition in fields beyond the scope of the patent itself, the license may violate Section 2 of the Sherman Act.

Antitrust issues may arise with cross-licenses, in which two or more companies agree to license each other on a package of patents, or pooling agreements, in which multiple patent holders license their patents to a third party, often a joint venture, which then issues further licenses for the pool of patents. These arrangements may be problematic when they involve competitors cross-licensing or pooling 'rival' patents, meaning that each patent performs the same function as the other without infringing the other patent. The following are examples of arrangements likely to be found illegal:

(a) Two competitors with rival patents agree to license each other, with one receiving exclusive rights to both patents in the eastern half of the US and the other retaining exclusive rights in the western half. A court would regard this arrangement as a sham license, designed to cover up a simple market allocation between horizontal competitors.

(b) Competitors with rival patents grant exclusive licences to their patents to a pool, managed by a joint venture that they control. The joint venture sets the royalties and other terms for licenses of patents in the pool. This arrangement accomplishes nothing more than the elimination of competition between the patent holders on licenses for their patents. A court would find it a *per se* violation of Section 1 of the Sherman Act.

Apart from such blatantly anti-competitive arrangements, courts will apply the Rule of Reason to cross-licensing and pooling agreements, and will find a violation only if the overall effect is to reduce competition. In many cases, the arrangements are found legal when they include 'blocking' patents, which are two or more patents each of which cannot be practised without infringing the other, and 'complementary' patents, which are two or more patents that must be practised to manufacture a particular product or to deliver a particular service. A cross-licensing or pooling arrangement is often the most efficient means of providing licenses to patents that are essential to effective competition.

The inclusion of rival patents in a cross-licensing or pooling arrangement is a factor suggesting an impairment of competition, but rival patents will not alone lead to a finding of illegality under the Rule of Reason. Other factors weighing towards a negative effect on competition are a high market share for the participants in the pool, the grant of exclusive patent rights to the pool, the inclusion of non-essential patents, and the inclusion of price and territorial terms that might impede competition between the licensors.

8.5.3 Patent tying

As discussed at **6.4.2**, a tying arrangement is an agreement to sell one product or service (the 'tying product') on the condition that the buyer also purchases a different product or service (the 'tied product'). For tying to violate Section 2 of the Sherman Act, the seller must have market power in the tying product. In many tying cases, the tying product is a patented product or service, or a patent license. A patent can be the basis for market power if it inhibits substantial competition for the tying product, but courts do not presume that patents necessarily have that effect (*Illinois Tool Works Inc v Independent Ink, Inc*, 547 US 28 (2006)). For example, if non-infringing products are readily available as a substitute for a patented product, proof of market power might fail.

8.5.4 Industry standards setting

In high-tech industries, firms often collaborate for industry standards on product specifications. Such standards can promote competition by ensuring that the products of different manufacturers are able to interconnect when necessary and that parts and accessories for a product can be developed by firms other than the original manufacturer. However, if an industry standard requires the use of technology covered by a patent, the adoption of that standard can create or enhance the monopoly power of the holder of that patent. To protect against that outcome, industry standards-setting organisations typically require that participants in the standards-setting process disclose all patents and patent applications applicable to any proposed standards (known as 'standard essential patents'), and that they commit to license on fair, reasonable and non-discriminatory (FRAND) terms all patents required to comply with the standards ultimately adopted. Antitrust issues have arisen when participants have failed to comply with these requirements for disclosure and FRAND licensing, in what is commonly known as a 'patent hold up'. A common example of a patent hold up is 'royalty stacking', a practice in which (i) the cumulative royalties paid for patents incorporated into a standard exceed the value of the feature implemented in the standard, and (ii) the aggregate royalties obtained for the various features of a product exceed the value of the product itself.

Appendices

Appendix 1

European Union Legislation

Treaty on the Functioning of the European Union

Article 101

1. The following shall be prohibited as incompatible with the internal market: all agreements between undertakings, decisions by associations of undertakings and concerted practices which may affect trade between Member States and which have as their object or effect the prevention, restriction or distortion of competition within the internal market, and in particular those which:

    (a)   directly or indirectly fix purchase or selling prices or any other trading conditions;

    (b)   limit or control production, markets, technical development, or investment;

    (c)   share markets or sources of supply;

    (d)   apply dissimilar conditions to equivalent transactions with other trading parties, thereby placing them at a competitive disadvantage;

    (e)   make the conclusion of contracts subject to acceptance by the other parties of supplementary obligations which, by their nature or according to commercial usage, have no connection with the subject of such contracts.

2. Any agreements or decisions prohibited pursuant to this article shall be automatically void.

3. The provisions of paragraph 1 may, however, be declared inapplicable in the case of:

    –   any agreement or category of agreements between undertakings,

    –   any decision or category of decisions by associations of undertakings,

    –   any concerted practice or category of concerted practices,

    which contributes to improving the production or distribution of goods or to promoting technical or economic progress, while allowing consumers a fair share of the resulting benefit, and which does not:

    (a)   impose on the undertakings concerned restrictions which are not indispensable to the attainment of these objectives;

    (b)   afford such undertakings the possibility of eliminating competition in respect of a substantial part of the products in question.

Article 102

Any abuse by one or more undertakings of a dominant position within the internal market or in a substantial part of it shall be prohibited as incompatible with the internal market in so far as it may affect trade between Member States.

Such abuse may, in particular, consist in:

(a)   directly or indirectly imposing unfair purchase or selling prices or other unfair trading conditions;

(b)   limiting production, markets or technical development to the prejudice of consumers;

(c)   applying dissimilar conditions to equivalent transactions with other trading parties, thereby placing them at a competitive disadvantage;

(d)   making the conclusion of contracts subject to acceptance by the other parties of supplementary obligations which, by their nature or according to commercial usage, have no connection with the subject of such contracts.

Appendix 2
UK Legislation

Competition Act 1998

The Chapter I prohibition

2.   Agreements etc. preventing, restricting or distorting competition

   (1)   Subject to section 3, agreements between undertakings, decisions by associations of undertakings or concerted practices which—

      (a)   may affect trade within the United Kingdom, and

      (b)   have as their object or effect the prevention, restriction or distortion of competition within the United Kingdom,

are prohibited unless they are exempt in accordance with the provisions of this Part.

   (2)   Subsection (1) applies, in particular, to agreements, decisions or practices which—

      (a)   directly or indirectly fix purchase or selling prices or any other trading conditions;

      (b)   limit or control production, markets, technical development or investment;

      (c)   share markets or sources of supply;

      (d)   apply dissimilar conditions to equivalent transactions with other trading parties, thereby placing them at a competitive disadvantage;

      (e)   make the conclusion of contracts subject to acceptance by the other parties of supplementary obligations which, by their nature or according to commercial usage, have no connection with the subject of such contracts.

   (3)   Subsection (1) applies only if the agreement, decision or practice is, or is intended to be, implemented in the United Kingdom.

   (4)   Any agreement or decision which is prohibited by subsection (1) is void.

   (5)   A provision of this Part which is expressed to apply to, or in relation to, an agreement is to be read as applying equally to, or in relation to, a decision by an association of undertakings or a concerted practice (but with any necessary modifications).

   (6)   Subsection (5) does not apply where the context otherwise requires.

   (7)   In this section 'the United Kingdom' means, in relation to an agreement which operates or is intended to operate only in a part of the United Kingdom, that part.

   (8)   The prohibition imposed by subsection (1) is referred to in this Act as 'the Chapter I prohibition'.

The Chapter II prohibition

18.   Abuse of dominant position

   (1)   Subject to section 19, any conduct on the part of one or more undertakings which amounts to the abuse of a dominant position in a market is prohibited if it may affect trade within the United Kingdom.

   (2)   Conduct may, in particular, constitute such an abuse if it consists in—

    (a)   directly, or indirectly imposing unfair purchase or selling prices or other unfair trading conditions;

    (b)   limiting production, markets or technical development to the prejudice of consumers;

    (c)   applying dissimilar conditions to equivalent transactions with other trading parties, thereby placing them at a competitive disadvantage;

    (d)   making the conclusion of contracts subject to acceptance by the other parties of supplementary obligations which, by their nature or according to commercial usage, have no connection with the subject of the contracts.

(3)   In this section—

'dominant position' means a dominant position within the United Kingdom; and

'the United Kingdom' means the United Kingdom or any part of it.

(4)   The prohibition imposed by subsection (1) is referred to in this Act as 'the Chapter II prohibition'.

Appendix 3

US Legislation

Sherman Act § 1, 15 USC § 1

Every contract, combination in the form of trust or otherwise, or conspiracy, in restraint of trade or commerce among the several States, or with foreign nations, is declared to be illegal. Every person who shall make any contract or engage in any combination or conspiracy hereby declared to be illegal shall be deemed guilty of a felony, and, on conviction thereof, shall be punished by fine not exceeding $100,000,000 if a corporation, or, if any other person, $1,000,000, or by imprisonment not exceeding 10 years, or by both said punishments, in the discretion of the court.

Sherman Act § 2, 15 USC § 2

Every person who shall monopolize, or attempt to monopolize, or combine or conspire with any other person or persons, to monopolize any part of the trade or commerce among the several States, or with foreign nations, shall be deemed guilty of a felony, and, on conviction thereof, shall be punished by fine not exceeding $100,000,000 if a corporation, or, if any other person, $1,000,000, or by imprisonment not exceeding 10 years, or by both said punishments, in the discretion of the court.

Appendix 4

Regulation 1 (extract)

The wording contained in this Appendix is taken from the *Official Journal* of the EU. As such it does not reflect the renumbering of treaty articles introduced by the Treaty on the Functioning of the European Union.

Council Regulation (EC) No 1/2003 of 16 December 2002 on the implementation of the rules on competition laid down in Articles 81 and 82 of the Treaty

THE COUNCIL OF THE EUROPEAN UNION

...

HAS ADOPTED THIS REGULATION:

CHAPTER I

PRINCIPLES

Article 1

Application of Articles 81 and 82 of the Treaty

1. Agreements, decisions and concerted practices caught by Article 81(1) of the Treaty which do not satisfy the conditions of Article 81(3) of the Treaty shall be prohibited, no prior decision to that effect being required.

2. Agreements, decisions and concerted practices caught by Article 81(1) of the Treaty which satisfy the conditions of Article 81(3) of the Treaty shall not be prohibited, no prior decision to that effect being required.

3. The abuse of a dominant position referred to in Article 82 of the Treaty shall be prohibited, no prior decision to that effect being required.

Article 2

Burden of proof

In any national or Community proceedings for the application of Articles 81 and 82 of the Treaty, the burden of proving an infringement of Article 81(1) or of Article 82 of the Treaty shall rest on the party or the authority alleging the infringement. The undertaking or association of undertakings claiming the benefit of Article 81(3) of the Treaty shall bear the burden of proving that the conditions of that paragraph are fulfilled.

Article 3

Relationship between Articles 81 and 82 of the Treaty and national competition laws

1. Where the competition authorities of the Member States or national courts apply national competition law to agreements, decisions by associations of undertakings or concerted practices within the meaning of Article 81(1) of the Treaty which may affect trade between Member States within the meaning of that provision, they shall also apply Article 81 of the Treaty to such agreements, decisions or concerted practices. Where the competition authorities of the Member States or national courts apply national competition law to any abuse prohibited by Article 82 of the Treaty, they shall also apply Article 82 of the Treaty.

2. The application of national competition law may not lead to the prohibition of agreements, decisions by associations of undertakings or concerted practices which may affect trade between Member States but which do not restrict competition within the meaning of Article 81(1) of the Treaty, or which fulfil the conditions of Article 81(3)

of the Treaty or which are covered by a Regulation for the application of Article 81(3) of the Treaty. Member States shall not under this Regulation be precluded from adopting and applying on their territory stricter national laws which prohibit or sanction unilateral conduct engaged in by undertakings.

3.   Without prejudice to general principles and other provisions of Community law, paragraphs 1 and 2 do not apply when the competition authorities and the courts of the Member States apply national merger control laws nor do they preclude the application of provisions of national law that predominantly pursue an objective different from that pursued by Articles 81 and 82 of the Treaty.

CHAPTER II
POWERS

Article 4
Powers of the Commission

For the purpose of applying Articles 81 and 82 of the Treaty, the Commission shall have the powers provided for by this Regulation.

Article 5
Powers of the competition authorities of the Member States

The competition authorities of the Member States shall have the power to apply Articles 81 and 82 of the Treaty in individual cases. For this purpose, acting on their own initiative or on a complaint, they may take the following decisions:

–   requiring that an infringement be brought to an end,

–   ordering interim measures,

–   accepting commitments,

–   imposing fines, periodic penalty payments or any other penalty provided for in their national law.

Where on the basis of the information in their possession the conditions for prohibition are not met they may likewise decide that there are no grounds for action on their part.

Article 6
Powers of the national courts

National courts shall have the power to apply Articles 81 and 82 of the Treaty.

CHAPTER III
COMMISSION DECISIONS

Article 7
Finding and termination of infringement

1.   Where the Commission, acting on a complaint or on its own initiative, finds that there is an infringement of Article 81 or of Article 82 of the Treaty, it may by decision require the undertakings and associations of undertakings concerned to bring such infringement to an end. For this purpose, it may impose on them any behavioural or structural remedies which are proportionate to the infringement committed and necessary to bring the infringement effectively to an end. Structural remedies can only be imposed either where there is no equally effective behavioural remedy or where any equally effective behavioural remedy would be more burdensome for the undertaking concerned than the structural remedy. If the Commission has a legitimate interest in doing so, it may also find that an infringement has been committed in the past.

2. Those entitled to lodge a complaint for the purposes of paragraph 1 are natural or legal persons who can show a legitimate interest and Member States.

Article 8
Interim measures

1. In cases of urgency due to the risk of serious and irreparable damage to competition, the Commission, acting on its own initiative may by decision, on the basis of a prima facie finding of infringement, order interim measures.

2. A decision under paragraph 1 shall apply for a specified period of time and may be renewed in so far this is necessary and appropriate.

Article 9
Commitments

1. Where the Commission intends to adopt a decision requiring that an infringement be brought to an end and the undertakings concerned offer commitments to meet the concerns expressed to them by the Commission in its preliminary assessment, the Commission may by decision make those commitments binding on the undertakings. Such a decision may be adopted for a specified period and shall conclude that there are no longer grounds for action by the Commission.

2. The Commission may, upon request or on its own initiative, reopen the proceedings:
    (a) where there has been a material change in any of the facts on which the decision was based;
    (b) where the undertakings concerned act contrary to their commitments; or
    (c) where the decision was based on incomplete, incorrect or misleading information provided by the parties.

Article 10
Finding of inapplicability

Where the Community public interest relating to the application of Articles 81 and 82 of the Treaty so requires, the Commission, acting on its own initiative, may by decision find that Article 81 of the Treaty is not applicable to an agreement, a decision by an association of undertakings or a concerted practice, either because the conditions of Article 81(1) of the Treaty are not fulfilled, or because the conditions of Article 81(3) of the Treaty are satisfied.

The Commission may likewise make such a finding with reference to Article 82 of the Treaty.

CHAPTER IV
COOPERATION

Article 11
Cooperation between the Commission and the competition authorities
of the Member States

1. The Commission and the competition authorities of the Member States shall apply the Community competition rules in close cooperation.

2. The Commission shall transmit to the competition authorities of the Member States copies of the most important documents it has collected with a view to applying Articles 7, 8, 9, 10 and Article 29(1). At the request of the competition authority of a Member State, the Commission shall provide it with a copy of other existing documents necessary for the assessment of the case.

3. The competition authorities of the Member States shall, when acting under Article 81 or Article 82 of the Treaty, inform the Commission in writing before or without delay after

commencing the first formal investigative measure. This information may also be made available to the competition authorities of the other Member States.

4. No later than 30 days before the adoption of a decision requiring that an infringement be brought to an end, accepting commitments or withdrawing the benefit of a block exemption Regulation, the competition authorities of the Member States shall inform the Commission. To that effect, they shall provide the Commission with a summary of the case, the envisaged decision or, in the absence thereof, any other document indicating the proposed course of action. This information may also be made available to the competition authorities of the other Member States. At the request of the Commission, the acting competition authority shall make available to the Commission other documents it holds which are necessary for the assessment of the case. The information supplied to the Commission may be made available to the competition authorities of the other Member States. National competition authorities may also exchange between themselves information necessary for the assessment of a case that they are dealing with under Article 81 or Article 82 of the Treaty.

5. The competition authorities of the Member States may consult the Commission on any case involving the application of Community law.

6. The initiation by the Commission of proceedings for the adoption of a decision under Chapter III shall relieve the competition authorities of the Member States of their competence to apply Articles 81 and 82 of the Treaty. If a competition authority of a Member State is already acting on a case, the Commission shall only initiate proceedings after consulting with that national competition authority.

Article 12
Exchange of information

1. For the purpose of applying Articles 81 and 82 of the Treaty the Commission and the competition authorities of the Member States shall have the power to provide one another with and use in evidence any matter of fact or of law, including confidential information.

2. Information exchanged shall only be used in evidence for the purpose of applying Article 81 or Article 82 of the Treaty and in respect of the subject-matter for which it was collected by the transmitting authority. However, where national competition law is applied in the same case and in parallel to Community competition law and does not lead to a different outcome, information exchanged under this Article may also be used for the application of national competition law.

3. Information exchanged pursuant to paragraph 1 can only be used in evidence to impose sanctions on natural persons where:
   - the law of the transmitting authority foresees sanctions of a similar kind in relation to an infringement of Article 81 or Article 82 of the Treaty or, in the absence thereof,
   - the information has been collected in a way which respects the same level of protection of the rights of defence of natural persons as provided for under the national rules of the receiving authority. However, in this case, the information exchanged cannot be used by the receiving authority to impose custodial sanctions.

Article 13
Suspension or termination of proceedings

1. Where competition authorities of two or more Member States have received a complaint or are acting on their own initiative under Article 81 or Article 82 of the Treaty against

the same agreement, decision of an association or practice, the fact that one authority is dealing with the case shall be sufficient grounds for the others to suspend the proceedings before them or to reject the complaint. The Commission may likewise reject a complaint on the ground that a competition authority of a Member State is dealing with the case.

2. Where a competition authority of a Member State or the Commission has received a complaint against an agreement, decision of an association or practice which has already been dealt with by another competition authority, it may reject it.

Article 14
Advisory Committee

1. The Commission shall consult an Advisory Committee on Restrictive Practices and Dominant Positions prior to the taking of any decision under Articles 7, 8, 9, 10, 23, Article 24(2) and Article 29(1).

2. For the discussion of individual cases, the Advisory Committee shall be composed of representatives of the competition authorities of the Member States. For meetings in which issues other than individual cases are being discussed, an additional Member State representative competent in competition matters may be appointed. Representatives may, if unable to attend, be replaced by other representatives.

3. The consultation may take place at a meeting convened and chaired by the Commission, held not earlier than 14 days after dispatch of the notice convening it, together with a summary of the case, an indication of the most important documents and a preliminary draft decision. In respect of decisions pursuant to Article 8, the meeting may be held seven days after the dispatch of the operative part of a draft decision. Where the Commission dispatches a notice convening the meeting which gives a shorter period of notice than those specified above, the meeting may take place on the proposed date in the absence of an objection by any Member State. The Advisory Committee shall deliver a written opinion on the Commission's preliminary draft decision. It may deliver an opinion even if some members are absent and are not represented. At the request of one or several members, the positions stated in the opinion shall be reasoned.

4. Consultation may also take place by written procedure. However, if any Member State so requests, the Commission shall convene a meeting. In case of written procedure, the Commission shall determine a time-limit of not less than 14 days within which the Member States are to put forward their observations for circulation to all other Member States. In case of decisions to be taken pursuant to Article 8, the time-limit of 14 days is replaced by seven days. Where the Commission determines a time-limit for the written procedure which is shorter than those specified above, the proposed time-limit shall be applicable in the absence of an objection by any Member State.

5. The Commission shall take the utmost account of the opinion delivered by the Advisory Committee. It shall inform the Committee of the manner in which its opinion has been taken into account.

6. Where the Advisory Committee delivers a written opinion, this opinion shall be appended to the draft decision. If the Advisory Committee recommends publication of the opinion, the Commission shall carry out such publication taking into account the legitimate interest of undertakings in the protection of their business secrets.

7. At the request of a competition authority of a Member State, the Commission shall include on the agenda of the Advisory Committee cases that are being dealt with by a competition authority of a Member State under Article 81 or Article 82 of the Treaty. The Commission may also do so on its own initiative. In either case, the Commission shall inform the competition authority concerned.

A request may in particular be made by a competition authority of a Member State in respect of a case where the Commission intends to initiate proceedings with the effect of Article 11(6).

The Advisory Committee shall not issue opinions on cases dealt with by competition authorities of the Member States. The Advisory Committee may also discuss general issues of Community competition law.

Article 15
Cooperation with national courts

1. In proceedings for the application of Article 81 or Article 82 of the Treaty, courts of the Member States may ask the Commission to transmit to them information in its possession or its opinion on questions concerning the application of the Community competition rules.

2. Member States shall forward to the Commission a copy of any written judgment of national courts deciding on the application of Article 81 or Article 82 of the Treaty. Such copy shall be forwarded without delay after the full written judgment is notified to the parties.

3. Competition authorities of the Member States, acting on their own initiative, may submit written observations to the national courts of their Member State on issues relating to the application of Article 81 or Article 82 of the Treaty. With the permission of the court in question, they may also submit oral observations to the national courts of their Member State. Where the coherent application of Article 81 or Article 82 of the Treaty so requires, the Commission, acting on its own initiative, may submit written observations to courts of the Member States. With the permission of the court in question, it may also make oral observations.

   For the purpose of the preparation of their observations only, the competition authorities of the Member States and the Commission may request the relevant court of the Member State to transmit or ensure the transmission to them of any documents necessary for the assessment of the case.

4. This Article is without prejudice to wider powers to make observations before courts conferred on competition authorities of the Member States under the law of their Member State.

Article 16
Uniform application of Community competition law

1. When national courts rule on agreements, decisions or practices under Article 81 or Article 82 of the Treaty which are already the subject of a Commission decision, they cannot take decisions running counter to the decision adopted by the Commission. They must also avoid giving decisions which would conflict with a decision contemplated by the Commission in proceedings it has initiated. To that effect, the national court may assess whether it is necessary to stay its proceedings. This obligation is without prejudice to the rights and obligations under Article 234 of the Treaty.

2. When competition authorities of the Member States rule on agreements, decisions or practices under Article 81 or Article 82 of the Treaty which are already the subject of a Commission decision, they cannot take decisions which would run counter to the decision adopted by the Commission.

CHAPTER V
POWERS OF INVESTIGATION

Article 17
Investigations into sectors of the economy and into types of agreements

1. Where the trend of trade between Member States, the rigidity of prices or other circumstances suggest that competition may be restricted or distorted within the common market, the Commission may conduct its inquiry into a particular sector of the economy or into a particular type of agreements across various sectors. In the course of that inquiry, the Commission may request the undertakings or associations of undertakings concerned to supply the information necessary for giving effect to Articles 81 and 82 of the Treaty and may carry out any inspections necessary for that purpose.

   The Commission may in particular request the undertakings or associations of undertakings concerned to communicate to it all agreements, decisions and concerted practices.

   The Commission may publish a report on the results of its inquiry into particular sectors of the economy or particular types of agreements across various sectors and invite comments from interested parties.

2. Articles 14, 18, 19, 20, 22, 23 and 24 shall apply mutatis mutandis.

Article 18
Requests for information

1. In order to carry out the duties assigned to it by this Regulation, the Commission may, by simple request or by decision, require undertakings and associations of undertakings to provide all necessary information.

2. When sending a simple request for information to an undertaking or association of undertakings, the Commission shall state the legal basis and the purpose of the request, specify what information is required and fix the time-limit within which the information is to be provided, and the penalties provided for in Article 23 for supplying incorrect or misleading information.

3. Where the Commission requires undertakings and associations of undertakings to supply information by decision, it shall state the legal basis and the purpose of the request, specify what information is required and fix the time-limit within which it is to be provided. It shall also indicate the penalties provided for in Article 23 and indicate or impose the penalties provided for in Article 24. It shall further indicate the right to have the decision reviewed by the Court of Justice.

4. The owners of the undertakings or their representatives and, in the case of legal persons, companies or firms, or associations having no legal personality, the persons authorised to represent them by law or by their constitution shall supply the information requested on behalf of the undertaking or the association of undertakings concerned. Lawyers duly authorised to act may supply the information on behalf of their clients. The latter shall remain fully responsible if the information supplied is incomplete, incorrect or misleading.

5. The Commission shall without delay forward a copy of the simple request or of the decision to the competition authority of the Member State in whose territory the seat of the undertaking or association of undertakings is situated and the competition authority of the Member State whose territory is affected.

6. At the request of the Commission the governments and competition authorities of the Member States shall provide the Commission with all necessary information to carry out the duties assigned to it by this Regulation.

Article 19
Power to take statements

1. In order to carry out the duties assigned to it by this Regulation, the Commission may interview any natural or legal person who consents to be interviewed for the purpose of collecting information relating to the subject-matter of an investigation.

2. Where an interview pursuant to paragraph 1 is conducted in the premises of an undertaking, the Commission shall inform the competition authority of the Member State in whose territory the interview takes place. If so requested by the competition authority of that Member State, its officials may assist the officials and other accompanying persons authorised by the Commission to conduct the interview.

Article 20
The Commission's powers of inspection

1. In order to carry out the duties assigned to it by this Regulation, the Commission may conduct all necessary inspections of undertakings and associations of undertakings.

2. The officials and other accompanying persons authorised by the Commission to conduct an inspection are empowered:

    (a) to enter any premises, land and means of transport of undertakings and associations of undertakings;

    (b) to examine the books and other records related to the business, irrespective of the medium on which they are stored;

    (c) to take or obtain in any form copies of or extracts from such books or records;

    (d) to seal any business premises and books or records for the period and to the extent necessary for the inspection;

    (e) to ask any representative or member of staff of the undertaking or association of undertakings for explanations on facts or documents relating to the subject-matter and purpose of the inspection and to record the answers.

3. The officials and other accompanying persons authorised by the Commission to conduct an inspection shall exercise their powers upon production of a written authorisation specifying the subject matter and purpose of the inspection and the penalties provided for in Article 23 in case the production of the required books or other records related to the business is incomplete or where the answers to questions asked under paragraph 2 of the present Article are incorrect or misleading. In good time before the inspection, the Commission shall give notice of the inspection to the competition authority of the Member State in whose territory it is to be conducted.

4. Undertakings and associations of undertakings are required to submit to inspections ordered by decision of the Commission. The decision shall specify the subject matter and purpose of the inspection, appoint the date on which it is to begin and indicate the penalties provided for in Articles 23 and 24 and the right to have the decision reviewed by the Court of Justice. The Commission shall take such decisions after consulting the competition authority of the Member State in whose territory the inspection is to be conducted.

5. Officials of as well as those authorised or appointed by the competition authority of the Member State in whose territory the inspection is to be conducted shall, at the request of that authority or of the Commission, actively assist the officials and other accompanying persons authorised by the Commission. To this end, they shall enjoy the powers specified in paragraph 2.

6. Where the officials and other accompanying persons authorised by the Commission find that an undertaking opposes an inspection ordered pursuant to this Article, the

Member State concerned shall afford them the necessary assistance, requesting where appropriate the assistance of the police or of an equivalent enforcement authority, so as to enable them to conduct their inspection.

7. If the assistance provided for in paragraph 6 requires authorisation from a judicial authority according to national rules, such authorisation shall be applied for. Such authorisation may also be applied for as a precautionary measure.

8. Where authorisation as referred to in paragraph 7 is applied for, the national judicial authority shall control that the Commission decision is authentic and that the coercive measures envisaged are neither arbitrary nor excessive having regard to the subject matter of the inspection. In its control of the proportionality of the coercive measures, the national judicial authority may ask the Commission, directly or through the Member State competition authority, for detailed explanations in particular on the grounds the Commission has for suspecting infringement of Articles 81 and 82 of the Treaty, as well as on the seriousness of the suspected infringement and on the nature of the involvement of the undertaking concerned. However, the national judicial authority may not call into question the necessity for the inspection nor demand that it be provided with the information in the Commission's file. The lawfulness of the Commission decision shall be subject to review only by the Court of Justice.

Article 21
Inspection of other premises

1. If a reasonable suspicion exists that books or other records related to the business and to the subject-matter of the inspection, which may be relevant to prove a serious violation of Article 81 or Article 82 of the Treaty, are being kept in any other premises, land and means of transport, including the homes of directors, managers and other members of staff of the undertakings and associations of undertakings concerned, the Commission can by decision order an inspection to be conducted in such other premises, land and means of transport.

2. The decision shall specify the subject matter and purpose of the inspection, appoint the date on which it is to begin and indicate the right to have the decision reviewed by the Court of Justice. It shall in particular state the reasons that have led the Commission to conclude that a suspicion in the sense of paragraph 1 exists. The Commission shall take such decisions after consulting the competition authority of the Member State in whose territory the inspection is to be conducted.

3. A decision adopted pursuant to paragraph 1 cannot be executed without prior authorisation from the national judicial authority of the Member State concerned. The national judicial authority shall control that the Commission decision is authentic and that the coercive measures envisaged are neither arbitrary nor excessive having regard in particular to the seriousness of the suspected infringement, to the importance of the evidence sought, to the involvement of the undertaking concerned and to the reasonable likelihood that business books and records relating to the subject matter of the inspection are kept in the premises for which the authorisation is requested. The national judicial authority may ask the Commission, directly or through the Member State competition authority, for detailed explanations on those elements which are necessary to allow its control of the proportionality of the coercive measures envisaged.

    However, the national judicial authority may not call into question the necessity for the inspection nor demand that it be provided with information in the Commission's file. The lawfulness of the Commission decision shall be subject to review only by the Court of Justice.

4. The officials and other accompanying persons authorised by the Commission to conduct an inspection ordered in accordance with paragraph 1 of this Article shall have the powers set out in Article 20(2)(a), (b) and (c). Article 20(5) and (6) shall apply mutatis mutandis.

Article 22
Investigations by competition authorities of Member States

1. The competition authority of a Member State may in its own territory carry out any inspection or other fact-finding measure under its national law on behalf and for the account of the competition authority of another Member State in order to establish whether there has been an infringement of Article 81 or Article 82 of the Treaty. Any exchange and use of the information collected shall be carried out in accordance with Article 12.

2. At the request of the Commission, the competition authorities of the Member States shall undertake the inspections which the Commission considers to be necessary under Article 20(1) or which it has ordered by decision pursuant to Article 20(4). The officials of the competition authorities of the Member States who are responsible for conducting these inspections as well as those authorised or appointed by them shall exercise their powers in accordance with their national law.

    If so requested by the Commission or by the competition authority of the Member State in whose territory the inspection is to be conducted, officials and other accompanying persons authorised by the Commission may assist the officials of the authority concerned.

CHAPTER VI
PENALTIES

Article 23
Fines

1. The Commission may by decision impose on undertakings and associations of undertakings fines not exceeding 1% of the total turnover in the preceding business year where, intentionally or negligently:

    (a) they supply incorrect or misleading information in response to a request made pursuant to Article 17 or Article 18(2);

    (b) in response to a request made by decision adopted pursuant to Article 17 or Article 18(3), they supply incorrect, incomplete or misleading information or do not supply information within the required time-limit;

    (c) they produce the required books or other records related to the business in incomplete form during inspections under Article 20 or refuse to submit to inspections ordered by a decision adopted pursuant to Article 20(4);

    (d) in response to a question asked in accordance with Article 20(2)(e),

    –   they give an incorrect or misleading answer,

    –   they fail to rectify within a time-limit set by the Commission an incorrect, incomplete or misleading answer given by a member of staff, or

    –   they fail or refuse to provide a complete answer on facts relating to the subject-matter and purpose of an inspection ordered by a decision adopted pursuant to Article 20(4);

    (e) seals affixed in accordance with Article 20(2)(d) by officials or other accompanying persons authorised by the Commission have been broken.

2.   The Commission may by decision impose fines on undertakings and associations of undertakings where, either intentionally or negligently:

(a)   they infringe Article 81 or Article 82 of the Treaty; or

(b)   they contravene a decision ordering interim measures under Article 8; or

(c)   they fail to comply with a commitment made binding by a decision pursuant to Article 9.

For each undertaking and association of undertakings participating in the infringement, the fine shall not exceed 10% of its total turnover in the preceding business year.

Where the infringement of an association relates to the activities of its members, the fine shall not exceed 10% of the sum of the total turnover of each member active on the market affected by the infringement of the association.

3.   In fixing the amount of the fine, regard shall be had both to the gravity and to the duration of the infringement.

4.   When a fine is imposed on an association of undertakings taking account of the turnover of its members and the association is not solvent, the association is obliged to call for contributions from its members to cover the amount of the fine.

Where such contributions have not been made to the association within a time-limit fixed by the Commission, the Commission may require payment of the fine directly by any of the undertakings whose representatives were members of the decision-making bodies concerned of the association.

After the Commission has required payment under the second subparagraph, where necessary to ensure full payment of the fine, the Commission may require payment of the balance by any of the members of the association which were active on the market on which the infringement occurred.

However, the Commission shall not require payment under the second or the third subparagraph from undertakings which show that they have not implemented the infringing decision of the association and either were not aware of its existence or have actively distanced themselves from it before the Commission started investigating the case.

The financial liability of each undertaking in respect of the payment of the fine shall not exceed 10% of its total turnover in the preceding business year.

5.   Decisions taken pursuant to paragraphs 1 and 2 shall not be of a criminal law nature.

Article 24
Periodic penalty payments

1.   The Commission may, by decision, impose on undertakings or associations of undertakings periodic penalty payments not exceeding 5 % of the average daily turnover in the preceding business year per day and calculated from the date appointed by the decision, in order to compel them:

(a)   to put an end to an infringement of Article 81 or Article 82 of the Treaty, in accordance with a decision taken pursuant to Article 7;

(b)   to comply with a decision ordering interim measures taken pursuant to Article 8;

(c)   to comply with a commitment made binding by a decision pursuant to Article 9;

(d)   to supply complete and correct information which it has requested by decision taken pursuant to Article 17 or Article 18(3);

(e)   to submit to an inspection which it has ordered by decision taken pursuant to Article 20(4).

2. Where the undertakings or associations of undertakings have satisfied the obligation which the periodic penalty payment was intended to enforce, the Commission may fix the definitive amount of the periodic penalty payment at a figure lower than that which would arise under the original decision. Article 23(4) shall apply correspondingly.

CHAPTER VII
LIMITATION PERIODS

Article 25
Limitation periods for the imposition of penalties

1. The powers conferred on the Commission by Articles 23 and 24 shall be subject to the following limitation periods:
    (a) three years in the case of infringements of provisions concerning requests for information or the conduct of inspections;
    (b) five years in the case of all other infringements.
2. Time shall begin to run on the day on which the infringement is committed. However, in the case of continuing or repeated infringements, time shall begin to run on the day on which the infringement ceases.
3. Any action taken by the Commission or by the competition authority of a Member State for the purpose of the investigation or proceedings in respect of an infringement shall interrupt the limitation period for the imposition of fines or periodic penalty payments. The limitation period shall be interrupted with effect from the date on which the action is notified to at least one undertaking or association of undertakings which has participated in the infringement. Actions which interrupt the running of the period shall include in particular the following:
    (a) written requests for information by the Commission or by the competition authority of a Member State;
    (b) written authorisations to conduct inspections issued to its officials by the Commission or by the competition authority of a Member State;
    (c) the initiation of proceedings by the Commission or by the competition authority of a Member State;
    (d) notification of the statement of objections of the Commission or of the competition authority of a Member State.
4. The interruption of the limitation period shall apply for all the undertakings or associations of undertakings which have participated in the infringement.
5. Each interruption shall start time running afresh. However, the limitation period shall expire at the latest on the day on which a period equal to twice the limitation period has elapsed without the Commission having imposed a fine or a periodic penalty payment. That period shall be extended by the time during which limitation is suspended pursuant to paragraph 6.
6. The limitation period for the imposition of fines or periodic penalty payments shall be suspended for as long as the decision of the Commission is the subject of proceedings pending before the Court of Justice.

Article 26
Limitation period for the enforcement of penalties

1. The power of the Commission to enforce decisions taken pursuant to Articles 23 and 24 shall be subject to a limitation period of five years.
2. Time shall begin to run on the day on which the decision becomes final.
3. The limitation period for the enforcement of penalties shall be interrupted:

(a) by notification of a decision varying the original amount of the fine or periodic penalty payment or refusing an application for variation;

(b) by any action of the Commission or of a Member State, acting at the request of the Commission, designed to enforce payment of the fine or periodic penalty payment.

4. Each interruption shall start time running afresh.

5. The limitation period for the enforcement of penalties shall be suspended for so long as:

(a) time to pay is allowed;

(b) enforcement of payment is suspended pursuant to a decision of the Court of Justice.

CHAPTER VIII
HEARINGS AND PROFESSIONAL SECRECY

Article 27
Hearing of the parties, complainants and others

1. Before taking decisions as provided for in Articles 7, 8, 23 and Article 24(2), the Commission shall give the undertakings or associations of undertakings which are the subject of the proceedings conducted by the Commission the opportunity of being heard on the matters to which the Commission has taken objection. The Commission shall base its decisions only on objections on which the parties concerned have been able to comment. Complainants shall be associated closely with the proceedings.

2. The rights of defence of the parties concerned shall be fully respected in the proceedings. They shall be entitled to have access to the Commission's file, subject to the legitimate interest of undertakings in the protection of their business secrets. The right of access to the file shall not extend to confidential information and internal documents of the Commission or the competition authorities of the Member States. In particular, the right of access shall not extend to correspondence between the Commission and the competition authorities of the Member States, or between the latter, including documents drawn up pursuant to Articles 11 and 14. Nothing in this paragraph shall prevent the Commission from disclosing and using information necessary to prove an infringement.

3. If the Commission considers it necessary, it may also hear other natural or legal persons. Applications to be heard on the part of such persons shall, where they show a sufficient interest, be granted. The competition authorities of the Member States may also ask the Commission to hear other natural or legal persons.

4. Where the Commission intends to adopt a decision pursuant to Article 9 or Article 10, it shall publish a concise summary of the case and the main content of the commitments or of the proposed course of action. Interested third parties may submit their observations within a time limit which is fixed by the Commission in its publication and which may not be less than one month. Publication shall have regard to the legitimate interest of undertakings in the protection of their business secrets.

Article 28
Professional secrecy

1. Without prejudice to Articles 12 and 15, information collected pursuant to Articles 17 to 22 shall be used only for the purpose for which it was acquired.

2. Without prejudice to the exchange and to the use of information foreseen in Articles 11, 12, 14, 15 and 27, the Commission and the competition authorities of the Member

States, their officials, servants and other persons working under the supervision of these authorities as well as officials and civil servants of other authorities of the Member States shall not disclose information acquired or exchanged by them pursuant to this Regulation and of the kind covered by the obligation of professional secrecy. This obligation also applies to all representatives and experts of Member States attending meetings of the Advisory Committee pursuant to Article 14.

CHAPTER IX
EXEMPTION REGULATIONS

Article 29
Withdrawal in individual cases

1. Where the Commission, empowered by a Council Regulation, such as Regulations 19/65/EEC, (EEC) No 2821/71, (EEC) No 3976/87, (EEC) No 1534/91 or (EEC) No 479/92, to apply Article 81(3) of the Treaty by regulation, has declared Article 81(1) of the Treaty inapplicable to certain categories of agreements, decisions by associations of undertakings or concerted practices, it may, acting on its own initiative or on a complaint, withdraw the benefit of such an exemption Regulation when it finds that in any particular case an agreement, decision or concerted practice to which the exemption Regulation applies has certain effects which are incompatible with Article 81(3) of the Treaty.

2. Where, in any particular case, agreements, decisions by associations of undertakings or concerted practices to which a Commission Regulation referred to in paragraph 1 applies have effects which are incompatible with Article 81(3) of the Treaty in the territory of a Member State, or in a part thereof, which has all the characteristics of a distinct geographic market, the competition authority of that Member State may withdraw the benefit of the Regulation in question in respect of that territory.

Appendix 5

Notice on Agreements of Minor Importance (extract)

COMMUNICATION FROM THE COMMISSION

Notice on agreements of minor importance which do not appreciably restrict competition under Article 101(1) of the Treaty on the Functioning of the European Union (De Minimis Notice) (2014/C 291/01)

I.

1. Article 101(1) of the Treaty on the Functioning of the European Union prohibits agreements between undertakings which may affect trade between Member States and which have as their object or effect the prevention, restriction or distortion of competition within the internal market. The Court of Justice of the European Union has clarified that that provision is not applicable where the impact of the agreement on trade between Member States or on competition is not appreciable.

2. The Court of Justice has also clarified that an agreement which may affect trade between Member States and which has as its object the prevention, restriction or distortion of competition within the internal market constitutes, by its nature and independently of any concrete effects that it may have, an appreciable restriction of competition. This Notice therefore does not cover agreements which have as their object the prevention, restriction or distortion of competition within the internal market.

3. In this Notice the Commission indicates, with the help of market share thresholds, the circumstances in which it considers that agreements which may have as their effect the prevention, restriction or distortion of competition within the internal market do not constitute an appreciable restriction of competition under Article 101 of the Treaty. This negative definition of appreciability does not imply that agreements between undertakings which exceed the thresholds set out in this Notice constitute an appreciable restriction of competition. Such agreements may still have only a negligible effect on competition and may therefore not be prohibited by Article 101(1) of the Treaty.

4. Agreements may also fall outside Article 101(1) of the Treaty because they are not capable of appreciably affecting trade between Member States. This Notice does not indicate what constitutes an appreciable effect on trade between Member States. Guidance to that effect is to be found in the Commission's Notice on effect on trade, in which the Commission quantifies, with the help of the combination of a 5% market share threshold and a EUR 40 million turnover threshold, which agreements are in principle not capable of appreciably affecting trade between Member States. Such agreements normally fall outside Article 101(1) of the Treaty even if they have as their object the prevention, restriction or distortion of competition.

5. In cases covered by this Notice, the Commission will not institute proceedings either upon a complaint or on its own initiative. In addition, where the Commission has instituted proceedings but undertakings can demonstrate that they have assumed in good faith that the market shares mentioned in points 8, 9, 10 and 11 were not exceeded, the Commission will not impose fines. Although not binding on them, this Notice is also intended to give guidance to the courts and competition authorities of the Member States in their application of Article 101 of the Treaty.

6. The principles set out in this Notice also apply to decisions by associations of undertakings and to concerted practices.

7. This Notice is without prejudice to any interpretation of Article 101 of the Treaty which may be given by the Court of Justice of the European Union.

II.

8. The Commission holds the view that agreements between undertakings which may affect trade between Member States and which may have as their effect the prevention, restriction or distortion of competition within the internal market, do not appreciably restrict competition within the meaning of Article 101(1) of the Treaty:

    (a)   if the aggregate market share held by the parties to the agreement does not exceed 10% on any of the relevant markets affected by the agreement, where the agreement is made between undertakings which are actual or potential competitors on any of those markets (agreements between competitors); or

    (b)   if the market share held by each of the parties to the agreement does not exceed 15% on any of the relevant markets affected by the agreement, where the agreement is made between undertakings which are not actual or potential competitors on any of those markets (agreements between non-competitors).

9. In cases where it is difficult to classify the agreement as either an agreement between competitors or an agreement between non-competitors the 10% threshold is applicable.

13. In view of the clarification of the Court of Justice referred to in point 2, this Notice does not cover agreements which have as their object the prevention, restriction or distortion of competition within the internal market. The Commission will thus not apply the safe harbour created by the market share thresholds set out in points 8, 9, 10 and 11 to such agreements. For instance, as regards agreements between competitors, the Commission will not apply the principles set out in this Notice to, in particular, agreements containing restrictions which, directly or indirectly, have as their object: a) the fixing of prices when selling products to third parties; b) the limitation of output or sales; or c) the allocation of markets or customers. Likewise, the Commission will not apply the safe harbour created by those market share thresholds to agreements containing any of the restrictions that are listed as hardcore restrictions in any current or future Commission block exemption regulation, which are considered by the Commission to generally constitute restrictions by object.

14. The safe harbour created by the market share thresholds set out in points 8, 9, 10 and 11 is particularly relevant for categories of agreements not covered by any Commission block exemption regulation. The safe harbour is also relevant for agreements covered by a Commission block exemption regulation to the extent that those agreements contain a so-called excluded restriction, that is a restriction not listed as a hardcore restriction but nonetheless not covered by the Commission block exemption regulation.

...

Appendix 6
Vertical Block Exemption Regulation

Commission Regulation (EU) 2022/720 of 10 May 2022 on the application of Article 101(3) of the Treaty on the Functioning of the European Union to categories of vertical agreements and concerted practices

THE EUROPEAN COMMISSION,

Having regard to the Treaty on the Functioning of the European Union,

Having regard to Regulation No 19/65/EEC of the Council of 2 March 1965 on the application of Article 85(3) of the Treaty to certain categories of agreements and concerted practices, and in particular Article 1 thereof,

Having published a draft of this Regulation,

After consulting the Advisory Committee on Restrictive Practices and Dominant Positions,

Whereas:

(1)   Regulation No 19/65/EEC empowers the Commission to apply Article 101 of the Treaty by regulation to certain categories of vertical agreements and corresponding concerted practices falling within Article 101(1) of the Treaty.

(2)   Commission Regulation (EU) No 330/2010 defines a category of vertical agreements that the Commission regarded as normally satisfying the conditions laid down in Article 101(3) of the Treaty. Experience with the application of Regulation (EU) No 330/2010, which expires on 31 May 2022, has been positive overall, as shown by the evaluation of that Regulation. Taking into account that experience as well as new market developments, such as the growth of e-commerce, and new or more prevalent types of vertical agreements, it is appropriate to adopt a new block exemption regulation.

(3)   The category of agreements which can be regarded as normally satisfying the conditions laid down in Article 101(3) of the Treaty includes vertical agreements for the purchase or sale of goods or services where those agreements are concluded between non-competing undertakings, between certain competitors or by certain associations of retailers of goods. It also includes vertical agreements containing ancillary provisions on the assignment or use of intellectual property rights. The term 'vertical agreements' should be understood to include the corresponding concerted practices.

(4)   For the application of Article 101(3) of the Treaty by regulation, it is not necessary to define those vertical agreements which are capable of falling within Article 101(1) of the Treaty. In the individual assessment of agreements under Article 101(1) of the Treaty, account has to be taken of several factors, in particular the market structure on the supply and purchase side.

(5)   The benefit of the block exemption established by this Regulation should be limited to vertical agreements for which it can be assumed with sufficient certainty that they satisfy the conditions of Article 101(3) of the Treaty.

(6)   Certain types of vertical agreements can improve economic efficiency within a chain of production or distribution by facilitating better coordination between the participating undertakings. In particular, they can lead to a reduction in the transaction and distribution costs of the parties and to an optimisation of their sales and investment levels.

(7)   The likelihood that such efficiency-enhancing effects will outweigh any anti-competitive effects due to restrictions contained in vertical agreements depends on the

degree of market power of the parties to the agreement and, in particular, on the extent to which those undertakings face competition from other suppliers of goods or services regarded by their customers as interchangeable or substitutable for one another, by reason of the products' characteristics, their prices and their intended use.

(8)   It can be presumed that, where the market share held by each of the undertakings party to the agreement on the relevant market does not exceed 30%, vertical agreements which do not contain certain types of severe restrictions of competition generally lead to an improvement in production or distribution and allow consumers a fair share of the resulting benefits.

(9)   Above the market share threshold of 30 %, there can be no presumption that vertical agreements falling within the scope of Article 101(1) of the Treaty will usually give rise to objective advantages of such a character and size as to compensate for the disadvantages that they create for competition. At the same time, there is no presumption that those vertical agreements are either caught by Article 101(1) of the Treaty or that they fail to satisfy the conditions of Article 101(3) of the Treaty.

(10) The online platform economy plays an increasingly important role in the distribution of goods and services. Undertakings active in the online platform economy make it possible to do business in new ways, some of which are not easy to categorise using concepts associated with vertical agreements in the traditional economy. In particular, online intermediation services allow undertakings to offer goods or services to other undertakings or to final consumers, with a view to facilitating the initiation of direct transactions between undertakings or between undertakings and final consumers. Agreements relating to the provision of online intermediation services are vertical agreements and should therefore be able to benefit from the block exemption established by this Regulation, subject to the conditions set out in this Regulation.

(11) The definition of online intermediation services used in Regulation (EU) 2019/1150 of the European Parliament and of the Council should be adapted for the purpose of the present Regulation. In particular, to reflect the scope of Article 101 of the Treaty, the definition used in the present Regulation should refer to undertakings. It should also include online intermediation services that facilitate the initiation of direct transactions between undertakings, as well as those that facilitate the initiation of direct transactions between undertakings and final consumers.

(12) Dual distribution refers to the scenario where a supplier sells goods or services not only at the upstream level but also at the downstream level, thereby competing with its independent distributors. In that scenario, in the absence of hardcore restrictions, and provided that the buyer does not compete with the supplier at the upstream level, the potential negative impact of the vertical agreement on the competitive relationship between the supplier and buyer at the downstream level is less important than the potential positive impact of the vertical agreement on competition in general at the upstream or downstream level. This Regulation should therefore exempt vertical agreements entered into in such scenarios of dual distribution.

(13) The exchange of information between a supplier and buyer can contribute to the pro-competitive effects of vertical agreements, in particular the optimisation of production and distribution processes. However, in dual distribution, the exchange of certain types of information may raise horizontal concerns. Therefore, this Regulation should only exempt information exchange between a supplier and a buyer in a dual distribution scenario where the information exchange is both directly related to the implementation of the vertical agreement and necessary to improve the production or distribution of the contract goods or services.

(14) The rationale for exempting vertical agreements in scenarios of dual distribution does not apply to vertical agreements relating to the provision of online intermediation services where the provider of the online intermediation services is also a competing undertaking on the relevant market for the sale of the intermediated goods or services. Providers of online intermediation services that have such a hybrid function may have the ability and the incentive to influence the outcome of competition on the relevant market for the sale of the intermediated goods or services. This Regulation should therefore not exempt such vertical agreements.

(15) This Regulation should not exempt vertical agreements containing restrictions which are likely to restrict competition and harm consumers or which are not indispensable to the attainment of the efficiency-enhancing effects. In particular, the benefit of the block exemption established by this Regulation should not apply to vertical agreements containing certain types of severe restrictions of competition, such as minimum and fixed resale prices and certain types of territorial protection, including the prevention of the effective use of the internet to sell or certain restrictions of online advertising. Accordingly, restrictions of online sales and online advertising should benefit from the block exemption established by this Regulation, provided that they do not, directly or indirectly, in isolation or in combination with other factors controlled by the parties, have the object of preventing the effective use of the internet by the buyer or its customers to sell the contract goods or services to particular territories or customers, or of preventing the use of an entire online advertising channel, such as price comparison services or search engine advertising. For instance, online sales restrictions should not benefit from the block exemption established by this Regulation where their objective is to significantly diminish the aggregate volume of online sales of the contract goods or services in the relevant market or the possibility for consumers to buy the contract goods or services online. The categorisation of a restriction as hardcore within the meaning of Article 4, point (e) may take into account the content and context of the restriction, but should not depend on market-specific circumstances or the individual characteristics of the parties.

(16) This Regulation should not exempt restrictions for which it cannot be assumed with sufficient certainty that they satisfy the conditions of Article 101(3) of the Treaty. In particular, to ensure access to and to prevent collusion on the relevant market, certain conditions should be attached to the block exemption. To this end, the exemption of non-compete obligations should be limited to obligations which do not exceed a duration of five years. Obligations causing the members of a selective distribution system not to sell the brands of particular competing suppliers should likewise be excluded from the benefit of this Regulation. The benefit of this Regulation should not apply to retail parity obligations causing buyers of online intermediation services not to offer, sell or resell goods or services to end users under more favourable conditions via competing online intermediation services.

(17) The market share limitation, the non-exemption of certain vertical agreements and the conditions provided for in this Regulation generally ensure that the agreements to which the block exemption applies do not enable the participating undertakings to eliminate competition in respect of a substantial part of the goods or services in question.

(18) The Commission may withdraw the benefit of this Regulation, pursuant to Article 29(1) of Council Regulation (EC) No 1/2003, where it finds in a particular case that an agreement to which the block exemption established by this Regulation applies nevertheless has effects which are incompatible with Article 101(3) of the Treaty. The competition authority of a Member State may withdraw the benefit of this Regulation where the conditions of Article 29(2) of Regulation (EC) No 1/2003 are fulfilled.

(19) Where the Commission or the competition authority of a Member State withdraws the benefit of this Regulation, it has the burden of proving that the vertical agreement in question falls within the scope of Article 101(1) of the Treaty, and that the agreement fails to fulfil at least one of the four conditions of Article 101(3) of the Treaty.

(20) In determining whether the benefit of this Regulation should be withdrawn pursuant to Article 29 of Regulation (EC) No 1/2003, the anti-competitive effects that may derive from the existence of parallel networks of vertical agreements that have similar effects, which significantly restrict access to a relevant market or competition therein, are of particular importance. Such cumulative effects may in particular arise in the case of exclusive distribution, exclusive supply, selective distribution, parity obligations or non-compete obligations.

(21) In order to strengthen the supervision of parallel networks of vertical agreements which have similar anti-competitive effects and which cover more than 50% of a given market, the Commission may by regulation declare this Regulation inapplicable to vertical agreements containing specific restraints relating to the market concerned, thereby restoring the full application of Article 101 of the Treaty to such agreements,

HAS ADOPTED THIS REGULATION:

Article 1 Definitions

1. For the purposes of this Regulation, the following definitions shall apply:

    (a) 'vertical agreement' means an agreement or concerted practice between two or more undertakings, each of which operates, for the purposes of the agreement or the concerted practice, at a different level of the production or distribution chain, and relating to the conditions under which the parties may purchase, sell or resell certain goods or services;

    (b) 'vertical restraint' means a restriction of competition in a vertical agreement falling within the scope of Article 101(1) of the Treaty;

    (c) 'competing undertaking' means an actual or potential competitor; 'actual competitor' means an undertaking that is active on the same relevant market; 'potential competitor' means an undertaking that, in the absence of the vertical agreement, would, on realistic grounds and not just as a mere theoretical possibility, be likely, within a short period of time, to make the necessary additional investments or incur other necessary costs to enter the relevant market;

    (d) 'supplier' includes an undertaking that provides online intermediation services;

    (e) 'online intermediation services' means information society services within the meaning of Article 1(1), point (b), of Directive (EU) 2015/1535 of the European Parliament and of the Council which allow undertakings to offer goods or services:

        (i)   to other undertakings, with a view to facilitating the initiating of direct transactions between those undertakings, or

        (ii) to final consumers, with a view to facilitating the initiating of direct transactions between those undertakings and final consumers,

        irrespective of whether and where the transactions are ultimately concluded;

    (f) 'non-compete obligation' means any direct or indirect obligation causing the buyer not to manufacture, purchase, sell or resell goods or services which compete with the contract goods or services, or any direct or indirect obligation on the buyer to purchase from the supplier or from another undertaking designated by the supplier more than 80% of the buyer's total purchases of the contract goods or services and their substitutes on the relevant market, calculated on the basis of the value or, where such is standard industry practice, the volume of its purchases in the preceding calendar year;

(g) 'selective distribution system' means a distribution system where the supplier undertakes to sell the contract goods or services, either directly or indirectly, only to distributors selected on the basis of specified criteria and where these distributors undertake not to sell such goods or services to unauthorised distributors within the territory reserved by the supplier to operate that system;

(h) 'exclusive distribution system' means a distribution system where the supplier allocates a territory or group of customers exclusively to itself or to a maximum of five buyers and restricts all its other buyers from actively selling into the exclusive territory or to the exclusive customer group;

(i) 'intellectual property rights' includes industrial property rights, know-how, copyright and neighbouring rights;

(j) 'know-how' means a package of non-patented practical information, resulting from experience and testing by the supplier, which is secret, substantial and identified; 'secret' means that the know-how is not generally known or easily accessible; 'substantial' means that the know-how is significant and useful to the buyer for the use, sale or resale of the contract goods or services; 'identified' means that the know-how is described in a sufficiently comprehensive manner so as to make it possible to verify that it fulfils the criteria of secrecy and substantiality;

(k) 'buyer' includes an undertaking which, under an agreement falling within Article 101(1) of the Treaty, sells goods or services on behalf of another undertaking;

(l) 'active sales' means actively targeting customers by visits, letters, emails, calls or other means of direct communication or through targeted advertising and promotion, offline or online, for instance by means of print or digital media, including online media, price comparison services or advertising on search engines targeting customers in particular territories or customer groups, operating a website with a top-level domain corresponding to particular territories, or offering on a website languages that are commonly used in particular territories, where such languages are different from the ones commonly used in the territory in which the buyer is established;

(m) 'passive sales' means sales made in response to unsolicited requests from individual customers, including delivery of goods or services to the customer, without the sale having been initiated by actively targeting the particular customer, customer group or territory, and including sales resulting from participating in public procurement or responding to private invitations to tender.

2. For the purposes of this Regulation, the terms 'undertaking', 'supplier' and 'buyer' shall include their respective connected undertakings.

'Connected undertakings' means:

(a) undertakings in which a party to the agreement, directly or indirectly:

    (i) has the power to exercise more than half the voting rights, or

    (ii) has the power to appoint more than half the members of the supervisory board, board of management or bodies legally representing the undertaking, or

    (iii) has the right to manage the undertaking's affairs; or

(b) undertakings which directly or indirectly have, over a party to the agreement, the rights or powers listed in point (a); or

(c)   undertakings in which an undertaking referred to in point (b) has, directly or indirectly, the rights or powers listed in point (a); or

(d)   undertakings in which a party to the agreement together with one or more of the undertakings referred to in points (a), (b) or (c), or in which two or more of the latter undertakings, jointly have the rights or powers listed in point (a); or

(e)   undertakings in which the rights or the powers listed in point (a) are jointly held by:

    (i)   parties to the agreement or their respective connected undertakings referred to in points (a) to (d), or

    (ii)   one or more of the parties to the agreement or one or more of their connected undertakings referred to in points (a) to (d) and one or more third parties.

Article 2 Exemption

1.   Pursuant to Article 101(3) of the Treaty and subject to the provisions of this Regulation, it is hereby declared that Article 101(1) of the Treaty shall not apply to vertical agreements. This exemption shall apply to the extent that such agreements contain vertical restraints.

2.   The exemption provided for in paragraph 1 shall apply to vertical agreements entered into between an association of undertakings and an individual member, or between such an association and an individual supplier, only if all the members of the association are retailers of goods and if no individual member of the association, together with its connected undertakings, has a total annual turnover exceeding EUR 50 million. Vertical agreements entered into by such associations shall be covered by this Regulation without prejudice to the application of Article 101 of the Treaty to horizontal agreements concluded between the members of the association or decisions adopted by the association.

3.   The exemption provided for in paragraph 1 shall apply to vertical agreements containing provisions which relate to the assignment to the buyer or use by the buyer of intellectual property rights, provided that those provisions do not constitute the primary object of such agreements and are directly related to the use, sale or resale of goods or services by the buyer or its customers. The exemption applies on the condition that, in relation to the contract goods or services, those provisions do not contain restrictions of competition having the same object as vertical restraints which are not exempted under this Regulation.

4.   The exemption provided for in paragraph 1 shall not apply to vertical agreements entered into between competing undertakings. However, that exemption shall apply where competing undertakings enter into a non-reciprocal vertical agreement and one of the following applies:

(a)   the supplier is active at an upstream level as a manufacturer, importer, or wholesaler and at a downstream level as an importer, wholesaler, or retailer of goods, while the buyer is an importer, wholesaler, or retailer at the downstream level and not a competing undertaking at the upstream level where it buys the contract goods; or

(b)   the supplier is a provider of services at several levels of trade, while the buyer provides its services at the retail level and is not a competing undertaking at the level of trade where it purchases the contract services.

5.   The exceptions set out in paragraph 4, points (a) and (b) shall not apply to the exchange of information between the supplier and the buyer that is either not directly related to the implementation of the vertical agreement or is not necessary to improve the

production or distribution of the contract goods or services, or which fulfils neither of those two conditions.

6.   The exceptions set out in paragraph 4, points (a) and (b) shall not apply to vertical agreements relating to the provision of online intermediation services where the provider of the online intermediation services is a competing undertaking on the relevant market for the sale of the intermediated goods or services.

7.   This Regulation shall not apply to vertical agreements the subject matter of which falls within the scope of any other block exemption regulation, unless otherwise provided for in such a regulation.

Article 3 Market share threshold

1.   The exemption provided for in Article 2 shall apply on condition that the market share held by the supplier does not exceed 30% of the relevant market on which it sells the contract goods or services and the market share held by the buyer does not exceed 30% of the relevant market on which it purchases the contract goods or services.

2.   For the purposes of paragraph 1, where in a multi-party agreement an undertaking buys the contract goods or services from one undertaking that is a party to the agreement and sells the contract goods or services to another undertaking that is also a party to the agreement, the market share of the first undertaking must respect the market share threshold provided for in that paragraph both as a buyer and a supplier in order for the exemption provided for in Article 2 to apply.

Article 4 Restrictions that remove the benefit of the block exemption - hardcore restrictions

The exemption provided for in Article 2 shall not apply to vertical agreements which, directly or indirectly, in isolation or in combination with other factors under the control of the parties, have as their object:

(a)   the restriction of the buyer's ability to determine its sale price, without prejudice to the possibility of the supplier to impose a maximum sale price or recommend a sale price, provided that they do not amount to a fixed or minimum sale price as a result of pressure from, or incentives offered by, any of the parties;

(b)   where the supplier operates an exclusive distribution system, the restriction of the territory into which, or of the customers to whom, the exclusive distributor may actively or passively sell the contract goods or services, except:

(i)   the restriction of active sales by the exclusive distributor and its direct customers, into a territory or to a customer group reserved to the supplier or allocated by the supplier exclusively to a maximum of five other exclusive distributors;

(ii)   the restriction of active or passive sales by the exclusive distributor and its customers to unauthorised distributors located in a territory where the supplier operates a selective distribution system for the contract goods or services;

(iii)   the restriction of the exclusive distributor's place of establishment;

(iv)   the restriction of active or passive sales to end users by an exclusive distributor operating at the wholesale level of trade;

(v)   the restriction of the exclusive distributor's ability to actively or passively sell components, supplied for the purposes of incorporation, to customers who would use them to manufacture the same type of goods as those produced by the supplier;

(c)   where the supplier operates a selective distribution system,

(i)   the restriction of the territory into which, or of the customers to whom, the members of the selective distribution system may actively or passively sell the contract goods or services, except:

        (1)   the restriction of active sales by the members of the selective distribution system and their direct customers, into a territory or to a customer group reserved to the supplier or allocated by the supplier exclusively to a maximum of five exclusive distributors;

        (2)   the restriction of active or passive sales by the members of the selective distribution system and their customers to unauthorised distributors located within the territory where the selective distribution system is operated;

        (3)   the restriction of the place of establishment of the members of the selective distribution system;

        (4)   the restriction of active or passive sales to end users by members of the selective distribution system operating at the wholesale level of trade;

        (5)   the restriction of the ability to actively or passively sell components, supplied for the purposes of incorporation, to customers who would use them to manufacture the same type of goods as those produced by the supplier;

    (ii)   the restriction of cross-supplies between the members of the selective distribution system operating at the same or different levels of trade;

    (iii)   the restriction of active or passive sales to end users by members of the selective distribution system operating at the retail level of trade, without prejudice to points (c)(i)(1) and (3);

(d)   where the supplier operates neither an exclusive distribution system nor a selective distribution system, the restriction of the territory into which, or of the customers to whom, the buyer may actively or passively sell the contract goods or services, except:

    (i)   the restriction of active sales by the buyer and its direct customers into a territory or to a customer group reserved to the supplier or allocated by the supplier exclusively to a maximum of five exclusive distributors;

    (ii)   the restriction of active or passive sales by the buyer and its customers to unauthorised distributors located in a territory where the supplier operates a selective distribution system for the contract goods or services;

    (iii)   the restriction of the buyer's place of establishment;

    (iv)   the restriction of active or passive sales to end users by a buyer operating at the wholesale level of trade;

    (v)   the restriction of the buyer's ability to actively or passively sell components, supplied for the purposes of incorporation, to customers who would use them to manufacture the same type of goods as those produced by the supplier;

(e)   the prevention of the effective use of the internet by the buyer or its customers to sell the contract goods or services, as it restricts the territory into which or the customers to whom the contract goods or services may be sold within the meaning of points (b), (c) or (d), without prejudice to the possibility of imposing on the buyer:

    (i)   other restrictions of online sales; or

    (ii)   restrictions of online advertising that do not have the object of preventing the use of an entire online advertising channel;

(f)   the restriction, agreed between a supplier of components and a buyer who incorporates those components, of the supplier's ability to sell the components as spare parts to end users or to repairers, wholesalers or other service providers not entrusted by the buyer with the repair or servicing of its goods.

Article 5 Excluded restrictions

1. The exemption provided for in Article 2 shall not apply to the following obligations contained in vertical agreements:

    (a) any direct or indirect non-compete obligation, the duration of which is indefinite or exceeds 5 years;

    (b) any direct or indirect obligation causing the buyer, after termination of the agreement, not to manufacture, purchase, sell or resell goods or services;

    (c) any direct or indirect obligation causing the members of a selective distribution system not to sell the brands of particular competing suppliers;

    (d) any direct or indirect obligation causing a buyer of online intermediation services not to offer, sell or resell goods or services to end users under more favourable conditions via competing online intermediation services;

2. By way of derogation from paragraph 1, point (a), the time limitation of five years shall not apply where the contract goods or services are sold by the buyer from premises and land owned by the supplier or leased by the supplier from third parties not connected with the buyer, provided that the duration of the non-compete obligation does not exceed the period of occupancy of the premises and land by the buyer.

3. By way of derogation from paragraph 1, point (b), the exemption provided for in Article 2 shall apply to any direct or indirect obligation causing the buyer, after termination of the agreement, not to manufacture, purchase, sell or resell goods or services where all of the following conditions are fulfilled:

    (a) the obligation relates to goods or services which compete with the contract goods or services;

    (b) the obligation is limited to the premises and land from which the buyer has operated during the contract period;

    (c) the obligation is indispensable to protect know-how transferred by the supplier to the buyer;

    (d) the duration of the obligation is limited to a period of one year after termination of the agreement.

Paragraph 1, point (b) shall be without prejudice to the possibility of imposing a restriction which is unlimited in time on the use and disclosure of know-how which has not entered the public domain.

Article 6 Withdrawal in individual cases

1. The Commission may withdraw the benefit of this Regulation, pursuant to Article 29(1) of Regulation (EC) No 1/2003, where it finds in any particular case that a vertical agreement to which the exemption provided for in Article 2 of this Regulation applies nevertheless has effects which are incompatible with Article 101(3) of the Treaty. Such effects may occur, for example, where the relevant market for the supply of online intermediation services is highly concentrated and competition between the providers of such services is restricted by the cumulative effect of parallel networks of similar agreements that restrict buyers of the online intermediation services from offering, selling or reselling goods or services to end users under more favourable conditions on their direct sales channels.

2. The competition authority of a Member State may withdraw the benefit of this Regulation where the conditions of Article 29(2) of Regulation (EC) No 1/2003 are fulfilled.

Article 7 Non-application of this Regulation

Pursuant to Article 1a of Regulation No 19/65/EEC, the Commission may by regulation declare that, where parallel networks of similar vertical restraints cover more than 50% of a relevant market, this Regulation shall not apply to vertical agreements containing specific restraints relating to that market.

Article 8 Application of the market share threshold

For the purposes of applying the market share thresholds provided for in Article 3 the following rules shall apply:

(a)   the market share of the supplier shall be calculated on the basis of market sales value data and the market share of the buyer shall be calculated on the basis of market purchase value data. If market sales value or market purchase value data are not available, estimates based on other reliable market information, including market sales and purchase volumes, may be used to establish the market share of the undertaking concerned;

(b)   the market shares shall be calculated on the basis of data relating to the preceding calendar year;

(c)   the market share of the supplier shall include any goods or services supplied to vertically integrated distributors for the purposes of sale;

(d)   if a market share is initially not more than 30%, but subsequently rises above that level, the exemption provided for in Article 2 shall continue to apply for a period of two consecutive calendar years following the year in which the 30% threshold was first exceeded;

(e)   the market share held by the undertakings referred to in Article 1(2), second subparagraph, point (e) shall be apportioned equally to each undertaking having the rights or the powers listed in point (a) of that subparagraph.

Article 9 Application of the turnover threshold

1.   For the purpose of calculating total annual turnover within the meaning of Article 2(2), the turnover achieved during the previous financial year by the relevant party to the vertical agreement and the turnover achieved by its connected undertakings in respect of all goods and services, excluding all taxes and other duties, shall be added together. For this purpose, no account shall be taken of dealings between the party to the vertical agreement and its connected undertakings or between its connected undertakings.

2.   The exemption provided for in Article 2 shall remain applicable where, for any period of two consecutive financial years, the total annual turnover threshold is exceeded by no more than 10%.

Article 10 Transitional period

The prohibition laid down in Article 101(1) of the Treaty shall not apply during the period from 1 June 2022 to 31 May 2023 in respect of agreements already in force on 31 May 2022 which do not satisfy the conditions for exemption provided for in this Regulation but which, on 31 May 2022, satisfied the conditions for exemption provided for in Regulation (EU) No 330/2010.

Article 11 Period of validity

This Regulation shall enter into force on 1 June 2022.

It shall expire on 31 May 2034.

This Regulation shall be binding in its entirety and directly applicable in all Member States.

Appendix 7

Vertical Agreements Block Exemption Order

Competition Act 1998 (Vertical Agreements Block Exemption) Order 2022 (SI 2022/516)

1. **Citation and commencement**

   This Order—

   (a) may be cited as the Competition Act 1998 (Vertical Agreements Block Exemption) Order 2022, and

   (b) comes into force on 1st June 2022.

2. **Interpretation**

   (1) In this Order—

   "block exemption" means the exemption from the Chapter 1 prohibition arising by virtue of this Order for the category of agreements specified in this Order;

   "buyer" means the purchaser of the contract goods or services and includes an undertaking which, under an agreement to which the Chapter 1 prohibition applies, sells goods or services on behalf of another undertaking;

   "connected undertakings", in relation to a party to an agreement, means—

   (a) undertakings in relation to which the party to the agreement, directly or indirectly—

       (i) has the power to exercise more than half the voting rights,

       (ii) has the power to appoint more than half the members of the supervisory board, board of management or bodies legally representing the undertaking, or

       (iii) has the right to manage the undertaking's affairs;

   (b) undertakings which directly or indirectly have, in relation to the party to the agreement, any of the rights or powers listed in paragraph (a);

   (c) undertakings in relation to which an undertaking referred to in paragraph (b) has, directly or indirectly, any of the rights or powers listed in paragraph (a);

   (d) undertakings in relation to which the party to the agreement together with one or more of the undertakings referred to in paragraph (a), (b) or (c), or in relation to which two or more of the undertakings referred to in paragraph (b) or (c), jointly have any of the rights or powers listed in paragraph (a);

   (e) undertakings in relation to which any of the rights or the powers listed in paragraph (a) are jointly held by—

       (i) parties to the agreement or their respective connected undertakings referred to in paragraphs (a) to (d), or

       (ii) one or more of the parties to the agreement or one or more of their respective connected undertakings referred to in paragraphs (a) to (d) and one or more third parties;

   "the contract goods or services" has the meaning given in article 3(2);

   "customer", in relation to a buyer, means an undertaking not party to the agreement which purchases the contract goods or services from a buyer which is party to the agreement;

"excluded restriction" has the meaning given in article 10(2);

"hardcore restriction" has the meaning given in article 8(2);

"know-how" means a package of non-patented practical information, resulting from experience and testing by the supplier, which is—

(a)   not generally known or easily accessible,

(b)   significant and useful to the buyer for the use, sale or resale of the contract goods or services, and

(c)   described in a sufficiently comprehensive manner so as to make it possible to verify that it fulfils the criteria in paragraphs (a) and (b);

"online intermediation service" means a service that allows undertakings to offer goods or services to other undertakings or to end users with a view to facilitating direct transactions between such undertakings or between such undertakings and end users, irrespective of whether and where those transactions are ultimately concluded and that constitutes an information society service within the meaning of Article 1(1)(b) of Directive (EU) 2015/1535 of the European Parliament and of the Council of 9 September 2015 laying down a procedure for the provision of information on the field of technical regulations and of rules on Information Society services (codification);

"selective distribution system" means a distribution system where the supplier undertakes to sell the contract goods or services, either directly or indirectly, only to distributors selected on the basis of specified criteria and where these distributors undertake not to sell such goods or services to distributors not authorised by the supplier within the geographical area reserved by the supplier in the agreement in order to operate that system;

"supplier" includes an undertaking that provides online intermediation services irrespective of whether it is a party to the transaction it facilitates;

"vertical agreement" has the meaning given in article 3(2);

"vertical restraint" means a restriction on competition in a vertical agreement to which the Chapter 1 prohibition applies.

(2)   In this Order, references to "the agreement" are to be read as references to the vertical agreement claiming the benefit of the block exemption.

(3)   For the purposes of this Order, the terms "undertaking", "supplier" and "buyer" include their respective connected undertakings.

3.   Block Exemption

(1)   The category of agreements identified in paragraph (2) as vertical agreements is specified for the purposes of section 6 of the Competition Act 1998.

(2)   Subject to paragraphs (3), (4), (5) and (6), for the purposes of this Order vertical agreements are agreements or concerted practices entered into between two or more undertakings each of which operates, for the purposes of the agreement or the concerted practice concerned, at a different level of the production or distribution chain, and relating to the conditions under which the parties may purchase, sell, or resell certain goods or services ("the contract goods or services").

(3)   Vertical agreements entered into between an association of undertakings and its members, or between such an association and its suppliers, are specified provided—

(a)   all members of the association are retailers of goods, and

(b)   subject to article 4(2), the annual turnover of each individual member of the association, when combined with the annual turnover of its respective connected undertakings, does not exceed £44 million.

(4)   Vertical agreements containing provisions which relate to the assignment to the buyer or use by the buyer of intellectual property rights are specified provided that—

(a)   those provisions do not constitute the primary object of such agreements and are directly related to the use, sale or resale of goods or services by the buyer or its customers, and

(b)   in relation to the contract goods or services, those provisions do not contain restrictions of competition having the same object as vertical restraints which are not exempted by virtue of this Order.

(5)   Vertical agreements entered into between competing undertakings are specified only to the extent that they are non-reciprocal, and the supplier—

(a)   is a manufacturer and a distributor of goods, while the buyer is a distributor and not a competing undertaking at the manufacturing level,

(b)   is a provider of services at several levels of trade, while the buyer provides its goods or services at the retail level and is not a competing undertaking at the level of trade where it purchases the contract services,

(c)   is a wholesaler and a distributor of goods, while the buyer is a distributor and not a competing undertaking at the wholesale level, or

(d)   is an importer and a distributor of goods, while the buyer is a distributor and not a competing undertaking at the level of trade where it purchases the goods or at the importation level.

(6)   This Order does not apply to—

(a)   vertical agreements the subject matter of which falls within the scope of any retained block exemption regulation or of any block exemption order, unless otherwise provided for in such a regulation or order;

(b)   rent and lease agreements where no goods or services are being sold by the supplier to the buyer.

(7)   In this article—

"actual competitor" means an undertaking active on the same relevant market;

"competing undertaking" means an actual competitor or a potential competitor;

"intellectual property rights" includes industrial property rights, know-how, copyright and neighbouring rights;

"potential competitor" means an undertaking that, in the absence of the agreement, would, on realistic grounds and not just as a mere theoretical possibility, be likely to undertake, within a short period of time, the necessary additional investments or other necessary switching costs to enter the relevant market.

4.   Calculation of annual turnover

(1)   For the purpose of calculating the combined annual turnover within the meaning of article 3(3)—

(a)   the turnover achieved during the previous financial year by the relevant member of the association and the turnover achieved by its connected undertakings in respect of all goods and services, excluding all taxes and other duties, are to be added together;

(b)   no account is to be taken of dealings between the member of the association and its connected undertakings or between its connected undertakings.

(2)   The block exemption remains applicable where, for any period of two consecutive financial years, the combined annual turnover does not exceed the combined annual turnover threshold by more than 10%.

Conditions and consequences of breach of conditions

5.   **Block exemption subject to conditions and obligation**

The block exemption has effect subject to the conditions and the obligation specified in articles 6 to 12.

6.   **Market share thresholds**

(1)   The block exemption applies on condition that—

(a)   the market share held by the undertaking which is party to the agreement and which is a supplier does not exceed 30% of the relevant market on which it sells the contract goods or services, and

(b)   the market share held by the undertaking which is party to the agreement and which is a buyer does not exceed 30% of the relevant market on which it purchases the contract goods or services.

(2)   For the purposes of paragraph (1), where in an agreement involving more than two parties an undertaking purchases the contract goods or services from one undertaking which is party to the agreement and sells the contract goods or services to another undertaking which is party to the agreement, the market share of the first undertaking must respect the market share threshold provided for in that paragraph both as a buyer and a supplier.

7.   **Rules for applying market share thresholds**

(1)   For the purposes of applying the market share thresholds provided for in article 6 the following rules apply—

(a)   the market share—

(i)   of the supplier is to be calculated on the basis of market sales value data (including sales to all vertically integrated distributors for the purposes of resale), and

(ii)   of the buyer is to be calculated on the basis of market purchase value data, and where market sales value or market purchase value data are not available, estimates based on other reliable market information, including market sales and purchase volumes, may be used to establish the market share of the undertaking concerned;

(b)   the market share is to be calculated on the basis of data relating to the preceding calendar year.

(2)   If a market share is initially not more than 30% but subsequently rises above that level without exceeding 35%, the block exemption continues to apply for a period of two consecutive calendar years following the year in which the 30% market share threshold was first exceeded.

(3)   If a market share is initially not more than 30% but subsequently rises to more than 35%, the block exemption continues to apply for one calendar year following the year in which the level of 35% was first reached.

(4)   The benefit of paragraphs (2) and (3) may not be combined so as to exceed a period of two calendar years.

(5)   The market share held by the undertakings referred to in paragraph (e) of the definition of "connected undertakings" in article 2(1) are to be apportioned

equally to each undertaking having the rights or the powers listed in paragraph (a) of that definition.

8. **Hardcore restrictions**

    (1)   The block exemption applies to the agreement on condition that it does not contain a hardcore restriction.

    (2)   A hardcore restriction is one or more provisions which, directly or indirectly, in isolation or in combination with other factors under the control of the parties, have as their object—

    (a)   the restriction of the buyer's ability to determine its onward sale price, without prejudice to the possibility of the supplier imposing a maximum sale price or recommending a sale price, provided that any such provisions do not amount to a fixed or minimum sale price as a result of pressure from, or incentives offered by, any of the parties;

    (b)   where the supplier operates an exclusive distribution system, the restriction of the geographical area into which, or of the customer groups to whom, one or a limited number of buyers, to which an exclusive geographical area or customer group has been allocated, may actively sell or passively sell the contract goods or services, but are not excepted restrictions set out in paragraph (3);

    (c)   where the supplier operates a selective distribution system—

    (i)   the restriction of the geographical area into which, or of the customer groups to whom, the members of the selective distribution system may actively sell or passively sell the contract goods or services, but are not excepted restrictions set out in paragraph (4),

    (ii)   the restriction of cross-supplies between the members of the selective distribution system operating at the same or different levels of trade, or

    (iii) the restriction of active sales or passive sales to end users by members of the selective distribution system operating at the retail level of trade, except in the situation set out in paragraph (4)(a);

    (d)   where the supplier operates neither an exclusive nor a selective distribution system, the restriction of the geographical area into which, or of the customer group to whom, a buyer may actively sell or passively sell the contract goods or services, but are not excepted restrictions set out in paragraph (5);

    (e)   the restriction, agreed between a supplier of components and a buyer who incorporates those components, of the supplier's ability to sell the components as spare parts to end-users or to repairers, wholesalers or other service providers not entrusted by the buyer with the repair or servicing of its goods;

    (f)   a wide retail parity obligation or measure that has the same effect as a wide retail parity obligation (which includes any course of action, including entering into agreements or engaging in concerted practices, which has the object of replicating the anti-competitive effects of a wide retail parity obligation).

    (3)   The excepted restrictions referred to in paragraph (2)(b) are—

    (a)   the restriction of active sales by the exclusive distributor, or the exclusive distributor and its customers that have entered into a distribution agreement with the supplier or with a party that was given distribution rights by the supplier, into a geographical area or to a customer group reserved to the supplier or allocated by the supplier exclusively to one or a limited number of other buyers,

(b)   the restriction of active sales or passive sales by the exclusive distributor, or the exclusive distributor and its customers to unauthorised distributors located in a geographical area where the supplier operates a selective distribution system for the contract goods or services,

(c)   the restriction of the exclusive distributor's place of establishment,

(d)   the restriction of active sales or passive sales to end users by an exclusive distributor operating at the wholesale level of trade, and

(e)   the restriction of the exclusive distributor's ability to actively sell or passively sell components, supplied for the purposes of incorporation to a product, to customers who would use them to manufacture the same type of goods as those produced by the supplier.

(4)   The excepted restrictions referred to in paragraph (2)(c)(i) are—

(a)   the restriction of active sales by the members of the selective distribution system, or the members of the selective distribution system and their customers that have entered into a distribution agreement with the supplier or with a party that was given distribution rights by the supplier, into a geographical area or to a customer group reserved to the supplier or allocated by the supplier exclusively to one or a limited number of buyers,

(b)   the restriction of active sales or passive sales by the members of the selective distribution system or their customers to unauthorised distributors located within the geographical area where the selective distribution system is operated,

(c)   the restriction of the place of establishment of the members of the selective distribution system,

(d)   the restriction of active sales or passive sales to end users by members of the selective distribution system operating at the wholesale level of trade, and

(e)   the restriction of the ability to actively sell or passively sell components, supplied for the purposes of incorporation into a product, to customers who would use them to manufacture the same type of goods as those produced by the supplier.

(5)   The excepted restrictions referred to in paragraph (2)(d) are—

(a)   the restriction of active sales by the buyer, or the buyer and its customers that have entered into a distribution agreement with the supplier or with a party that was given distribution rights by the supplier, into a geographical area or to a customer group reserved to the supplier or allocated by the supplier exclusively to one or a limited number of buyers,

(b)   the restriction of active sales or passive sales by the buyer or its customers to unauthorised distributors located in a geographical area where the supplier operates a selective distribution system for the contract goods or services,

(c)   the restriction of the buyer's place of establishment,

(d)   the restriction of active sales or passive sales to end users by a buyer operating at the wholesale level of trade, and

(e)   the restriction of the buyer's ability to actively sell or passively sell components, supplied for the purposes of incorporation into a product, to customers who would use them to manufacture the same type of goods as those produced by the supplier.

(6) In paragraph (2), a reference to a restriction of an active sale or passive sale, or to a restriction of actively selling or passively selling, in relation to the selling of goods and services online, includes a restriction that, directly or indirectly, in isolation or combination with other factors, has as its object—

(a) the prevention of buyers or their customers effectively using the internet for the purposes of selling their goods or services online or from effectively using one or more online advertising channels,

(b) the restriction of the geographical area into which or the customer group to whom the buyers may sell the contract goods or services, or

(c) in the case of selective distribution, the restriction of active sales or passive sales to end users by members of the selective distribution system operating at the retail level of trade.

(7) In this article—

"active sales" means—

(a) actively targeting customers by for instance calls, e-mails, letters, visits or other direct means of communication,

(b) targeted advertising and promotion, by means of print or digital media, offline or online, including online media, digital comparison tools or advertising on search engines targeting customers in specific geographical areas or customer groups,

(c) advertisement or promotion that is only attractive for the buyer if it (in addition to reaching other customers) reaches a specific group of customers or customers in a specific geographical area (and is considered active selling to that customer group or customers in that geographical area),

(d) offering on a website language options different to the ones commonly used in the geographical area in which the distributor is established, or

(e) using a domain name corresponding to a geographical area other than the one in which the distributor is established,

and the expressions "actively sell" and "actively selling" should be construed accordingly;

"digital comparison tools" means online intermediation services used by end users to compare prices, quality or other characteristics of, and potentially to switch or purchase, goods or services from a range of businesses;

"exclusive distribution system" means a distribution system where the supplier allocates a geographical area or customer group exclusively to itself or to one or a limited number of buyers, determined in proportion to the allocated geographical area or customer group in such a way as to secure certain volumes of business that preserves their investment efforts, and restricts other buyers from actively selling into the exclusive geographical area or to the exclusive customer group;

"passive sales" means—

(a) sales in response to unsolicited requests from individual customers, including delivery of goods or services to such customers without the sale having been initiated through advertising actively targeting the particular customer group or geographical area,

(b) general advertising or promotion that reaches customers in other distributors' geographical areas or customer groups (whether exclusive or not) but which is a reasonable way to reach customers not in those other distributors' geographical areas or customer groups (whether exclusive or not), for instance to reach customers in a supplier's own geographical area, or

(c)   participating in a public procurement exercise undertaken in accordance with—

(i)   in England, Wales or Northern Ireland, the Defence and Security Public Contracts Regulations 2011, the Public Contracts Regulations 2015, the Concession Contracts Regulations 2016 or the Utilities Contracts Regulations 2016, and

(ii)   in Scotland, the Defence and Security Public Contracts Regulations 2011, the Public Contracts (Scotland) Regulations 2015, the Concession Contracts (Scotland) Regulations 2016 or the Utilities Contracts Regulations 2016,

and the expressions "passively sell" and "passively selling" should be construed accordingly;

"wide retail parity obligation" means a restriction by reference to any of the supplier's indirect sales channels (whether online or offline, for instance online platforms or other intermediaries), which ensures that the prices or other terms and conditions at which the supplier's goods or services are offered to end users on a sales channel are no worse than those offered by the supplier on another sales channel.

9.   Effect of breach of conditions in article 6 or 8

Breach of either of the conditions imposed by article 6 or 8 has the effect of cancelling the block exemption in respect of that vertical agreement.

10.   Excluded restrictions

(1)   The block exemption applies to the agreement on condition that it does not contain an excluded restriction.

(2)   Subject to paragraphs (3) and (4), an excluded restriction means—

(a)   any non-compete obligation, the duration of which is indefinite or exceeds five years (and a non-compete obligation which is automatically renewable beyond a period of five years is deemed to have been concluded for an indefinite duration);

(b)   any direct or indirect obligation causing the buyer, after termination of the agreement, not to manufacture, purchase, sell or resell any goods or services;

(c)   any direct or indirect obligation causing the members of a selective distribution system not to sell the brands of particular competing suppliers.

(3)   The time limitation of five years in paragraph (2)(a) does not apply where the contract goods or services are sold by the buyer from premises, land or a vehicle owned by the supplier or leased by the supplier from third parties not connected with the buyer, provided that the duration of the non-compete obligation does not exceed the period of occupancy of the premises or land, or possession of the vehicle, by the buyer.

(4)   As regards paragraph (2)(b)—

(a)   any direct or indirect obligation causing the buyer, after termination of the agreement, not to manufacture, purchase, sell or resell goods or services is not an excluded restriction, provided that the following conditions are fulfilled—

(i)   the obligation relates to goods or services which compete with the contract goods or services,

        (ii)   the obligation is limited to the premises, land or vehicle from which the buyer has operated during the contract period,

        (iii) the obligation is indispensable to protect know-how transferred by the supplier to the buyer, and

        (iv) the duration of the obligation is limited to a period of one year after termination of the agreement, and

    (b)   any restriction which is indispensable to protect know-how transferred by the supplier to the buyer which has not entered the public domain, whether or not it is time limited, is not an excluded restriction.

(5)   In this article, "non-compete obligation" means any direct or indirect obligation causing the buyer not to manufacture, purchase, sell or resell goods or services which compete with the contract goods or services, or any direct or indirect obligation on the buyer to purchase from the supplier or from another undertaking designated by the supplier more than 80% of the buyer's total purchases of the contract goods or services and their substitutes on the relevant market, calculated on the basis of the value or, where such is standard industry practice, the volume of its purchases in the preceding calendar year.

11. Effect of breach of condition in article 10

Breach of the condition imposed by article 10 has the effect, as regards a vertical agreement which contains an excluded restriction—

(a)   which is not severable from the agreement, of cancelling the block exemption in respect of that agreement;

(b)   which is severable from the agreement, of cancelling the block exemption in respect of that excluded restriction only.

12. Obligation to provide information

(1)   A person must supply to the CMA such information in connection with the agreements to which it is a party as the CMA may require—

    (a)   within a period of ten working days commencing with the relevant day, or

    (b)   within such longer period of working days commencing with the relevant day as the CMA may, having regard to the particular circumstances of the case, agree with the person in writing.

(2)   If there is a failure to comply with the obligation imposed by paragraph (1) without reasonable excuse, the CMA may, subject first to giving notice in writing of its proposal and considering any representations made to it, by notice in writing cancel the block exemption in respect of any vertical agreement to which the request for information under paragraph (1) relates.

(3)   In this article—

"relevant day" means—

    (a)   the day on which a person receives notice in writing to provide information under paragraph (1), or

    (b)   where notice to provide information under paragraph (1) is given by publication pursuant to article 14(b), the day on which the notice is published;

"working day" means a day which is not a Saturday, Sunday or any other day on which the CMA is closed for business.

Cancellation and notices

13. **Cancellation in individual cases**

   (1)   If the CMA considers that a particular vertical agreement is not one which is exempt from the Chapter 1 prohibition as a result of section 9 of the Competition Act 1998, it may, subject to paragraph (2), by notice in writing cancel the block exemption in respect of that vertical agreement.

   (2)   If the CMA proposes to cancel the block exemption in accordance with this Article, it must first give notice in writing of its proposal and must consider any representations made to it.

14. **Notices in writing**

   For the purposes of articles 12 and 13, notice in writing is to be given by—

   (a)   the CMA giving notice in writing of its request for information, decision or proposal to those persons whom it can reasonably identify as being parties to the relevant vertical agreement, or

   (b)   where it is not reasonably practicable for the CMA to comply with paragraph (a), the CMA publishing its request for information, decision or proposal in—

      (i)   the register maintained by the CMA under rule 20 of the CMA's rules set out in the Schedule to the Competition Act 1998 (Competition and Markets Authority's Rules) Order 2014,

      (ii)   the London, Edinburgh and Belfast Gazettes,

      (iii)   at least one national daily newspaper, and

      (iv)   if there is in circulation an appropriate trade journal which is published at intervals not exceeding one month, in such trade journal, stating the facts on which it bases the request, decision or proposal, and its reasons for making it.

Transitional provision and expiry

15. **Transitional provision**

   (1)   In this article, a "pre-existing vertical agreement" means an agreement or concerted practice entered into before 1st June 2022 which on 1st June 2022—

   (a)   does not fall into the category specified in article 3, or satisfy the conditions provided for in this Order, and

   (b)   immediately before that date satisfied the conditions for exemption provided for in Commission Regulation (EU) No 330/2010 of 20 April 2010 on the application of Article 101(3) of the Treaty on the Functioning of the European Union to categories of vertical agreements and concerted practices.

   (2)   A pre-existing vertical agreement is to be treated as a vertical agreement specified in article 3 and meeting the conditions provided for in this Order until 1st June 2023.

   (3)   Articles 12 to 14 apply to a pre-existing vertical agreement as they apply to a vertical agreement.

16. **Expiry**

   This Order ceases to have effect on 1st June 2028.

Appendix 8

Merger Regulation (extracts)

Council Regulation (EC) No 139/2004 of 20 January 2004 on the control of concentrations between undertakings (the Merger Regulation)

THE COUNCIL OF THE EUROPEN UNION

...

Whereas:

...

(6) A specific legal instrument is therefore necessary to permit effective control of all concentrations in terms of their effect on the structure of competition in the Community and to be the only instrument applicable to such concentrations. ...

...

(8) The provisions to be adopted in this Regulation should apply to significant structural changes, the impact of which on the market goes beyond the national borders of any one Member State. Such concentrations should, as a general rule, be reviewed exclusively at Community level, in application of a 'one-stop shop' system and in compliance with the principle of subsidiarity. Concentrations not covered by this Regulation come, in principle, within the jurisdiction of the Member States.

...

(20) It is expedient to define the concept of concentration in such a manner as to cover operations bringing about a lasting change in the control of the undertakings concerned and therefore in the structure of the market. It is therefore appropriate to include, within the scope of this Regulation, all joint ventures performing on a lasting basis all the functions of an autonomous economic entity. It is moreover appropriate to treat as a single concentration transactions that are closely connected in that they are linked by condition or take the form of a series of transactions in securities taking place within a reasonably short period of time.

(21) This Regulation should also apply where the undertakings concerned accept restrictions directly related to, and necessary for, the implementation of the concentration. Commission decisions declaring concentrations compatible with the common market in application of this Regulation should automatically cover such restrictions, without the Commission having to assess such restrictions in individual cases. At the request of the undertakings concerned, however, the Commission should, in cases presenting novel or unresolved questions giving rise to genuine uncertainty, expressly assess whether or not any restriction is directly related to, and necessary or, the implementation of the concentration. A case presents a novel or unresolved question giving rise to genuine uncertainty if the question is not covered by the relevant Commission notice in force or a published Commission decision.

...

(32) Concentrations which, by reason of the limited market share of the undertakings concerned, are not liable to impede effective competition may be presumed to be compatible with the common market. Without prejudice to Articles 81 and 82 of the Treaty, an indication to this effect exists, in particular, where the market share of the undertakings concerned does not exceed 25% either in the common market or in a substantial part of it.

...

HAS ADOPTED THIS REGULATION:

Article 1

Scope

1. Without prejudice to Article 4(5) and Article 22, this Regulation shall apply to all concentrations with a Community dimension as defined in this Article.

2. A concentration has a Community dimension where:

   (a) the combined aggregate worldwide turnover of all the undertakings concerned is more than EUR 5000 million; and

   (b) the aggregate Community-wide turnover of each of at least two of the undertakings concerned is more than EUR 250 million,

   unless each of the undertakings concerned achieves more than two-thirds of its aggregate Community-wide turnover within one and the same Member State.

3. A concentration that does not meet the thresholds laid down in paragraph 2 has a Community dimension where:

   (a) the combined aggregate worldwide turnover of all the undertakings concerned is more than EUR 2500 million;

   (b) in each of at least three Member States, the combined aggregate turnover of all the undertakings concerned is more than EUR 100 million;

   (c) in each of at least three Member States included for the purpose of point (b), the aggregate turnover of each of at least two of the undertakings concerned is more than EUR 25 million; and

   (d) the aggregate Community-wide turnover of each of at least two of the undertakings concerned is more than EUR 100 million,

   unless each of the undertakings concerned achieves more than two-thirds of its aggregate Community-wide turnover within one and the same Member State.

...

Article 2

Appraisal of concentrations

1. Concentrations within the scope of this Regulation shall be appraised in accordance with the objectives of this Regulation and the following provisions with a view to establishing whether or not they are compatible with the common market.

   In making this appraisal, the Commission shall take into account:

   (a) the need to maintain and develop effective competition within the common market in view of, among other things, the structure of all the markets concerned and the actual or potential competition from undertakings located either within or outwith the Community;

   (b) the market position of the undertakings concerned and their economic and financial power, the alternatives available to suppliers and users, their access to supplies or markets, any legal or other barriers to entry, supply and demand trends for the relevant goods and services, the interests of the intermediate and ultimate consumers, and the development of technical and economic progress provided that it is to consumers' advantage and does not form an obstacle to competition.

2. A concentration which would not significantly impede effective competition in the common market or in a substantial part of it, in particular as a result of the creation or

strengthening of a dominant position, shall be declared compatible with the common market.

3.   A concentration which would significantly impede effective competition, in the common market or in a substantial part of it, in particular as a result of the creation or strengthening of a dominant position, shall be declared incompatible with the common market.

4.   To the extent that the creation of a joint venture constituting a concentration pursuant to Article 3 has as its object or effect the coordination of the competitive behaviour of undertakings that remain independent, such coordination shall be appraised in accordance with the criteria of Article 81(1) and (3) of the Treaty, with a view to establishing whether or not the operation is compatible with the common market.

5.   In making this appraisal, the Commission shall take into account in particular:

–   whether two or more parent companies retain, to a significant extent, activities in the same market as the joint venture or in a market which is downstream or upstream from that of the joint venture or in a neighbouring market closely related to this market,

–   whether the coordination which is the direct consequence of the creation of the joint venture affords the undertakings concerned the possibility of eliminating competition in respect of a substantial part of the products or services in question.

Article 3
Definition of concentration

1.   A concentration shall be deemed to arise where a change of control on a lasting basis results from:

(a)   the merger of two or more previously independent undertakings or parts of undertakings, or

(b)   the acquisition, by one or more persons already controlling at least one undertaking, or by one or more undertakings, whether by purchase of securities or assets, by contract or by any other means, of direct or indirect control of the whole or parts of one or more other undertakings.

2.   Control shall be constituted by rights, contracts or any other means which, either separately or in combination and having regard to the considerations of fact or law involved, confer the possibility of exercising decisive influence on an undertaking, in particular by:

(a)   ownership or the right to use all or part of the assets of an undertaking;

(b)   rights or contracts which confer decisive influence on the composition, voting or decisions of the organs of an undertaking.

3.   Control is acquired by persons or undertakings which:

(a)   are holders of the rights or entitled to rights under the contracts concerned; or

(b)   while not being holders of such rights or entitled to rights under such contracts, have the power to exercise the rights deriving therefrom.

4.   The creation of a joint venture performing on a lasting basis all the functions of an autonomous economic entity shall constitute a concentration within the meaning of paragraph 1(b).

...

Article 4
Prior notification of concentrations and pre-notification referral at the request
of the notifying parties

1. Concentrations with a Community dimension defined in this Regulation shall be notified to the Commission prior to their implementation and following the conclusion of the agreement, the announcement of the public bid, or the acquisition of a controlling interest.

    Notification may also be made where the undertakings concerned demonstrate to the Commission a good faith intention to conclude an agreement or, in the case of a public bid, where they have publicly announced an intention to make such a bid, provided that the intended agreement or bid would result in a concentration with a Community dimension.

    For the purposes of this Regulation, the term 'notified concentration' shall also cover intended concentrations notified pursuant to the second subparagraph. For the purposes of paragraphs 4 and 5 of this Article, the term 'concentration' includes intended concentrations within the meaning of the second subparagraph.

2. A concentration which consists of a merger within the meaning of Article 3(1)(a) or in the acquisition of joint control within the meaning of Article 3(1)(b) shall be notified jointly by the parties to the merger or by those acquiring joint control as the case may be. In all other cases, the notification shall be effected by the person or undertaking acquiring control of the whole or parts of one or more undertakings.

    ...

4. Prior to the notification of a concentration within the meaning of paragraph 1, the persons or undertakings referred to in paragraph 2 may inform the Commission, by means of a reasoned submission, that the concentration may significantly affect competition in a market within a Member State which presents all the characteristics of a distinct market and should therefore be examined, in whole or in part, by that Member State.

    The Commission shall transmit this submission to all Member States without delay. The Member State referred to in the reasoned submission shall, within 15 working days of receiving the submission, express its agreement or disagreement as regards the request to refer the case. Where that Member State takes no such decision within this period, it shall be deemed to have agreed.

    Unless that Member State disagrees, the Commission, where it considers that such a distinct market exists, and that competition in that market may be significantly affected by the concentration, may decide to refer the whole or part of the case to the competent authorities of that Member State with a view to the application of that State's national competition law.

    The decision whether or not to refer the case in accordance with the third subparagraph shall be taken within 25 working days starting from the receipt of the reasoned submission by the Commission. The Commission shall inform the other Member States and the persons or undertakings concerned of its decision. If the Commission does not take a decision within this period, it shall be deemed to have adopted a decision to refer the case in accordance with the submission made by the persons or undertakings concerned.

    If the Commission decides, or is deemed to have decided, pursuant to the third and fourth subparagraphs, to refer the whole of the case, no notification shall be made pursuant to paragraph 1 and national competition law shall apply. Article 9(6) to (9) shall apply mutatis mutandis.

5. With regard to a concentration as defined in Article 3 which does not have a Community dimension within the meaning of Article 1 and which is capable of being reviewed under the national competition laws of at least three Member States, the persons or undertakings referred to in paragraph 2 may, before any notification to the competent authorities, inform the Commission by means of a reasoned submission that the concentration should be examined by the Commission.

The Commission shall transmit this submission to all Member States without delay.

Any Member State competent to examine the concentration under its national competition law may, within 15 working days of receiving the reasoned submission, express its disagreement as regards the request to refer the case.

Where at least one such Member State has expressed its disagreement in accordance with the third subparagraph within the period of 15 working days, the case shall not be referred. The Commission shall, without delay, inform all Member States and the persons or undertakings concerned of any such expression of disagreement.

Where no Member State has expressed its disagreement in accordance with the third subparagraph within the period of 15 working days, the concentration shall be deemed to have a Community dimension and shall be notified to the Commission in accordance with paragraphs 1 and 2. In such situations, no Member State shall apply its national competition law to the concentration.

...

Article 5
Calculation of turnover

1. Aggregate turnover within the meaning of this Regulation shall comprise the amounts derived by the undertakings concerned in the preceding financial year from the sale of products and the provision of services falling within the undertakings' ordinary activities after deduction of sales rebates and of value added tax and other taxes directly related to turnover ...

2. By way of derogation from paragraph 1, where the concentration consists of the acquisition of parts, whether or not constituted as legal entities, of one or more undertakings, only the turnover relating to the parts which are the subject of the concentration shall be taken into account with regard to the seller or sellers.

...

4. Without prejudice to paragraph 2, the aggregate turnover of an undertaking concerned within the meaning of this Regulation shall be calculated by adding together the respective turnovers of the following:
   (a)   the undertaking concerned;
   (b)   those undertakings in which the undertaking concerned, directly or indirectly:
      (i)   owns more than half the capital or business assets, or
      (ii)   has the power to exercise more than half the voting rights, or
      (iii) has the power to appoint more than half the members of the supervisory board, the administrative board or bodies legally representing the undertakings, or
      (iv)   has the right to manage the undertakings' affairs;
   (c)   those undertakings which have in the undertaking concerned the rights or powers listed in (b);
   (d)   those undertakings in which an undertaking as referred to in (c) has the rights or powers listed in (b);

(e)   those undertakings in which two or more undertakings as referred to in (a) to (d) jointly have the rights or powers listed in (b).

5.   Where undertakings concerned by the concentration jointly have the rights or powers listed in paragraph 4(b), in calculating the aggregate turnover of the undertakings concerned for the purposes of this Regulation:

(a)   no account shall be taken of the turnover resulting from the sale of products or the provision of services between the joint undertaking and each of the undertakings concerned or any other undertaking connected with any one of them, as set out in paragraph 4(b) to (e);

(b)   account shall be taken of the turnover resulting from the sale of products and the provision of services between the joint undertaking and any third undertakings. This turnover shall be apportioned equally amongst the undertakings concerned.

Article 6
Examination of the notification and initiation of proceedings

1.   The Commission shall examine the notification as soon as it is received.

(a)   Where it concludes that the concentration notified does not fall within the scope of this Regulation, it shall record that finding by means of a decision.

(b)   Where it finds that the concentration notified, although falling within the scope of this Regulation, does not raise serious doubts as to its compatibility with the common market, it shall decide not to oppose it and shall declare that it is compatible with the common market.

A decision declaring a concentration compatible shall be deemed to cover restrictions directly related and necessary to the implementation of the concentration.

(c)   Without prejudice to paragraph 2, where the Commission finds that the concentration notified falls within the scope of this Regulation and raises serious doubts as to its compatibility with the common market, it shall decide to initiate proceedings. Without prejudice to Article 9, such proceedings shall be closed by means of a decision as provided for in Article 8(1) to (4), unless the undertakings concerned have demonstrated to the satisfaction of the Commission that they have abandoned the concentration.

2.   Where the Commission finds that, following modification by the undertakings concerned, a notified concentration no longer raises serious doubts within the meaning of paragraph 1(c), it shall declare the concentration compatible with the common market pursuant to paragraph 1(b).

The Commission may attach to its decision under paragraph 1(b) conditions and obligations intended to ensure that the undertakings concerned comply with the commitments they have entered into vis-à-vis the Commission with a view to rendering the concentration compatible with the common market.

...

Article 7
Suspension of concentrations

1.   A concentration with a Community dimension as defined in Article 1, or which is to be examined by the Commission pursuant to Article 4(5), shall not be implemented either before its notification or until it has been declared compatible with the common market pursuant to a decision under Articles 6(1)(b), 8(1) or 8(2), or on the basis of a presumption according to Article 10(6).

...

Article 8
Powers of decision of the Commission

1. Where the Commission finds that a notified concentration fulfils the criterion laid down in Article 2(2) and, in the cases referred to in Article 2(4), the criteria laid down in Article 81(3) of the Treaty, it shall issue a decision declaring the concentration compatible with the common market.

   A decision declaring a concentration compatible shall be deemed to cover restrictions directly related and necessary to the implementation of the concentration.

2. Where the Commission finds that, following modification by the undertakings concerned, a notified concentration fulfils the criterion laid down in Article 2(2) and, in the cases referred to in Article 2(4), the criteria laid down in Article 81(3) of the Treaty, it shall issue a decision declaring the concentration compatible with the common market.

   The Commission may attach to its decision conditions and obligations intended to ensure that the undertakings concerned comply with the commitments they have entered into vis-à-vis the Commission with a view to rendering the concentration compatible with the common market.

   A decision declaring a concentration compatible shall be deemed to cover restrictions directly related and necessary to the implementation of the concentration.

3. Where the Commission finds that a concentration fulfils the criterion defined in Article 2(3) or, in the cases referred to in Article 2(4), does not fulfil the criteria laid down in Article 81(3) of the Treaty, it shall issue a decision declaring that the concentration is incompatible with the common market.

...

Article 9
Referral to the competent authorities of the Member States

1. The Commission may, by means of a decision notified without delay to the undertakings concerned and the competent authorities of the other Member States, refer a notified concentration to the competent authorities of the Member State concerned in the following circumstances.

2. Within 15 working days of the date of receipt of the copy of the notification, a Member State, on its own initiative or upon the invitation of the Commission, may inform the Commission, which shall inform the undertakings concerned, that:

   (a) a concentration threatens to affect significantly competition in a market within that Member State, which presents all the characteristics of a distinct market, or

   (b) a concentration affects competition in a market within that Member State, which presents all the characteristics of a distinct market and which does not constitute a substantial part of the common market.

3. If the Commission considers that, having regard to the market for the products or services in question and the geographical reference market within the meaning of paragraph 7, there is such a distinct market and that such a threat exists, either:

   (a) it shall itself deal with the case in accordance with this Regulation; or

   (b) it shall refer the whole or part of the case to the competent authorities of the Member State concerned with a view to the application of that State's national competition law.

Article 10
Time limits for initiating proceedings and for decisions

1. Without prejudice to Article 6(4), the decisions referred to in Article 6(1) shall be taken within 25 working days at most. That period shall begin on the working day following

that of the receipt of a notification or, if the information to be supplied with the notification is incomplete, on the working day following that of the receipt of the complete information.

That period shall be increased to 35 working days where the Commission receives a request from a Member State in accordance with Article 9(2)or where, the undertakings concerned offer commitments pursuant to Article 6(2) with a view to rendering the concentration compatible with the common market.

2.   Decisions pursuant to Article 8(1) or (2) concerning notified concentrations shall be taken as soon as it appears that the serious doubts referred to in Article 6(1)(c) have been removed, particularly as a result of modifications made by the undertakings concerned, and at the latest by the time limit laid down in paragraph 3.

3.   Without prejudice to Article 8(7), decisions pursuant to Article 8(1) to (3) concerning notified concentrations shall be taken within not more than 90 working days of the date on which the proceedings are initiated. That period shall be increased to 105 working days where the undertakings concerned offer commitments pursuant to Article 8(2), second subparagraph, with a view to rendering the concentration compatible with the common market, unless these commitments have been offered less than 55 working days after the initiation of proceedings.

The periods set by the first subparagraph shall likewise be extended if the notifying parties make a request to that effect not later than 15 working days after the initiation of proceedings pursuant to Article 6(1)(c). The notifying parties may make only one such request. Likewise, at any time following the initiation of proceedings, the periods set by the first subparagraph may be extended by the Commission with the agreement of the notifying parties. The total duration of any extension or extensions effected pursuant to this subparagraph shall not exceed 20 working days.

...

Article 21
Application of the Regulation and jurisdiction

1.   This Regulation alone shall apply to concentrations as defined in Article 3, and Council Regulations (EC) No 1/2003(8), (EEC) No 1017/68(9), (EEC) No 4056/86(10) and (EEC) No 3975/87(11) shall not apply, except in relation to joint ventures that do not have a Community dimension and which have as their object or effect the coordination of the competitive behaviour of undertakings that remain independent.

2.   Subject to review by the Court of Justice, the Commission shall have sole jurisdiction to take the decisions provided for in this Regulation.

3.   No Member State shall apply its national legislation on competition to any concentration that has a Community dimension.

The first subparagraph shall be without prejudice to any Member State's power to carry out any enquiries necessary for the application of Articles 4(4), 9(2) or after referral, pursuant to Article 9(3), first subparagraph, indent (b), or Article 9(5), to take the measures strictly necessary for the application of Article 9(8).

4.   Notwithstanding paragraphs 2 and 3, Member States may take appropriate measures to protect legitimate interests other than those taken into consideration by this Regulation and compatible with the general principles and other provisions of Community law.

Public security, plurality of the media and prudential rules shall be regarded as legitimate interests within the meaning of the first subparagraph.

Any other public interest must be communicated to the Commission by the Member State concerned and shall be recognised by the Commission after an assessment of its compatibility with the general principles and other provisions of Community law before the measures referred to above may be taken. The Commission shall inform the Member State concerned of its decision within 25 working days of that communication.

Article 22
Referral to the Commission

1.   One or more Member States may request the Commission to examine any concentration as defined in Article 3 that does not have a Community dimension within the meaning of Article 1 but affects trade between Member States and threatens to significantly affect competition within the territory of the Member State or States making the request.

Such a request shall be made at most within 15 working days of the date on which the concentration was notified, or if no notification is required, otherwise made known to the Member State concerned.

2.   The Commission shall inform the competent authorities of the Member States and the undertakings concerned of any request received pursuant to paragraph 1 without delay.

Any other Member State shall have the right to join the initial request within a period of 15 working days of being informed by the Commission of the initial request.

All national time limits relating to the concentration shall be suspended until, in accordance with the procedure set out in this Article, it has been decided where the concentration shall be examined. As soon as a Member State has informed the Commission and the undertakings concerned that it does not wish to join the request, the suspension of its national time limits shall end.

...

5.   The Commission may inform one or several Member States that it considers a concentration fulfils the criteria in paragraph 1. In such cases, the Commission may invite that Member State or those Member States to make a request pursuant to paragraph 1.

Appendix 9
Jurisdictional Notice (extracts)

The wording contained in this Appendix is taken from the *Official Journal* of the EU. As such it does not reflect the renumbering of treaty articles introduced by the Treaty on the Functioning of the European Union (see 1.3.1.1).

Commission Consolidated Jurisdictional Notice under Council Regulation (EC) No 139/2004 on the control of concentrations between undertakings (2008/C 95/01)

...

NOTION OF UNDERTAKING CONCERNED

General

(129) From the point of view of determining jurisdiction, the undertakings concerned are those participating in a concentration, i.e. a merger or an acquisition of control as foreseen in Article 3(1). The individual and aggregate turnover of those undertakings will be decisive in determining whether the thresholds are met.

...

Mergers

(132) In a merger the undertakings concerned are each of the merging entities.

Acquisition of control

(133) In the remaining cases, it is the concept of 'acquiring control' that will determine which are the undertakings concerned. On the acquiring side, there can be one or more undertakings acquiring sole or joint control. On the acquired side, there can be one or more undertakings as a whole or parts thereof. As a general rule, each of these undertakings will be an undertaking concerned within the meaning of the Merger Regulation.

TURNOVER CALCULATION AND FINANCIAL ACCOUNTS

The general rule

(169) The Commission seeks to base itself upon the most accurate and reliable figures available. Generally, the Commission will refer to accounts which relate to the closest financial year to the date of the transaction and which are audited under the standard applicable to the undertaking in question and compulsory for the relevant financial year. An adjustment of the audited figures should only take place if this is required by the provisions of the Merger Regulation, including the cases explained in more detail in paragraph 172.

...

(172) Notwithstanding the foregoing paragraphs, an adjustment must always be made to account for permanent changes in the economic reality of the undertakings concerned, such as acquisitions or divestments which are not or not fully reflected in the audited accounts ...

ATTRIBUTION OF TURNOVER UNDER ARTICLE 5(4)

Identification of undertakings whose turnover is taken into account

(175) When an undertaking concerned by a concentration belongs to a group, not only the turnover of the undertaking concerned is considered, but the Merger Regulation requires to also take into account the turnover of those undertakings with which the undertaking

concerned has links consisting in the rights or powers listed in Article 5(4) in order to determine whether the thresholds contained in Article 1 of the Merger Regulation are met. The aim is again to capture the total volume of the economic resources that are being combined through the operation irrespective of whether the economic activities are carried out directly by the undertaking concerned or whether they are undertaken indirectly via undertakings with which the undertaking concerned possesses the links described in Article 5(4).

Allocation of turnover of the undertakings identified

(185) In general, as long as the test under Article 5(4)(b) is fulfilled, the whole turnover of the subsidiary in question will be taken into account regardless of the actual shareholding which the undertaking concerned holds in the subsidiary. In the chart, the whole turnover of the subsidiaries called b of the undertaking concerned a will be taken into account.

(186) However, the Merger Regulation includes specific rules for joint ventures. Article 5(5)(b) provides that for joint ventures between two or more undertakings concerned, the turnover of the joint venture (as far as the turnover is generated from activities with third parties as set out above in paragraph 168) should be apportioned equally amongst the undertakings concerned, irrespective of their share of the capital or the voting rights.

GEOGRAPHIC ALLOCATION OF TURNOVER

...

General rule

(196) The Merger Regulation does not discriminate between 'products sold' and 'services provided' for the geographic allocation of turnover. In both cases, the general rule is that turnover should be attributed to the place where the customer is located. The underlying principle is that turnover should be allocated to the location where competition with alternative suppliers takes place. This location is normally also the place where the characteristic action under the contract in question is to be performed, *i.e.* where the service is actually provided and the product is actually delivered. In the case of Internet transactions, it may be difficult for the undertakings to determine the location of the customer at the time when the contract is concluded via the Internet. If the product or the service itself is not supplied via the Internet, focusing on the place where the characteristic action under the contract is performed may avoid those difficulties. In the following, the sale of goods and the provision of services are dealt with separately as they exhibit certain different features in terms of allocation of turnover.

Appendix 10

Technology Transfer Block Exemption Regulation

Commission Regulation (EU) No 316/2014 of 21 March 2014 on the application of Article 101(3) of the Treaty on the Functioning of the European Union to categories of technology transfer agreements

(Text with EEA relevance)

THE EUROPEAN COMMISSION,

Having regard to the Treaty on the Functioning of the European Union,

Having regard to Regulation No 19/65/EEC of the Council of 2 March 1965 on application of Article 85(3) of the Treaty to certain categories of agreements and concerted practices, and in particular Article 1 thereof,

Having published a draft of this Regulation,

After consulting the Advisory Committee on Restrictive Practices and Dominant Positions,

Whereas:

(1)   Regulation No 19/65/EEC empowers the Commission to apply Article 101(3) of the Treaty by regulation to certain categories of technology transfer agreements and corresponding concerted practices to which only two undertakings are party which fall within Article 101(1) of the Treaty.

(2)   Pursuant to Regulation No 19/65/EEC, the Commission has, in particular, adopted Commission Regulation (EC) No 772/2004. Regulation (EC) No 772/2004 defines categories of technology transfer agreements which the Commission regarded as normally satisfying the conditions laid down in Article 101(3) of the Treaty. In view of the overall positive experience with the application of that Regulation, which expires on 30 April 2014, and taking into account further experience acquired since its adoption, it is appropriate to adopt a new block exemption regulation.

(3)   This Regulation should meet the two requirements of ensuring effective protection of competition and providing adequate legal security for undertakings. The pursuit of those objectives should take account of the need to simplify administrative supervision and the legislative framework to as great an extent as possible.

(4)   Technology transfer agreements concern the licensing of technology rights. Such agreements will usually improve economic efficiency and be pro-competitive as they can reduce duplication of research and development, strengthen the incentive for the initial research and development, spur incremental innovation, facilitate diffusion and generate product market competition.

(5)   The likelihood that such efficiency-enhancing and pro-competitive effects will outweigh any anti-competitive effects due to restrictions contained in technology transfer agreements depends on the degree of market power of the undertakings concerned and, therefore, on the extent to which those undertakings face competition from undertakings owning substitute technologies or undertakings producing substitute products.

(6)   This Regulation should cover only technology transfer agreements between a licensor and a licensee. It should cover such agreements even if the agreement contains conditions relating to more than one level of trade, for instance requiring the licensee to

set up a particular distribution system and specifying the obligations the licensee must or may impose on resellers of the products produced under the licence. However, such conditions and obligations should comply with the competition rules applicable to supply and distribution agreements set out in Commission Regulation (EU) No 330/2010. Supply and distribution agreements concluded between a licensee and buyers of its contract products should not be exempted by this Regulation.

(7)   This Regulation should only apply to agreements where the licensor permits the licensee and/or one or more of its sub-contractors to exploit the licensed technology rights, possibly after further research and development by the licensee and/or its sub-contractors, for the purpose of producing goods or services. It should not apply to licensing in the context of research and development agreements which are covered by Commission Regulation (EU) No 1217/2010 or to licensing in the context of specialisation agreements which are covered by Commission Regulation (EU) No 1218/2010. It should also not apply to agreements, the purpose of which is the mere reproduction and distribution of software copyright protected products as such agreements do not concern the licensing of a technology to produce but are more akin to distribution agreements. Nor should it apply to agreements to set up technology pools, that is to say, agreements for the pooling of technologies with the purpose of licensing them to third parties, or to agreements whereby the pooled technology is licensed out to those third parties.

(8)   For the application of Article 101(3) of the Treaty by regulation, it is not necessary to define those technology transfer agreements that are capable of falling within Article 101(1) of the Treaty. In the individual assessment of agreements pursuant to Article 101(1), account has to be taken of several factors, and in particular the structure and the dynamics of the relevant technology and product markets.

(9)   The benefit of the block exemption established by this Regulation should be limited to those agreements which can be assumed with sufficient certainty to satisfy the conditions of Article 101(3) of the Treaty. In order to attain the benefits and objectives of technology transfer, this Regulation should not only cover the transfer of technology as such but also other provisions contained in technology transfer agreements if, and to the extent that, those provisions are directly related to the production or sale of the contract products.

(10)   For technology transfer agreements between competitors it can be presumed that, where the combined share of the relevant markets accounted for by the parties does not exceed 20% and the agreements do not contain certain severely anti-competitive restrictions, they generally lead to an improvement in production or distribution and allow consumers a fair share of the resulting benefits.

(11)   For technology transfer agreements between non-competitors it can be presumed that, where the individual share of the relevant markets accounted for by each of the parties does not exceed 30% and the agreements do not contain certain severely anti-competitive restrictions, they generally lead to an improvement in production or distribution and allow consumers a fair share of the resulting benefits.

(12)   If the applicable market-share threshold is exceeded on one or more product or technology markets, the block exemption should not apply to the agreement for the relevant markets concerned.

(13)   There can be no presumption that, above those market-share thresholds, technology transfer agreements fall within the scope of Article 101(1) of the Treaty. For instance, exclusive licensing agreements between non-competing undertakings often fall outside the scope of Article 101(1). There can also be no presumption that, above those market-share thresholds, technology transfer agreements falling within the scope of Article

101(1) will not satisfy the conditions for exemption. However, it can also not be presumed that they will usually give rise to objective advantages of such a character and size as to compensate for the disadvantages which they create for competition.

(14) This Regulation should not exempt technology transfer agreements containing restrictions which are not indispensable to the improvement of production or distribution. In particular, technology transfer agreements containing certain severely anti-competitive restrictions, such as the fixing of prices charged to third parties, should be excluded from the benefit of the block exemption established by this Regulation irrespective of the market shares of the undertakings concerned. In the case of such hardcore restrictions the whole agreement should be excluded from the benefit of the block exemption.

(15) In order to protect incentives to innovate and the appropriate application of intellectual property rights, certain restrictions should be excluded from the benefit of the block exemption. In particular certain grant back obligations and non-challenge clauses should be excluded. Where such a restriction is included in a licence agreement only the restriction in question should be excluded from the benefit of the block exemption.

(16) The market-share thresholds and the non-exemption of technology transfer agreements containing the severely anti-competitive restrictions and the excluded restrictions provided for in this Regulation will normally ensure that the agreements to which the block exemption applies do not enable the participating undertakings to eliminate competition in respect of a substantial part of the products in question.

(17) The Commission may withdraw the benefit of this Regulation, pursuant to Article 29(1) of Council Regulation (EC) No 1/2003, where it finds in a particular case that an agreement to which the exemption provided for in this Regulation applies nevertheless has effects which are incompatible with Article 101(3) of the Treaty. This may occur in particular where the incentives to innovate are reduced or where access to markets is hindered.

(18) The competition authority of a Member State may withdraw the benefit of this Regulation pursuant to Article 29(2) of Regulation (EC) No 1/2003 in respect of the territory of that Member State, or a part thereof where, in a particular case, an agreement to which the exemption provided for in this Regulation applies nevertheless has effects which are incompatible with Article 101(3) of the Treaty in the territory of that Member State, or in a part thereof, and where such territory has all the characteristics of a distinct geographic market.

(19) In order to strengthen supervision of parallel networks of technology transfer agreements which have similar restrictive effects and which cover more than 50% of a given market, the Commission may by regulation declare this Regulation inapplicable to technology transfer agreements containing specific restrictions relating to the market concerned, thereby restoring the full application of Article 101 of the Treaty to such agreements,

HAS ADOPTED THIS REGULATION:

Article 1
Definitions

1. For the purposes of this Regulation, the following definitions shall apply:

    (a) 'agreement' means an agreement, a decision of an association of undertakings or a concerted practice;

    (b) 'technology rights' means know-how and the following rights, or a combination thereof, including applications for or applications for registration of those rights:

        (i)   patents,

        (ii)   utility models,

        (iii) design rights,

        (iv) topographies of semiconductor products,

        (v)   supplementary protection certificates for medicinal products or other products for which such supplementary protection certificates may be obtained,

        (vi) plant breeder's certificates and

        (vii) software copyrights;

(c)   'technology transfer agreement' means:

        (i)   a technology rights licensing agreement entered into between two undertakings for the purpose of the production of contract products by the licensee and/or its sub-contractor(s),

        (ii)   an assignment of technology rights between two undertakings for the purpose of the production of contract products where part of the risk associated with the exploitation of the technology remains with the assignor;

(d)   'reciprocal agreement' means a technology transfer agreement where two undertakings grant each other, in the same or separate contracts, a technology rights licence, and where those licences concern competing technologies or can be used for the production of competing products;

(e)   'non-reciprocal agreement' means a technology transfer agreement where one undertaking grants another undertaking a technology rights licence, or where two undertakings grant each other such a licence but where those licences do not concern competing technologies and cannot be used for the production of competing products;

(f)   'product' means goods or a service, including both intermediary goods and services and final goods and services;

(g)   'contract product' means a product produced, directly or indirectly, on the basis of the licensed technology rights;

(h)   'intellectual property rights' includes industrial property rights, in particular patents and trademarks, copyright and neighbouring rights;

(i)   'know-how' means a package of practical information, resulting from experience and testing, which is:

        (i)   secret, that is to say, not generally known or easily accessible,

        (ii)   substantial, that is to say, significant and useful for the production of the contract products, and

        (iii) identified, that is to say, described in a sufficiently comprehensive manner so as to make it possible to verify that it fulfils the criteria of secrecy and substantiality;

(j)   'relevant product market' means the market for the contract products and their substitutes, that is to say all those products which are regarded as interchangeable or substitutable by the buyer, by reason of the products' characteristics, their prices and their intended use;

(k)   'relevant technology market' means the market for the licensed technology rights and their substitutes, that is to say all those technology rights which are regarded as interchangeable or substitutable by the licensee, by reason of the technology rights' characteristics, the royalties payable in respect of those rights and their intended use;

(l)   'relevant geographic market' means the area in which the undertakings concerned are involved in the supply of and demand for products or the licensing of technology rights, in which the conditions of competition are sufficiently homogeneous and which can be distinguished from neighbouring areas because the conditions of competition are appreciably different in those areas;

(m)   'relevant market' means the combination of the relevant product or technology market with the relevant geographic market;

(n)   'competing undertakings' means undertakings which compete on the relevant market, that is to say:

    (i)   competing undertakings on the relevant market where the technology rights are licensed, that is to say, undertakings which license out competing technology rights (actual competitors on the relevant market),

    (ii)   competing undertakings on the relevant market where the contract products are sold, that is to say, undertakings which, in the absence of the technology transfer agreement, would both be active on the relevant market(s) on which the contract products are sold (actual competitors on the relevant market) or which, in the absence of the technology transfer agreement, would, on realistic grounds and not just as a mere theoretical possibility, in response to a small and permanent increase in relative prices, be likely to undertake, within a short period of time, the necessary additional investments or other necessary switching costs to enter the relevant market(s) (potential competitors on the relevant market);

(o)   'selective distribution system' means a distribution system where the licensor undertakes to license the production of the contract products, either directly or indirectly, only to licensees selected on the basis of specified criteria and where those licensees undertake not to sell the contract products to unauthorised distributors within the territory reserved by the licensor to operate that system;

(p)   'exclusive licence' means a licence under which the licensor itself is not permitted to produce on the basis of the licensed technology rights and is not permitted to license the licensed technology rights to third parties, in general or for a particular use or in a particular territory;

(q)   'exclusive territory' means a given territory within which only one undertaking is allowed to produce the contract products, but where it is nevertheless possible to allow another licensee to produce the contract products within that territory only for a particular customer where the second licence was granted in order to create an alternative source of supply for that customer;

(r)   'exclusive customer group' means a group of customers to which only one party to the technology transfer agreement is allowed to actively sell the contract products produced with the licensed technology.

2.   For the purposes of this Regulation, the terms 'undertaking', 'licensor' and 'licensee' shall include their respective connected undertakings.

'Connected undertakings' means:

(a)   undertakings in which a party to the technology transfer agreement, directly or indirectly:

    (i)   has the power to exercise more than half the voting rights, or

(ii)   has the power to appoint more than half the members of the supervisory board, board of management or bodies legally representing the undertaking, or

(ii)   has the right to manage the undertaking's affairs;

(b)   undertakings which directly or indirectly have, over a party to the technology transfer agreement, the rights or powers listed in point (a);

(c)   undertakings in which an undertaking referred to in point (b) has, directly or indirectly, the rights or powers listed in point (a);

(d)   undertakings in which a party to the technology transfer agreement together with one or more of the undertakings referred to in points (a), (b) or (c), or in which two or more of the latter undertakings, jointly have the rights or powers listed in point (a);

(e)   undertakings in which the rights or the powers listed in point (a) are jointly held by:

(i)   parties to the technology transfer agreement or their respective connected undertakings referred to in points (a) to (d), or

(ii)   one or more of the parties to the technology transfer agreement or one or more of their connected undertakings referred to in points (a) to (d) and one or more third parties.

Article 2
Exemption

1.   Pursuant to Article 101(3) of the Treaty and subject to the provisions of this Regulation, Article 101(1) of the Treaty shall not apply to technology transfer agreements.

2.   The exemption provided for in paragraph 1 shall apply to the extent that technology transfer agreements contain restrictions of competition falling within the scope of Article 101(1) of the Treaty. The exemption shall apply for as long as the licensed technology rights have not expired, lapsed or been declared invalid or, in the case of know-how, for as long as the know-how remains secret. However, where know-how becomes publicly known as a result of action by the licensee, the exemption shall apply for the duration of the agreement.

3.   The exemption provided for in paragraph 1 shall also apply to provisions, in technology transfer agreements, which relate to the purchase of products by the licensee or which relate to the licensing or assignment of other intellectual property rights or know-how to the licensee, if, and to the extent that, those provisions are directly related to the production or sale of the contract products.

Article 3
Market-share thresholds

1.   Where the undertakings party to the agreement are competing undertakings, the exemption provided for in Article 2 shall apply on condition that the combined market share of the parties does not exceed 20% on the relevant market(s).

2.   Where the undertakings party to the agreement are not competing undertakings, the exemption provided for in Article 2 shall apply on condition that the market share of each of the parties does not exceed 30% on the relevant market(s).

Article 4
Hardcore restrictions

1.   Where the undertakings party to the agreement are competing undertakings, the exemption provided for in Article 2 shall not apply to agreements which, directly or

indirectly, in isolation or in combination with other factors under the control of the parties, have as their object any of the following:

(a) the restriction of a party's ability to determine its prices when selling products to third parties;

(b) the limitation of output, except limitations on the output of contract products imposed on the licensee in a non-reciprocal agreement or imposed on only one of the licensees in a reciprocal agreement;

(c) the allocation of markets or customers except:

  (i) the obligation on the licensor and/or the licensee, in a non-reciprocal agreement, not to produce with the licensed technology rights within the exclusive territory reserved for the other party and/or not to sell actively and/or passively into the exclusive territory or to the exclusive customer group reserved for the other party,

  (ii) the restriction, in a non-reciprocal agreement, of active sales by the licensee into the exclusive territory or to the exclusive customer group allocated by the licensor to another licensee provided the latter was not a competing undertaking of the licensor at the time of the conclusion of its own licence,

  (iii) the obligation on the licensee to produce the contract products only for its own use provided that the licensee is not restricted in selling the contract products actively and passively as spare parts for its own products,

  (iv) the obligation on the licensee, in a non-reciprocal agreement, to produce the contract products only for a particular customer, where the licence was granted in order to create an alternative source of supply for that customer;

(d) the restriction of the licensee's ability to exploit its own technology rights or the restriction of the ability of any of the parties to the agreement to carry out research and development, unless such latter restriction is indispensable to prevent the disclosure of the licensed know-how to third parties.

2. Where the undertakings party to the agreement are not competing undertakings, the exemption provided for in Article 2 shall not apply to agreements which, directly or indirectly, in isolation or in combination with other factors under the control of the parties, have as their object any of the following:

(a) the restriction of a party's ability to determine its prices when selling products to third parties, without prejudice to the possibility of imposing a maximum sale price or recommending a sale price, provided that it does not amount to a fixed or minimum sale price as a result of pressure from, or incentives offered by, any of the parties;

(b) the restriction of the territory into which, or of the customers to whom, the licensee may passively sell the contract products, except:

  (i) the restriction of passive sales into an exclusive territory or to an exclusive customer group reserved for the licensor,

  (ii) the obligation to produce the contract products only for its own use provided that the licensee is not restricted in selling the contract products actively and passively as spare parts for its own products,

  (iii) the obligation to produce the contract products only for a particular customer, where the licence was granted in order to create an alternative source of supply for that customer,

  (iv) the restriction of sales to end-users by a licensee operating at the wholesale level of trade,

        (v)   the restriction of sales to unauthorised distributors by the members of a selective distribution system;

      (c)   the restriction of active or passive sales to end-users by a licensee which is a member of a selective distribution system and which operates at the retail level, without prejudice to the possibility of prohibiting a member of the system from operating out of an unauthorised place of establishment.

3.   Where the undertakings party to the agreement are not competing undertakings at the time of the conclusion of the agreement but become competing undertakings afterwards, paragraph 2 and not paragraph 1 shall apply for the full life of the agreement unless the agreement is subsequently amended in any material respect. Such an amendment includes the conclusion of a new technology transfer agreement between the parties concerning competing technology rights.

Article 5

Excluded restrictions

1.   The exemption provided for in Article 2 shall not apply to any of the following obligations contained in technology transfer agreements:

      (a)   any direct or indirect obligation on the licensee to grant an exclusive licence or to assign rights, in whole or in part, to the licensor or to a third party designated by the licensor in respect of its own improvements to, or its own new applications of, the licensed technology;

      (b)   any direct or indirect obligation on a party not to challenge the validity of intellectual property rights which the other party holds in the Union, without prejudice to the possibility, in the case of an exclusive licence, of providing for termination of the technology transfer agreement in the event that the licensee challenges the validity of any of the licensed technology rights.

2.   Where the undertakings party to the agreement are not competing undertakings, the exemption provided for in Article 2 shall not apply to any direct or indirect obligation limiting the licensee's ability to exploit its own technology rights or limiting the ability of any of the parties to the agreement to carry out research and development, unless such latter restriction is indispensable to prevent the disclosure of the licensed know-how to third parties.

Article 6

Withdrawal in individual cases

1.   The Commission may withdraw the benefit of this Regulation, pursuant to Article 29(1) of Regulation (EC) No 1/2003, where it finds in any particular case that a technology transfer agreement to which the exemption provided for in Article 2 of this Regulation applies nevertheless has effects which are incompatible with Article 101(3) of the Treaty, and in particular where:

      (a)   access of third parties' technologies to the market is restricted, for instance by the cumulative effect of parallel networks of similar restrictive agreements prohibiting licensees from using third parties' technologies;

      (b)   access of potential licensees to the market is restricted, for instance by the cumulative effect of parallel networks of similar restrictive agreements prohibiting licensors from licensing to other licensees or because the only technology owner licensing out relevant technology rights concludes an exclusive license with a licensee who is already active on the product market on the basis of substitutable technology rights.

2. Where, in any particular case, a technology transfer agreement to which the exemption provided for in Article 2 of this Regulation applies has effects which are incompatible with Article 101(3) of the Treaty in the territory of a Member State, or in a part thereof, which has all the characteristics of a distinct geographic market, the competition authority of that Member State may withdraw the benefit of this Regulation, pursuant to Article 29(2) of Regulation (EC) No 1/2003, in respect of that territory, under the same circumstances as those set out in paragraph 1 of this Article.

Article 7
Non-application of this Regulation

1. Pursuant to Article 1a of Regulation (EC) No 19/65/EEC, the Commission may by regulation declare that, where parallel networks of similar technology transfer agreements cover more than 50% of a relevant market, this Regulation is not to apply to technology transfer agreements containing specific restrictions relating to that market.

2. A regulation pursuant to paragraph 1 shall not become applicable earlier than six months following its adoption.

Article 8
Application of the market-share thresholds

For the purposes of applying the market-share thresholds laid down in Article 3 the following rules shall apply:

(a) the market share shall be calculated on the basis of market sales value data; if market sales value data are not available, estimates based on other reliable market information, including market sales volumes, may be used to establish the market share of the undertaking concerned;

(b) the market share shall be calculated on the basis of data relating to the preceding calendar year;

(c) the market share held by the undertakings referred to in point (e) of the second subparagraph of Article 1(2) shall be apportioned equally to each undertaking having the rights or the powers listed in point (a) of the second subparagraph of Article 1(2);

(d) the market share of a licensor on a relevant market for the licensed technology rights shall be calculated on the basis of the presence of the licensed technology rights on the relevant market(s) (that is the product market(s) and the geographic market(s)) where the contract products are sold, that is on the basis of the sales data relating to the contract products produced by the licensor and its licensees combined;

(e) if the market share referred to in Article 3(1) or (2) is initially not more than 20% or 30% respectively, but subsequently rises above those levels, the exemption provided for in Article 2 shall continue to apply for a period of two consecutive calendar years following the year in which the 20% threshold or 30% threshold was first exceeded.

Article 9
Relationship with other block exemption regulations

This Regulation shall not apply to licensing arrangements in research and development agreements which fall within the scope of Regulation (EU) No 1217/2010 or in specialisation agreements which fall within the scope of Regulation (EU) No 1218/2010.

Article 10
Transitional period

The prohibition laid down in Article 101(1) of the Treaty shall not apply from 1 May 2014 until 30 April 2015 to agreements already in force on 30 April 2014 which do not satisfy the conditions for exemption provided for in this Regulation but which, on 30 April 2014, satisfied the conditions for exemption provided for in Regulation (EC) No 772/2004.

Article 11

Period of validity

This Regulation shall enter into force on 1 May 2014.

It shall expire on 30 April 2026.

This Regulation shall be binding in its entirety and directly applicable in all Member States.

Done at Brussels, 21 March 2014.

Index